CIVILISING GRASS

CIVILISING GRASS

The Art of the Lawn on the South African Highveld

Jonathan Cane

WITS UNIVERSITY PRESS

Published in South Africa by:
Wits University Press
1 Jan Smuts Avenue
Johannesburg 2001

www.witspress.co.za

First published 2019

http://dx.doi.org.10.18772/12019073108

978-1-77614-310-8 (Paperback)
978-1-77614-311-5 (Web PDF)
978-1-77614-312-2 (EPUB)
978-1-77614-313-9 (Mobi)

Project manager: Lisa Compton
Copyeditor: Alison Lockhart
Proofreader: Lisa Compton
Indexer: Sanet le Roux
Cover design: Jonathan Cane
Typesetter: Newgen
Typeset in 10.5 point Plantin

To Gerrit, who taught me to write,
and to André, who was patient

The front lawn lay spread like a huge welcome mat, inviting me into the nooks and crannies of their private spaces. But I was afraid ...

— Ivan Vladislavić, *Flashback Hotel: Early Stories*

I envisioned all sorts of dramatic deaths: a woman strangling herself to death after being overwhelmed by hot flashes in one of the kerosene lamp-lit tunnels of the asylum; another one drowning in her night sweat; a man standing for hours on end against the wall in another tunnel masturbating himself to death; men and women writhing on the sprawling lawns dying from melancholia.

— Zakes Mda, *Cion*

CONTENTS

List of Plates

8. P. H. Connell et al., *Native Township General Site Layout*, 1938. (Courtesy of the Dean of the Faculty of Engineering and the Built Environment, University of the Witwatersrand.)

9. D. M. Calderwood, *NE 51/9*, 1953. (From D. M. Calderwood, 'Native Housing in South Africa', PhD thesis, University of the Witwatersrand, 1953. Courtesy of Wits University Press.)

10. D. M. Calderwood, *Proposed New Residential Centre*, 1953. (From D. M. Calderwood, 'Native Housing in South Africa', PhD thesis, University of the Witwatersrand, 1953. Courtesy of Wits University Press.)

11. D. M. Calderwood, *Analysis of 50′ x 70′ plots*, 1953. (From D. M. Calderwood, 'Native Housing in South Africa', PhD thesis, University of the Witwatersrand, 1953. Courtesy of Wits University Press.)

12. Joane Pim, site of the garden of the Western Deep Levels hospital for mine workers in 1964. (Image from Joane Pim, *Beauty is Necessary* [Cape Town: Purnell & Sons, 1971].)

13. The hospital garden three years later. (Image from Joane Pim, *Beauty is Necessary* [Cape Town: Purnell & Sons, 1971].)

14. Roelof Uytenbogaardt, *Nederduitse Gereformeerde Kerk (NGK) Welkom Wes*. (Original in possession of University of Cape Town Libraries. Courtesy UCT, Special Collections.)

15. Jane Alexander, *Security/Segurança*, 2006. (© 2018 Jane Alexander/DALRO. Photograph: Juan Guerra.)

16. Lungiswa Gqunta, *Lawn 1*, 2016. (Image courtesy of Lungiswa Gqunta and Whatiftheworld Gallery.)

17. Kemang Wa Lehulere, *Do not go far they say*, 2015. (© Kemang Wa Lehulere. Courtesy of Stevenson, Cape Town and Johannesburg.)

Acknowledgements

I want to acknowledge the financial support of my family; the postdoctoral fellowship that I held for 2016–18 through the Wits City Institute, as part of the Andrew W. Mellon Foundation's Programme in Critical Architecture and Urbanism, funded by the Foundation's prestigious international Architecture, Urbanism and the Humanities Initiative; and the Wits School of the Arts Merit Award and PhD Completion Grants (2014–15).

The Wits City Institute's Director and Chair in Critical Architecture and Urbanism Noëleen Murray created a stimulating and supportive space for writing. Professors Gerrit Olivier and David Bunn at the University of the Witwatersrand provided the intellectual direction for the project, initially as doctoral supervisors, then later as readers and interlocutors in the making of this book.

Sao Mendes from the Wits School of Arts, Suzette Jansen van Rensburg and Janie Johnson from the University of Witwatersrand libraries, and Clive Kirkwood from the University of Cape Town's Special Collections made it possible for me to work in all corners of the world. Roshan Cader from Wits University Press and project manager Lisa Compton and editor Alison Lockhart made this book possible. Zen Marie helped me to see the lawn with fresh eyes at the Zoo Lake Bowling Club, and André Prado read, edited, proofed, sacrificed and supported my writing for too many years.

Author's Note

The South African linguistic landscape is fraught with discursive danger. This book, deliberately perched precariously between the dangerous and the critical in its writing, seeks to contribute to the surfacing of the brutality of South Africa's everyday language, while at the same time addressing the sensitivities of racialised wording as it is produced and reproduced. Where an offensive term, like 'garden boy', could be avoided altogether or replaced with a potentially less offensive term, like 'gardener', without affecting the clarity of argument, it has been done. The tension between, on the one hand, a paid garden labourer (sometimes called a 'garden boy') and, on the other hand, a property owner, considered by some as the 'real' gardener, is central to Chapter 2. These subject positions were not and are not now purely linguistic. In other instances, like housing planning discourse, historically specific racial classifications – 'urban Native' (Connell et al. 1939) before 1950 and 'urban Bantu' (NBRI 1954) thereafter – reflected not only racial assumptions by white planners, but also a set of real, ontological grounds of possibility. Of course, no matter how brutal certain linguistic acts were, people found ways to resist and subvert them and this book hopes to be attentive to these tensions and contestations.

Scare quotes around troubling words such as 'boy', 'garden boy', 'houseboy', 'shamba-boy', 'maid', 'native', 'Bantu', 'kaffir', 'master', 'madam', 'dyke' and 'poor white' are used sparingly, except where they are being discussed explicitly as a concept or linguistic term – the notion of the 'urban Native'.

Similarly, names of cities, homelands, provinces, countries and terms that would have been used in specific historical times remain as they were.

Some of the sources cited and terms used in this book are in Afrikaans. In each instance, translations are provided in the text. All translations from Afrikaans are my own and reference is made to the original sources.

Introduction: The Lawn is Singing

There is a way in which the dryness of the winter veld, when the sun is very harsh and the grass is bleached very white, or else is very black from veld fires, corresponds to the tonal range of a white sheet of paper and charcoal and charcoal dust – in a way more immediately even than oil paint. There was a way in which the winter veld fires, in which the grass is burned to black stubble, made drawings of themselves. You could rub a sheet of paper across the landscape itself, and you would come up with a charcoal drawing.

— William Kentridge, 'Meeting the World Halfway: A Johannesburg Biography'

William Kentridge (2010) observes that for much of his childhood in Johannesburg he felt that he 'had been cheated of a landscape'. He explains that he wanted a landscape of 'forests, of trees, of brooks' but instead he had 'dry veld, beyond the green gardens of the city'. The 'veld' is a particularly South African notion. Originally a Dutch word meaning 'field' or 'countryside', in Afrikaans it describes a field, pasture, plain, territory or ground, and in South African botany it is used to describe a set of vegetation found in southern Africa.

I felt this too when I was growing up in Johannesburg – without a landscape. I recall sitting in the back seat of my parents' car watching fires burn across the winter veld, casting palls of smoke across the highways. I longed for green. I remember dreaming of planting lawns over the mine dumps and along the so-called green belts. The same fires would also burn the open grass veld next to our home, and the white men who owned homes in the suburb would beat the fire with sacks while my mother (and myself, when I had grown older) would spray water on the roof and lawns. Mostly, catastrophe was averted, but sometimes the fire would nick the lawn from over the precast concrete walls, scarring it black.

The lawn, consistently and perfectly mown, was a great joy to my father but also a cause for concern. On weekdays the gardeners – Laxton, after him Sam, then Benjamin and Hanock – would mow, fertilise, water, seed, spread compost and repair broken sprinklers. On weekends my shirtless father would mow his lawn. With the help of apartheid, my father's family, who at the time of the Great Depression had been *bywoners* (white Afrikaans tenant farmers, displaced from their own property, often associated with 'poor whites'), were lifted from penury and had taken on, with great commitment, the struggle to become 'good whites' (Teppo 2004). Among a number of other banal domestic practices that allowed them to lay claim to a viable white location, the lawn – its propagation, design, maintenance, appreciation and use – provided a territory and a backdrop for their (mis)adventures in white heteropatriarchy.

My mother, who during periods of my father's absence energetically fulfilled his lawn duties, was Rhodesian, as were her parents. They too were committed lawn subjects, at home and on the sports field. Internationally successful sportsmen and women, they excelled in field hockey and lawn bowls. Indeed, I have many childhood memories of my grandparents, decked out all in white and padding softly on lettuce-green turf.

The banal brutality of these kinds of scenes has not been lost on careful artistic and academic observers.

The lawn in theory

Internationally, from the late 1990s onwards, critics have provided thorough treatments of the lawn phenomenon. The bulk of the research focuses on the United States, with some research from the United Kingdom and ex-British colonies.[1] These studies put the lawn on the research agenda and opened up lines of inquiry into the lawn as a botanical, cultural, political and aesthetic object of analysis. The varied and interdisciplinary approaches have drawn on methods from environmental history, urban political economy, cultural history, urban studies, sociology and visual studies, producing a rich and provocative literature. These studies have done the hard work of tracing the histories of technological developments such as the invention and global spread of the lawnmower and the introduction and mass uptake of pesticides and fertilisers. They have asked questions about the meaning of the lawn; about the cultural values encoded in it; about how and what it signifies. Further, they have explored the lawn as a representational domain embodied in fine art, design, landscape architecture, architectural plans, advertising, ephemera, legal proceedings, poetry and so on. Some writers have also advanced a critique of the lawn from a Marxist standpoint, showing convincingly how environmentally destructive lawn economies structure supposedly personal landscape preferences. Notably, the discipline of political ecology has shown how lawns are part of a cyborg world – part natural/part social, part technical/part cultural – where non-humans play active roles in socio-natural processes. Finally, many studies have offered spirited political alternatives to the hegemony of the lawn while also acknowledging the powerful hold the lawn discourse exercises over the possibilities for speaking and acting against the lawn.[2]

As W. J. T. Mitchell formulated it in *Landscape and Power*, landscapes should be considered 'verbs', unfinished processes, inconclusive attempts at fixing a permanent vision of nature, rather than as 'nouns', which can be surveyed, owned or possessed. This theorisation attempted to address the way power functions in and through landscape, moving away from the notion that landscape *represents* power towards the idea that landscape is part of the operation of power. Drawing on Louis Althusser's notion of interpellation, Mitchell suggests that the landscape is 'not an object to be seen or text to be read, but … a process by which social and subjective identities are formed' (1994b: 1). The landscape interpellates us, he argues; that is to say, the landscape is presumed to have the power to call out to us, to hail us, as Althusser put it, and in so doing it forms us as its subjects. This counterintuitive explanation of power shifts attention away from the presumed agency of individual selfhood to a structural reading of ideology.

Since the 1994 edition of *Landscape and Power* there has been something of a re-evaluation of the verb thesis. Historian Jill Casid (2011) has argued that while Mitchell's 'verb thesis' contributed to a shift in thinking about landscapes as productive and active (especially with regard to imperialism and colonisation), it did not sufficiently consider performative accounts of power, nor did it account for the production of women, queers and disabled subjects.

In the preface to the second edition of *Landscape and Power* (2002: vii) Mitchell writes that given the chance to retitle the book he would now call it *Space, Place, and Landscape.* 'If one wanted to continue to insist,' says Mitchell, 'on power as the key to the significance of landscape',

> one would have to acknowledge that it is a relatively weak power compared to that of armies, police forces, governments, and corporations. Landscape exerts a subtle power over people, eliciting a broad range of emotions and meanings that may be difficult to specify. This indeterminacy of affect seems, in fact, to be a crucial feature of whatever force landscape can have. As the background within which a figure, form, or narrative act emerges, landscape exerts a passive force of setting, scene, and sight. (2002: vii)

To understand this 'weakness', Mitchell suggests that it is necessary to take up the notion of desire: the Freudian/psychoanalytic picture of desire as lack or longing (2005: 61) and the image of desire as a process, an 'experimental, productive force' (Ross 2010: 66–67). It is the ambiguous formulation of desire as *want* that appears most productive in unsettling the power base of landscape. To ask what landscapes want 'is not just to attribute to them life and power and desire, but also to raise the question of what it is they *lack*, what they do not possess, what cannot be attributed to them' (Mitchell 2005: 10).

Casid's response to Mitchell is evocative because she pulls in an entirely different direction, insisting on what she calls the 'isness' – the presence – of landscape by foregrounding its recalcitrance, its refusal to recede: 'from landscape as a settled place or fixed point we instead encounter landscape in the performative, landscaping the relations of ground to figure, the potentials of bodies, and the interrelations of humans, animals, plants, and what we call the "environment"' (Casid 2011: 98).

The lawn is boring, it matters and we must say so

Casid's response is an attempt to put landscape into action 'under the performative'. She describes her project as 'landscape trouble'

(2008), signalling a move to inflect *landscape* with the qualities of a verb to account for landscape as an 'ongoing process of materialization' (2011: 98–99). In response to Mitchell's aphorism that 'Like life, landscape is boring; we must not say so' (1994a: 5), Casid retorts that, in fact, 'landscape matters (and is volatile, fascinating, and queer in the ways it matters and performs); we must say so' (2011: 100).[3] The queering of the landscape is a theoretical manoeuvre that not only seeks to highlight the work of lesbian, gay, bisexual, transgender, intersex, and queer (LGBTIQ) landscapers, gardeners, writers and artists but, further, seeks a critique of the very paradigm of heteronormativity, which dominates our ideas of 'nature'. Queer theory suggests that so-called natural environments and processes of growth are not apolitical; they are caught up in a unidirectional narrative of progress and flourishing, which does not sufficiently account for the volatile, fascinating and queer in the ways humans and non-humans matter themselves. Casid's performative conception also makes an aesthetic methodological stand against the primacy of landscape painting as the proper object of landscape studies and to include installation, performance art, sound, video and sculpture in the conversation. This is to reaffirm, in a different way, Mitchell's refusal of landscape as a genre of painting in favour of landscape as 'medium' (1994a: 5). It is also to insist that landscape's 'performance' is 'not just taking place, making place, or decaying or even destroying place ... but also and importantly its being and changing in and over time without final outcome despite the illusion of "isness" and the effects of naturalization' (Casid 2011: 103). The 'isness' of landscape – its presumed presence as stable, as finished – requires the appearance of being outside of time, or after time.

Casid's formulation suggests that landscape's symbolic consolidation of power exists in an abiding paradox because landscape does not actually have a 'final outcome'. The vitality of action, labour, process, movement in, on, through, by, in front of landscape is deeply threatening to the operation of the landscape idea, which is aimed at creating the illusion of permanence and stability. Landscape is always the attempt at transforming nature or land and the open-endedness of our relationship to these, into a space of ownership, possession, belonging; a stabilisation of the present and desired future formations of power into something seemingly permanent. In this sense, landscape must fail.

Scholarship should thus be far more interested in the disproportionate tendency to record, monumentalise and remember moments of success. Is it possible to claim that the imperial garden or, even more boldly, the imperial landscape (seen as processes and movements that are multidirectional and happening over time and space) is at its core already failing? Part of the 'strategic instrumentality' (Corner 1999: 4) of imperialist landscape is to arrest decay linguistically, aesthetically and materially, to present transient victories as evidence of permanence. The strategies of postcolonial, peripheral, queer landscape art and theory are to record the always failing garden/landscape as the norm, not the aberration, and to use failure as a tool of liberation. These minoritarian positions, the postcolonial and the queer, are concerned with life on the margins, and have seldom been under the illusion that 'success' belonged equally to (white) heterosexuals and (black) queers. Embracing failure as a liberatory approach, as proposed by Jack Halberstam in *The Queer Art of Failure* (2011), means reframing failure as 'alternative ways of knowing' and modes of 'unbeing and unbecoming' (2011: 23–24). These modes of flourishing and growing can potentially be outside of the time and space of productive, capitalist heteronormativity.

The lawn in South Africa

Six old white ladies with perms, in obligatory white bowling gear, cardigans and regulation flat-soled shoes, play bowls on a Saturday afternoon. It is winter, June 1980; some of the trees around the green have lost their leaves and it is likely that the East Rand Proprietary Mines (ERPM) bowling green is less than green – brown and dormant because of the cold, rainless winters that characterise the South African highveld. The highveld is a high-altitude plateau, especially in the north-east of South Africa, between 1 500 and 2 100 metres above sea level, which includes the Free State and Gauteng provinces, and portions of the surrounding areas: the western rim of Lesotho and portions of the Eastern Cape, Northern Cape, North West, Limpopo and Mpumalanga provinces. David Goldblatt's *Saturday afternoon: bowls on the East Rand Proprietary Mines green. June 1980* (1982; see Plate 1) is shot facing east; in the background is a double-storey terrace married quarters built by architect Herbert Baker in 1910 for the mines. If we look carefully, between the trees we see a distinctive

Baker chimney, brick with a subtle flourish on the crown (Van der Walt & Birkholtz 2012). Opened in 1915 – just after Johannesburg's oldest green, Kensington Bowls Club (1914) – the ERPM bowling green, like the gardens, fields and parks of Goldblatt's photographic work *In Boksburg* (1982), appears both flat and ordinary, unremarkable.[4] This banality is not incidental; neither is the flatness inconsequential. The flat lawn embodies centuries of expertise, hours of effort, substantial capital and a particular assemblage of desire and discernment.

As a photographer, Goldblatt was drawn to the boring and everyday, 'to the quiet and commonplace, where nothing "happened" and yet all was contained and immanent' (Dubow 1998: 24). In the everyday, he saw the conditions of possibility for apartheid's insanity and brutality, and like the British Marxist art historians, cultural critics and geographers of the 1970s and 1980s who studied the 'dark side of the landscape',[5] Goldblatt was drawn, repeatedly, to the seemingly innocent landscapes of South Africa. He made it clear that his interest in landscape had nothing to do with being a 'nature lover' but rather with 'the way we act with the land, work with the land, move on it, mark it' (O'Toole 2003).

The lawn is largely absent from Goldblatt's earlier work, *Some Afrikaners Photographed* (1975). The images he captured there are landscapes of no-lawn; the Afrikaners he photographed do not seem to garden, or have gardens, but instead dance, work, farm, flirt, sing. In a later work, *The Structure of Things Then* (1998), the lawns seem terribly permanent, enduring topographies of apartheid. *In Boksburg*, his exploration of a segregated suburb, includes as many as twenty lawns. Both in the private garden and the civic sphere, these brittle black-and-white lawns form the grounds for polite, respectable white subjectivities. For instance, *At a meeting of the Voortrekkers in the suburb of Whitfield, Boksburg* records a team of '*penkoppe*' (boys) and '*drawwertjies*' (girls) squatting on the lawn with their leader. In a similar way, *Flag-raising ceremony for Republic Day (31 May) at Christian Brothers College, Boksburg. 30 May 1980* depicts an everyday kind of political event, on a bleached Johannesburg lawn. In the domestic realm, Goldblatt observes kidney-shaped swimming pools rimmed with face-brick and lawn, precast concrete fences with neatly maintained grass, and, of course, mowing. In many of his photographs, the lawn is just caught in the corner of the frame. The tiny wedge of grass, bottom left in the photograph *Girl in her new tutu on the stoep*, is perhaps the most suggestive example of the lawn functioning in a supplementary, apparently unimportant way. Even in *Saturday afternoon: bowls*, where the lawn is in every practical sense necessary, even fundamental, it exists pictorially and ideologically as part of the background. The lawn seems to just be there.

It is the lawn's just-thereness that explains, partly, why it has remained largely inoculated against sustained critique, why it has remained almost entirely politically unchallenged and is still ecologically, aesthetically and infrastructurally hegemonic.

While the lawn's goodness, innocence and neutrality may have been convincing to most planners, artists and administrators, there have always been a small group of dissenters who have resisted the lawn in subtle and explicit ways, foregrounding the politics of its surface, offering alternatives to its dominance and taking a spade to its roots. For instance, in the eighteenth century Uvedale Price famously declared that the lawn was both boring and ugly, and entirely at odds with the picturesque principles that he felt were in good taste: 'The notion that a lawn, or any meadow or pasture ground near the house, ought to be kept quite open and clear from any kind of thickets, has been one very principle cause of the bareness I have so often had occasion to censure' (1810: 175).

In twentieth-century South Africa, at the same time that Goldblatt was capturing the long shadows of highveld winter, Mike Nicol's poem 'Returning' in *Staffrider* (1984: 6) foregrounds the 'brittle lawns' of white suburbia:

> Who returns to his winter suburb
> walks familiar streets in the brown afternoons,
> another itinerant passing wide of Alsatian and Doberman.
> No-one looks up: children chase their fantasies
> across brittle lawns. A year's growth has thickened gardens
> and spawned a new generation for the nannies on the
> pavements.
> Gardeners lurk behind hedges; a woman
> shifts her chair to catch the moving sun.
> The air carries intimations of despair:
> a shower of ash lodging black in the curtains,
> bodies massacred in room after room.[6]

The vitreousness of Nicol's lawns is in stark contrast to the discursive softness of the lawns in the literary and technical archive. Apart from the brittle lawns in 'Returning' and Lungiswa Gqunta's glassy installation *Lawn 1* (see Plate 16), which I discuss in Chapter 4, the lawn is overwhelmingly and consistently described as 'soft', an 'illustration of the *beautiful*' (Jackson Downing 1853: 62; see also Johnson 1979: 154; Martin 1983: 467; Omole 2011; Stapf 1921: 88). The beauty, tranquillity and naturalness of the lawn are ideas that arrived in South Africa as part of the baggage of British empire. Even kikuyu, the lawn grass that has become naturalised in South Africa, was originally from the East Africa Protectorate and sent via Pretoria to Kew Royal Botanic Gardens in London to be classified and propagated.

The ideal of the British lawn has been unexpectedly adaptable to the politics of the South African highveld, if not always to its climate. The flat, green lawn has been planted in locations as diverse as Pretoria's Union Buildings (1913), the Voortrekker Monument (1949) and Freedom Park (2004); elite private high schools such as St Stithians, St Andrews and Roedean; the post-apartheid sculpture installation *Long March to Freedom* at Tshwane's National Heritage Monument and the sculpture park at the Nirox Foundation at the Cradle of Humankind; and in Soweto, the Hector Pieterson Memorial and Museum has a dramatic axial line of lawn connecting the place where Pieterson was shot with the entrance to the museum. The lawn, here, is a peculiar vector from 16 June 1976 to the present.

The encounter between European landscape conventions and the South African environment, what Mary Louise Pratt calls the 'contact zone' (1991), is a territory in which scholars have sought to understand the problems of colonialism, dispossession, belonging, land and labour.

J. M. Coetzee set the terms for this debate with the publication of *White Writing: On the Culture of Letters in South Africa* (1988). His approach to the landscape was very much in line with the 'dark side' landscape critics from that period who argue that landscape is an ideological concept, a 'way of seeing' (Berger 1972), which 'mystifies, renders opaque, distorts, hides, occludes reality' (Wylie 2007: 69). Among other 'dark side' landscape critics, Raymond Williams (1975), John Barrell (1983) and Ann Bermingham (1986) argue that the landscape represents to certain people their imagined relationship with nature (Cosgrove 1984) and simultaneously hides the struggles, achievements and – importantly – the labour of the 'inhabitants' of that landscape (Daniels 1989). Coetzee extended and departed from these arguments in significant ways, particularly his concern with imperialism and racism.

In *White Writing*, Coetzee describes how South African landscape art and landscape from the nineteenth to the mid-twentieth century revolved around the question of 'finding a language to fit Africa, a language that will be authentically African' (1988: 7). He was concerned with the representational politics of 'the land itself' (10); work; visibility and the discourse of idleness; European schemas of thinking Africa, especially through the picturesque and the pastoral; and race, especially by marking and historicising whiteness. Zoë Wicomb and Jennifer Beningfield have pointed out how 'white writing' is 'something incomplete, not fully adapted to its environment, something in transition' (Wicomb 1998: 372), 'plagued by doubts and insecurities … conflicts, ambiguities and silences' (Beningfield 2006a: 18). These conflicts have animated a range of scholars, producing an eloquent and politically attuned body of literature (see Carruthers 2011; Darian-Smith, Gunner & Nuttall 1996; Foster 2008; Van Sittert 2003). *Blank____Architecture, Apartheid and After*, edited by Ivan Vladislavić and Hilton Judin (1998), marks a strand of theorisation, present also in 'Naturing the Nation' (Comaroff & Comaroff 2001), concerned with the question of *after*: what possible shapes could a *post*-apartheid and *post*colonial South Africa take?

However, apart from one brief study on the lawns of Kirstenbosch National Botanical Garden in Cape Town (Mogren 2012), the only piece of research that offers a sustained, critical view of the South African lawn is David Bunn's chapter '"Our Wattled Cot": Mercantile and Domestic Spaces in Thomas Pringle's African Landscapes' (1994). Published in the influential volume *Landscape and Power*, Bunn's study of attitudes in the 1820s to landscape in the Cape Colony is important for two reasons. The first is its attention to the colonial lawn landscape and the second is how it works as part of the broader argument Mitchell advanced in *Landscape and Power*.

While Bunn critiques the naturalisation of settler subjectivity in ways that are familiar, showing how the eighteenth-century English landscape garden was exported to the periphery, he also departs in a fundamental way from the theorisation of the landscape as symbolic or representational. What he argues is that far from landscape being a symbolic expression of human intention or simply an aesthetic appreciation, landscape is, in fact, the (somewhat) independent instrument of cultural power.

Civilising grass

This book presents five introductory theses on the South African lawn, outlined below.

1. The lawn is political

The South African lawn has remained largely invisible in plain sight. Naturalised and treated as the product of common sense, the lawn appears to exist outside of politics and is commonly thought of as 'neutral in struggles for power, which is tantamount to it being placed outside ideology' (Fairclough 1989: 92). The ideological dimensions of the lawn are, however, perceptible and the discourse from which it emerges is evident in the archive. The lawn discourse governs, for instance, its colour, shape, texture, height, incline, level, orientation, relationship to buildings and so on. It also exerts control over practices, including those related to ownership and the creation, maintenance, usage, destruction, transfer and movement of the lawn. This discourse displays a strong tendency towards normative and value-based assessments of an individual lawn's compliance or non-compliance with the ideal lawn. Lawns are seldom the star of the show, even when they are. (This is partly why they remained for so long inoculated against critical inquiry.) Lawns recede into the background and are favoured as backgrounds for the *real* drama of life. Foregrounding the lawn is a political act of denaturalisation, leading to a reversal of the normative figure-ground relationship.

2. The lawn is moving

Conceptually, aesthetically, materially and ecologically the South African lawn comes from somewhere else. Indeed, it is also on its way somewhere else. Colonialism and imperialism facilitate the lawn's movement but also attempt to conceal that very movement. While colonial discourse relies on botanical transplantation and exchange, it also depends on the simultaneous impression of stasis to obscure its multidirectional and asymmetrical movements. The colonial landscape must not appear dynamic; it must seem stable, passive and immobile because timelessness and finishedness are fundamental requirements of the imperial landscape (see thesis 5). The lawn moves and grows rhizomatically: supposedly flat, even and soft, the lawn is not so much a *surface* as it is matter that connects, takes root and advances (down, up and outward). In this sense, the lawn is deep, not only because it tends to obscure what is beneath it but also because it is stubbornly knitted into and grounded in the earth. Following Gilles Deleuze and Félix Guattari, I argue that the lawn is a weed and a 'vegetable war machine' (Marks 2010).

3. The lawn is work

Lawns require labour, time and money. In the past, sheep and other animals trimmed the lawn by grazing, and in a science fiction future, 'mowbots' (Greene 1970) may well keep the lawn. However, since the eighteenth century, humans have kept the lawn. Which humans – what gender, age, race and sexuality, for what pay or reward, on which day, at what time, in what conditions, with what equipment and inputs – is determined by the lawn discourse. In South Africa, which humans keep the lawn (and under what conditions) has everything to do with race and class. Anxiety about racial idleness and the injunction to conceal labour that does not support claims of land ownership underpin representations of the lawn (Coetzee 1988). Hence, the manner in which work done to the lawn is presented and represented, acknowledged and denied, remembered and ignored is very revealing about the power at work in the landscape. In addition to the work required to keep the lawn, the lawn itself is also *at* work. To focus on the inner workings of the lawn itself is to accord it a certain vitality and to acknowledge its power to produce certain effects in human and other bodies (Bennett 2010). The lawn's work involves the complex process of producing subjects and perpetuating itself by extending rhizomatically over time and space – which is to say, colonising – without drawing too much attention to its fragility, its being-in-progress and its underlying aggression.

4. The lawn desires family

In a common-sense way, the lawn is strongly associated with children. For instance, it is quite typical for the literature to sincerely ask: but where would the children play if there was no lawn? Indeed, this question was especially vexing for white planners during the apartheid years, who worried about black children's safety and cleanliness while at play. The lawn is historically understood to be a hygienic, safe, healthy, clean, modern surface, safe from ticks, snakes, traffic and dust, and exerting a 'healthful' influence (Dreher 1997; Mellon 2009). These sanitary discourses are focused on the bodies of children, the poor, the indigent, the disabled, the racially inferior and the sexually deviant in an attempt to reform their unhealthy and unproductive modes of place making. Public parks, sports fields and domestic lawns emphasise the desirability of family, wholesomeness and middle-class respectability. In opposition to this normalising drive, so-called anti-social queer theorists encourage resistance to being incorporated into productive heteropatriarchy. According to this argument, the child is understood to be the embodiment of 'reproductive futurism', which ought to be countered by a negative queer oppositionality (Edelman 2004). The embrace of queer negativity is in direct opposition to the lawn's optimism and future orientation.

5. The lawn is a failure

The depressed, the hopeless, those without a stake are unlikely to make (good) lawns. Keeping a perfectly flat, even, green lawn is difficult and expensive work, easily compromised by extreme weather or low rainfall and so the successful lawn is often elusive, the cause of anxiety and insecurity. While the ideal lawn is understood to be fixed, permanent and durable, the lived lawn is really a mess: it is dying, flowering, rough, brown, bumpy, coarse, scratchy, dry, burnt, green, patchy, uneven and alive. It is an ideological function of the landscape medium to arrest complex processes and rhythms and to present them as stable. As a framing device, the lawn landscape was (and is) one of the tools at the disposal of the colonial and modern eye. And yet, at its heart, there is an internal contradiction because the lawn can, at best, only ever be a temporary victory. Essentially, the lawn is a landscape 'without final outcome' (Casid 2011: 103) and it is this open-endedness, this dynamic potential, that must be centred in a discussion of the colonial landscape. By queering the lawn we challenge the notion that it functions by way of injunction – No walking on the lawn! No blacks! No gays! – and that it is the binary opposite of the wilderness. The relation between the lawn and wildness is much more complicated; indeed, the lawn's relation to human and non-human actors is much more complex. The lawn is strangely suited to misuse and reuse and is constantly and consistently failing even as it persists and even as it is unusually resistant to critique.

Structure of the book

Civilising Grass consists of four chapters, which each deal with a particular aspect of lawns. These lawn moments, part of the larger lawn archive, are all located on the South African highveld, between the late nineteenth century and the present day. There is something discrete and somewhat unique about this geographic and historical selection. The discovery of gold, rapid industrialisation and crass commercialism, the Anglo-Boer War, the South African Union cemented in Pretoria, Nelson Mandela's inauguration as president of South Africa on the Union Building lawns, all played out in a climatic zone that, compared to the Western Cape and KwaZulu-Natal, is particularly unwelcoming to the arrival and imposition of the lawn. It seems to me that the highveld, particularly in winter, is perhaps the brownest landscape one could imagine – smog, veld, mine dumps and dust. And therefore, to even imagine (never mind actually plant and keep) a lawn in this place is to push the naturalness of the lawn trope to its most audacious limits.

However, I would argue that the findings of this book are relevant in general across South Africa and even in Zimbabwe, Zambia, Kenya and Tanzania because of their Anglo-colonial similarities. That said, one would expect future research to flesh out differences. For instance, a study on KwaZulu-Natal would have to reckon with the influence of Brazilian modernist landscaping and the valorisation of tropicality, as Sally-Ann Murray (2006) has pointed out, and a study of the Cape would have to take into account the specifics of Cape colonial history.

The archive for *Civilising Grass* is composed from two groups of texts: those I call 'scientific', for lack of a better term, and those I call 'artistic'. The distinction is not one that could hold up to any scrutiny; I could not possibly convince the reader that so-called scientific texts are not profoundly aesthetic, nor would I want to. To be deeply suspicious of any text that claims to be truth-telling is the inheritance of critical theory. And yet, in my archive, there is a coherent body of texts that claim to have something true to say about the lawn: *This* is how to mow it; *this* is how to plant from seed; *that* is too much water; *these* kinds of lawns are beautiful; *those* are unfashionable, uncivil, shameful and so on. These texts were written by experts – historians, administrators, scientists, botanists, teachers, gardeners, garden owners, garden writers, landscape architects and architects and they give shape to the discourses that govern the lawn. The writers often have uncomfortable things to say about 'garden boys', weeds, the poor and so on. They are overwhelmingly white – in fact, almost exclusively white – but many are women, and a couple are queer, too. They tend to write with little aesthetic or rhetorical finesse, but this lack of literary sensitivity can be read as signalling one of the ways a text of this kind makes a claim for facticity, strengthening its scientific pretensions and, possibly, its imagined lack of bias. What could be less political than advice on digging holes or choosing the right lawnmower?

If the first body of texts is characterised by its blindness to politics, the artistic texts are characterised by their blindness to the lawn. In these texts, the lawn is rarely the subject of the statement. And because the lawns I discuss are simply behind the sitter in the portrait, or in the foreground of the larger landscape or barely specified in architectural plans, they are difficult to track down and often unintended by the image-maker. This means locating lawns in artistic texts requires the collection of texts with the intuition that within the oeuvre of that author or artist there will be a lawn, somewhere. Those who have read Vladislavić, the biographer of Johannesburg, would expect to find a good many lawns in the geography of his writing, which they will. The same applies to the photographers Ernest Cole and David Goldblatt. But one would have had to have known to look there in the first place. The text collection was persistent and unsystematic – like cruising for sex in a park. The search term 'lawn' and permutations like *queer* lawn, *black* lawn, *apartheid* lawn, *green* lawn, *post/colonial* lawn, as well as translations like *grasperk* were put through digital databases and analogue searches. The first priority was South African and South African-focused texts, with an explicit intention to privilege texts by women, blacks and queers. I was willing to consider any medium: from poetry to pornography, online user comments to user-generated dictionaries, prophesies to painting, hate speech to children's homework exercises, physical places to paper plans.

In selecting the lawns for analysis I especially searched for moments in which, for instance, a literary lawn clashes with a lived lawn or where a historical archive overlays a set of spatial practices. Here it was useful to think about Henri Lefebvre's triadic conception of space, which suggests that far from being inert, neutral or pre-given, social space is a social product and every society produces its *own* space. *The Production of Space* shows that because of the 'illusion of transparency', space can appear 'luminous', 'innocent' and 'free of traps or secret places' (Lefebvre 1991: 27–28). Thus, it is possible and necessary to interpret social space as dialectically produced by representations of space, representational spaces and spatial practice (33).

Andy Merrifield explains that conceived space is dominant: expressed in numbers and systems of formalised signs, it functions in 'objectified plans and paradigms' (2006: 109). This kind of space finds its 'objective expression' in monuments and towers, in factories and office blocks, in the 'bureaucratic and political authoritarianism immanent to a repressive space' (Lefebvre 1991: 49). Spaces of representation (representational spaces) or 'lived space' are the 'nonspecialist world of argot rather than jargon', non-verbal symbols and signs (Merrifield 2006: 109), the 'clandestine or underground side of social life' (Lefebvre 1991: 33). Spatial practice or 'perceived space' includes the daily activity, which 'secretes that society's space' (38), like the 'pathways that spontaneously appear on a greensward as a result of walking patterns' (Mitchell 2002: ix) and 'routes and networks, patterns and interactions that connect places and people, images with reality, work with leisure' (Merrifield 2006: 110). This is the space of daily routine (Lefebvre 1991: 38).

As Lefebvre argues, relations between the three moments of the perceived, the conceived and the lived are 'never either simple or stable, nor are they "positive" in the sense in which this term might be opposed to "negative", to indecipherable, the unsaid, the prohibited, or the unconscious' (1991: 46). 'Space,' he argues, 'may be said to embrace a multitude of intersections' (33). The point should not be to dragoon the various spaces into domesticated intellectual submission. The goal of the present analysis is not to tame the profusion of unruly lawns.

Lefebvre's theory underpins my approach to imagined spaces, maps, photographs of geographic spaces, intentionally and unintentionally unbuilt architectural proposals, empty spaces on the page (in literature, theory and plans) and empty spaces on the ground, patterns of lived space, the imagining, creation and use of play spaces, patterns of foot traffic, uses, misuses, reappropriations, deployment, rejection of spaces on paper, in person, by the body, against and with other bodies, both dead and alive. These assemblages complicate authoritative representation: they recognise the limitations of discursive analysis and attempt (within limits) to trace its silences. The goal is, however, not simply to examine the spaces from different angles or see different sides of the story. Rather, it is to examine how landscape and power are at work in producing human and non-human subjects in a process that is complex, open-ended, fraught and messy.

In Chapter 1, I work towards an operational definition of the lawn. By way of a discursive analysis of a number of key 'scientific' or truth-claiming texts from 1260 to the present, based on an extensive survey of English (as well as a limited collection of Latin, French and Afrikaans) gardening and landscape texts, the chapter identifies modes or themes. What the discourse analysis shows is a highly regulated terrain, with clear patterns governing what is and is not sayable and doable with respect to the lawn. It also shows a remarkable persistence over the long term – sometimes against all empirical evidence to the contrary. The lawn is understood in overwhelmingly positive terms, except for some picturesque writers of the eighteenth century and later anti-lawn campaigners. The overwhelming historical consensus is that the lawn is a good, clean, healthy and modern surface, worth aspiring to and worth the vast amounts of energy, effort and worry required to keep it as it should – indeed, *must* – be.

However hegemonic it may be, the lawn discourse is not totalising, and this chapter begins to identify many ambivalences, silences and contradictions. To trace a discourse is to be attuned to what was unsayable and undoable. By its nature, an archive excludes numerous subaltern voices. The small representation of working-class black female and black male voices is an expected limitation to encounter in a discursive study in a country with South Africa's racial history. There is an acute need for primary empirical data on *lived* landscape from below, as it were, which would profoundly enrich our understanding of, and challenge our arguments about, the relationship between landscape and race. Apart from the absence of certain types of voices (a limitation of the methodology), the lawn (as a medium) itself functions in some instances as a kind of absence. As an ideal form, the lawn is often not fully accomplished, or indeed planted at all. Its normative and normalising frame can exercise its power even as a mental abstraction, a literary assumption or mode of seeing. Apart from these kinds of silences, certain internal contradictions unsettle the account of lawn landscape as fixed and permanent. One becomes aware of a kind of neurosis at the lawn's limits and boundaries. Many of these fears and anxieties are barely whispers but are nascent of a challenge from the margins.

Chapter 2 engages with the fundamental quality of the lawn: that it must be made and kept. It requires material inputs, competencies, tools, time, labour. In the South African context, these conditions of possibility are constituted by and constituting of racial inequality. The chapter builds an extensive discursive analysis of the 'garden boy' and his place in the lawn landscape, arguing that the figure of the garden boy is important, under-studied and quintessentially southern African. He demonstrates the complex relationship between raced and gendered human and non-human life that characterises the colonial landscape. The garden boy's subjection to his master/mistress, the stunting of his chronology, his abuse, his embodiment of white fear, his body as a machine, challenge the landscape's attempted effacement of labour. While obviously made, the lawn still manages to hide or forget the labour that must continuously make it, the process of its emergence, the tenuous accomplishment that requires consistent and constant attention. The tendency to erase black labour is made all the more obvious by the instances where white garden work is recorded and monumentalised. The meaning of these different acts and the disparities in their modes of representation draw attention to the problems of race and respectability as they manifest in the domestic space. This chapter also attempts to examine the relationship between white women and the lawn. In what could be called a 'Rhodesian' discourse, women memoirists and novelists attempt to write a place for themselves in relation to black labour and the garden landscape.

Chapter 3 investigates a period of optimism, early- to mid-twentieth century, during which the lawn signified, often in entirely unstated and unconscious ways, one of the promises of modernity. The utopian discourses that energised much of the planning and urban design by white planners, just before and during apartheid, drew inspiration from and were part of international debates that were consummately amenable to the kind of racial social engineering desired in South Africa. This chapter attempts to historicise the landscape preferences of these technocrats and to connect their (so far unstudied) garden designs with the broader, established literature on apartheid spatiality. That these official 'representations of space' never materialised in the ways that were imagined and hoped for is to be expected. Thus, this chapter emphasises the multifarious ways in which 'lived modernisms' (Le Roux 2014) disrupt the sites under investigation, producing dynamic, unexpected and dangerous spaces. The chapter examines three sites: first, an audacious and unbuilt high-rise township for 20 000 'urban natives', designed in 1939 by radical University of Witwatersrand students; second, the assemblage of spatial production in the black township of KwaThema, both historical and contemporary; and third, the landscape designs for the mining town of Welkom by Joane Pim and, as a contrapuntal reading, the landscape of the Welkom-Wes Nederduitse Gereformeerde Kerk by Roelof Uytenbogaardt. The case studies in this chapter provide a critique of the lawn's teleological orientation towards progress and instead suggest, borrowing from Bruno Latour, that the lawn has never been modern (1991).

Drawing on anti-social queer theory, Chapter 4 explores the notion of failure as a potential site of freedom from heteropatriarchal capitalism and its teleology. Doing bad things to and with the lawn means including into the archive narratives of inappropriate, tacky, sleazy, perverted, incorrect lawn keeping and usage. The chapter presents three particular examples. The first is an analysis of *Pennisetum clandestinum*, better known as kikuyu grass, a remarkably mobile botanical actor that, after being 'discovered' in what was then the East Africa Protectorate, travelled first as a cutting in a milk-tin to Pretoria, then to London and then back to South Africa and other parts of the world. Officially categorised as an 'excellent colonizer' (Quattrocchi 2006: 1637), kikuyu's vitality, mobility and aggressiveness offer a counterpoint to the dominant discourse that the lawn is peaceful, stable and immobile. The second example is Joubert Park in Johannesburg. The narrative of the park's decline from Edwardian promenading ground to post-apartheid blight provides an opportunity to question the supposed failure of modernity. Contrary to what is often imagined, the photographic records of the park demonstrate the versatility and amenability of the lawn to alternative and incorrect uses. The third case study, the lawn in Marlene van Niekerk's novel *Triomf* (1999), continues the elaboration of possible disruptions by and desecration of the landscape. Whereas the analysis of Joubert Park examines the threat of failing public space, the failing yard of the 'poor white' Benade family provides an opportunity to examine the possible repercussions of wrongful gardening for neighbourhood sociality. With the spectre of the 1994 elections and the end of apartheid hanging over the Benades, we witness obscene, funny, abject and violent effects in their garden. The landscape fails to contain the ambiguous claims of ownership and belonging to the land.

Chapter 1
The Lawn Discourse

(n.) A grassy place in front of my house that you should stay the fuck off of.

— TenInchPlaya, urbandictionary.com

In *Travels and Adventures in Southern Africa* George Thompson describes his arrival at the residence of his friend Mr Thornhill in the Eastern Cape. He remarks that it is 'one of the most beautiful spots in Albany, with lawns and copsewoods, laid out by the hand of Nature, that far surpass many a nobleman's park in England' (1827: 20). The image of the lawn provides Thompson with a familiar convention by which to order the landscape and bring it within a British frame. He is not content simply to note that the lawns and copsewoods are thoroughly English; he stresses that they would 'surpass' an English landscape garden.

Thompson's comment provides insight into the logic of British imperial adjudication and 'measurement' and also reveals the way in which landscape is in the service of class. The naturalness of the lawn appears as a sign 'of the aristocratic landowner's improving hand' (Bunn 1994: 152). Even in England where the lawn was thoroughly naturalised, commentators were well aware that vast amounts of labour and capital were involved in making and keeping lawns, although this was often downplayed or even purposefully hidden, as in the American example of Andrew Jackson Downing, who in the 1840s had his lawns mowed at night by 'invisible hands' so that family and guests would not have to witness this 'distasteful activity' (Jenkins 1994a).

It seems to me that this impulse is more pronounced in the colony and serves not only to keep out of the frame the 'invisible hands' but further to assert that the 'hand of Nature' is responsible. If the English landscape garden of this period strived for an affected naturalness that served as evidence of the naturalness of its owners, a landscape garden discovered in Africa that *actually* required no labour must surpass that of a nobleman's.

This chapter defines the concept of the lawn as a transplanted concept that crosses the colonial threshold. The idea of the lawn, with all that is connected to it, is confronted by a different physical reality, a place where the lawn does not exist, or does not yet exist, or has yet to find its place in a new environment; thus it is often imagined, conceptually placed within or read into the landscape, as something that is yet to be made. The discourse (which includes the sense of an ideal lawn) is largely shaped already but now has to be integrated with a new environment. Thus the concept of lawn hovers between the ideal and the real.

A non-event

> *The more they tried to make it just like home,*
> *the more they made everybody miss it.*
>
> — *Apocalypse Now* (Coppola 1979)

The challenge for a travel writer, who is a 'verbal painter', is that he or she 'must render momentously significant what is, especially from a narrative point of view, practically a non-event' (Pratt 2007: 198).

Captain William Cornwallis Harris was a British diplomat, adventurer, hunter, author and amateur painter whose book *Wild Sports of South Africa: Being the Narrative of an Expedition from the Cape of Good Hope* (1839) describes his adventures in the Transvaal. His precision made his records of African fauna useful in the imperial metropole and interesting as historical documents rather than literary creations. His florid landscape prose is a standard – that is to say, typical and unremarkable – representation of the lawn idea of this period.

In *Wild Sports of South Africa* Harris describes his escape from a fierce battle, then an evening's journey and thereafter the morning lifting the 'curtain' on the landscape. By his account, the view was not the 'dreary waste' such as he had just been travelling through, but rather an 'extensive park'. He describes the scene before him: 'A lawn, level as a billiard-table, was everywhere spread with a soft carpet of luxuriant green grass, spangled with flowers, and shaded by spreading acacia' (1839: 55). He populates the prelapsarian tableau with exotic animals and flowers that 'yielded [an] aromatic and overpowering perfume'.

This passage exemplifies Mary Louise Pratt's three standard elements of the imperial trope: 'the mastery of the landscape, the estheticizing adjectives, the broad panorama anchored in the seer' (2007: 205).

It is necessary to address Harris's deployment of a number of standard lawn tropes – levelness ('as a billiard-table'), softness ('a carpet'), 'luxuriant' greenness[1] – but I want to defer close analysis of these grammatical elements for now. It is enough to note at this point that his lawn possesses the attributes that would qualify it *as* a lawn and qualify it to be *found* as such. What I want to draw attention to is the strangeness of Harris's discovery: the arrival at a lawn that does not (yet) exist. It is an entirely literary construction of a cultivated terrain requiring no labour, though implying labour; a prefiguring of the lawns that were to come and the real hands that would get dirty digging. This 'lawn', this level, soft, green, luxuriant, decorated carpet, is 'only' veld, a field in drag. This passage demonstrates a conceptual transformation and appropriation of the landscape through the eye. Harris is making a lawn where there is none. In terms of colonial discourse, the already present lawn is a form of welcoming; an acknowledgement, so to speak, of the universality of the idiom.

I would like to highlight two syntactic characteristics in this passage. The first, which is only suggested, is that the lawn is set up in a binary relationship with the 'other' landscape – the 'dreary waste'. This binary of garden/wilderness is a central organising principle of lawn literature and is more explicitly articulated in passages from John Buchan's *The African Colony* (1903), discussed in more detail later in this chapter. The second aspect is the metaphor of the interior evoked by Harris in images of the billiard-table and the soft carpet. The archive contains many other instances of interior language to describe lawns; the carpet is only the most regularly occurring (Eliovson 1983: 59; Kellaway 1907: 55; Martin 1983: 467; Rogers 1995; Sheat 1956: 15; Waugh 1926: 83).[2] Thomas Meehan also tells us that a lawn is to the garden as 'a tapestry is to the parlor' (1868: 103); and *Home Gardening in South Africa* explains that a 'well-kept lawn improves the appearance of a garden as much as a rich carpet improves the appearance of a room' (Smith 1940: 216). The notion of the garden as an exterior room is an important concept that emerges in South Africa modernist planning discourse.

We know from historians that in eighteenth-century London 'it was taken for granted that any house of reasonable size should have a billiard room' (Polsky 1969: 22) and, while billiards could be played almost anywhere, for respectable gentlemen it was important to distance themselves from the morally deviant (who had more and more taken up billiards) and play at home or in upper-class meeting places. Harris's gentlemanly figuration of the lawn as an interior space – a domestic space – complicates simple notions about the gendering of domesticity and asks to what degree lawn can be thought of as an exemplar of wilderness domestication.

Before moving on to a more thorough elaboration of the lawn/wilderness binary in Buchan, I want to draw attention to the painterly quality of Harris's account. It is a description of a piece of land that has composed itself to be painted, a 'scene' that is decorated – 'spangled' and 'shaded'. This notion of self-presentation, where the mountains 'present themselves' and the country 'opens up', is typical of a colonial picturesque (Pratt 2007: 59). Landscape is 'mediated land, land that has been aesthetically processed,' notes Malcom Andrews. 'It is land that has arranged itself, or been arranged by the artistic vision, so that it is ready to sit for its portrait' (1999: 7). There are two strongly related ideas here. One is nature arranging itself; the other is nature being arranged by the artistic vision. While the description may be in terms of an artistic vision, the idea that nature presents itself as lawn or garden (that it does not have to be re-presented as such, or transformed into lawn/garden) would seem to strengthen the domestication of nature.

The archive is packed with picturesque explanations of the lawn as the 'groundwork' of the 'garden picture' (Waugh 1926: 83). Jackson Downing has this to say about the artistic nature of the lawn: 'As a general rule, the grass or surface of the lawn answers as the principal light, and the woods or plantations as the shadows, in the same manner in nature as in painting' (1849: 109). *Standard Garden Practice for Southern Africa* suggests that a lawn is an 'integral part of the garden picture' (Sheat 1956: 15); *Good Morning Gardeners* says that a lawn can be said 'to provide the canvas upon which the overall picture is painted' (Jeffs 1964: 9); and Wilhelm Miller talks about 'bold pictures on lawns' (1913: 227). The painterly framing of the lawn reaches its apex in suburban guides where flowers and shrubs become compositional elements in amateur garden paintings. *The Southern African Garden Manual*, for example, exhorts its readers to 'arrange shrub borders around the edge of the lawn … This will serve the same purpose as the frame to a picture' (1958: 20). Uvedale Price, in *Essays on the Picturesque*, offers one of the very few contrarian opinions: 'I have frequently heard it wondered at, that a green lawn, which is so charming in nature, should look so ill when painted … it does look miserably flat and insipid in a picture' (1794: 291).

The man on the hilltop

John Buchan was a young man when Lord Alfred Milner, high commissioner for South Africa and governor of the Cape, recruited him in 1901. He was twenty-six when he arrived to supervise the improvement of conditions in Anglo-Boer War concentration camps (Dubow 2006: 188). He stayed for two years, during which time he wrote *The African Colony: Studies in Reconstruction* (1903). After leaving the colonial service in South Africa, Buchan continued to write prolifically, publishing well over 100 titles. Some works like *The African Colony*, with a very small print run and a direct focus on policy makers, were not well known outside of bureaucratic circles. Other publications were immensely popular; the spy novel *The Thirty-nine Steps* (1915) was even adapted for film by Alfred Hitchcock in 1935. In addition to his literary career, Buchan continued in imperial public service, which culminated in a baronetcy as the governor-general of Canada.

Whether he was working as an author or bureaucrat, landscape was foundational for Buchan; the land was the place from which to speak. Romantic notions of belonging, even destiny, pervade his work and laid the grounds for a nationalist interpretation of the South African landscape as the natural location for national identity. In *Washed with Sun: Landscape and the Making of White South*

Africa Jeremy Foster comments on this entanglement: 'Strikingly lyrical passages of landscape description permeate all sections of *The African Colony*, leading one to ask whether it was intended as a sober political document promoting New Imperialism or a piece of impressionist landscape writing. The answer to this question is probably "both"' (2008: 121).

The African Colony makes the argument for a white South African national identity located not in language or even politics but rather *in* the landscape (Henshaw 2003: 13). In essence, it is a forceful argument for, explanation of and elaboration of Milner's economic and political policies and, indeed, a response to Milner's critics in London.

In Buchan's own words, *The African Colony* is a kind of 'Guide Book' in three parts. Part I, 'The Early Masters', is a collection of 'historical sketches' dealing with the 'native', 'uitlander' and 'Boer', which, while attempting to articulate a sympathetic history of the Boer – as potential co-labourer with the British, as possessing 'natural dignity beyond praise' and an 'antique kindliness' (Buchan 1903: 74) – succeeded in causing much offence in its descriptions of the Boer's 'mental sluggishness', 'blind faith' and 'meagre imagination' (70). Part II, 'Notes of Travel', offers a series of brief '*carnets de voyage*' or travelogues concerned with the 'configuration of the land'. These travel narratives 'are devoted almost entirely to descriptions of unimproved, sparsely inhabited rural districts' and not urban centres (Foster 2008: 122). Part II conforms to the rules that govern Victorian travel writing as laid out by Pratt in *Imperial Eyes* (2007). The most explicitly 'non-political' of the three sections, 'Notes of Travel' deploys what Pratt has termed 'strategies of innocence' – that is to say, 'strategies of representation whereby European bourgeois subjects seek to secure their innocence in the same moment as they assert European hegemony' (2007: 9). Part III, 'The Political Problem', offers a 'modest diagnosis' or what Buchan calls a 'highly controversial sketch' (1903: xvi) of the issues to be faced in South Africa. In prefacing his 'diffidence' with regard to this task, he apologises to his 'friends' (xviii) for his 'audacity' and frames his role as outside observer in terms of a landscape trope: 'A critic on a neighbouring hill-top will be a poor guide to the flora and fauna of the parish below; but he may be a good authority on its contours, on the height of its hills and the number of its rivers, and he may, perhaps, be a better judge of the magnitude of a thunderstorm coming out of the west than the parishioner in his garden' (xiii).

The passages I examine are from two different travelogues in Part II. Both are instances where Buchan deploys the lawn trope and in both cases he makes explicit reference to the conventions of Englishness. A binary between the inside/outside, garden/wilds and journey/arrival is set up in both passages. In the first instance, the 'contrast' Buchan suggests is 'between the common veld and [the] garden' (126); and in the second, between two different greens: the 'dull green', which he wishes would 'give place to tender green' (129).

A garden on the edge of the wilderness

The passage below is from 'The Wood Bush' (Buchan 1903: 113), the record of a journey dated January 1903. It describes a mid-summer afternoon in the lowveld, an area of which Buchan was exceedingly fond, which he called the 'true Hesperides' and the 'New Eden' (117). Buchan is astride his horse on the plateau of the Haenartsburg and describes the prospect below. He *is* the man on the hilltop, or what Pratt has called the 'seeing-man' (2007: 9):

> It is England, richer, softer, kindlier, a vast demesne laid out as no landscape gardener could ever contrive, waiting for a human life worthy of such an environment. But it is more – it is that most fascinating of all types of scenery, a garden on the edge of a wilderness. And such a wilderness! Over the brink of the meadow, four thousand feet down, stretch the steaming fever flats. From a cool fresh lawn you look clear over a hundred miles of nameless savagery. The first contrast which fascinates the traveller is between the common veld and this garden; but the deeper contrast, which is a perpetual delight to the dweller, is between his temperate home and the rude wilds beyond his park wall. (Buchan 1903: 126)

In the garden on the edge of the wilderness, Buchan is writing the lawn into being, providing a memory of a lawn which is not real, not *yet*. The 'lawn' Captain Harris wrote about was drawn from memories of British landscapes he had seen, as was Buchan's lawn. But Harris was not a bureaucrat, officially charged with solving problems of land resettlement and immigration. Buchan was officially empowered to look, with the clear intent to find places that were suitable, habitable. So, moved by the landscape, his search shifts towards finding a life 'worthy' of the environment, rather than the other way around. Buchan sees a lawn that does not exist but that, in part as a result of the text he wrote, would actually become a lawn.

Following the notion that for Buchan the lawn originates linguistically – it is first of all written – it is worth analysing the things the lawn *does* in this passage: firstly, it provides a place, on which to stand, from which to look, from which to write; and secondly, the lawn (that is to say, the 'lawn-contrast') fascinates and delights. This place comes about through a set of oppositions or contrasts and is the appropriate place from which to appreciate them. Essentially the binary in operation is between lawn and wilderness, which is underpinned by a more fundamental binary between civilised and uncivilised. This binary is elaborated descriptively as the 'inside' (garden, richer, softer, kindlier, cool, fresh, temperate, home), in opposition to the 'outside' (common veld, rude, steaming, nameless savagery). Aside from the explicit articulation of the South African wilderness as 'veld', set up against the garden, and the expected colonial racial language (savagery) and class language (rude/kindly), I want to draw attention to the passage's structuring of difference through temperature. While it may be sensible to claim that lawns *actually* do feel cooler than some other ground surfaces, especially in Africa, it is worth noting that the lawn's coolness is generally collocated with terms like hygiene, 'clean, cool' (Waugh 1926: 83) and cultivation, 'cool, green, cultivated' (Eliovson 1968: 113). It can hardly be claimed that Buchan's contrast between the 'cool, fresh, temperate' garden with 'steaming fever flats' is a description dealing with empirical notions of hot and cold. It is not that the 'steaming fever flats' are *bad* per se; their hotness is necessary. Without the heat the temperate garden would be rather boring. It is worth noting how often temperature is thought of as an *appearance* rather than a feeling; as both Sima Eliovson (1968: 113) and E. N. Anderson note, the lawn '*looks* cool' (1972: 180; emphasis added). Without the nameless (unnameable), sensual, uncivilised flats, the accomplishment of the garden would only be 'England', not 'richer, softer, kindlier', for that requires the comparative logic, richer (than), softer (than), kindlier (than). This relational grammar sets up repetitive contrasts that move from a simple contrast to a 'deeper' contrast. The simple contrast is for the traveller, but the deeper contrast, which is delightful, is reserved for the dweller.

In order for this logic to function, a boundary concept is required to mark what is 'in' and 'out' and, therefore, who or what is civilised, uncivilised, civilisable. Buchan's description demarcates and encloses the lawn with an 'edge', a 'brink', a 'park wall'.

One is struck that there already is a 'natural' border: the brink of the meadow. Buchan shrinks and domesticates the panoramic view, ending with the 'park wall'. Furthermore, the idea of garden and countryside forming an undivided whole differs from the physical and conceptual divisions that govern the Buchan passage. So, apart from the idea of a boundary between garden and wilderness, one also has the idea of the garden being united with the environment.

The notion that the lawn is bounded is both fundamental and implicit, just as it is mostly subtly articulated in the literature. That the lawn must end is a certainty; how it ends is a matter of taste. Price preferred 'a just gradation from highly embellished to simple nature: just as the polished lawn ... does afterwards to the wilder wood-walks and pastures' (1810: 165). The 'gradation' Price advocated was made possible by the innovation of the 'ha-ha', which was a sunken barrier or a ditch that kept the grazing animals out of the garden without interrupting the vistas. It first appears in *La théorie et la pratique du jardinage* by A. J. Dezallier d'Argenville (published in 1709), translated into English as *The Theory and Practice of Gardening* (published in 1712) and then taken up by nobleman Horace Walpole in *On Modern Gardening*, where he called it the 'Ha! Ha!', the 'capital stroke [in] the destruction of walls for boundaries' (1780: 59). That the ability of the ha-ha to hide boundaries and to 'create the illusion that the garden and the surrounding countryside was one and undivided' (Thacker 1985: 183) should have become so fashionable at the very moment of accelerated enclosures gives pause for thought. Later writers sometimes preferred a more explicit border 'of shrubbery [that] makes a lawn more beautiful, because it acts like the frame of a picture' (Miller 1913: 91).

The question of how to define the boundary of the lawn is fundamental to the definition of the concept of the North American lawn and has led to some fiery literary scuffles – such as the tiff that took place between Eugene Klapp, editor of *The House Beautiful* (1897), and Wilhelm Miller of *Garden Magazine* (1909). Klapp, drawing on French and British examples, made the argument for picturesque walls and fences in order to end the 'monotony' of American yard culture and to provide more privacy. Miller strongly disagreed, insisting that the lawn, connected to the public domain, is a gesture of civil solidarity: 'The American idea is to have the front yard of every small place composed of an unbroken lawn ... This frank, open treatment which subordinates the individual's rights to the park-like effect of the whole street, is fit expression of a democratic people. But such publicity is abhorrent to the English, with whom privacy is the dominant passion' (Miller 2000: 51).

The North American lawn is what Michael Pollan calls an 'egalitarian conceit' (1998: 4). The seemingly unbounded front lawn presents the illusion of a collective landscape, which is held in a kind of common. This common is, however, at odds with and structured by the competing claims of private ownership, which must be seen to be relinquished for the greater good of the park-like effect. Thus, public displays of private ownership take on an implicitly political character, a democratic ideal expressed through conformity. Lawn maintenance and lawn conformity, that is to say, the willingness and ability to blend your landscape, takes on a moral and civic quality.

In *American Green* Ted Steinberg supposes that the American lawn ideal was exported to Canada, Australia and New Zealand (2006: 62) but there is little evidence to support this claim. Instead, the literature supports the idea that the modern lawn is derived from and is a more or less successful approximation of the English lawn. Indeed, by the mid-nineteenth century, writers on both sides of the Atlantic ascribed, if not 'ownership', then certainly mastery of the lawn to the English. Even Jackson Downing, who is credited by some historians with 'importing' the English tradition to the United States (Macinnis 2009: 66), acknowledged that 'the unrivalled beauty of the "velvet lawns" of England has passed into proverb' (1849: 525). *The Gardeners' Magazine of Botany, Horticulture, Floriculture, and Natural Science* notes that 'smooth, polished turf is one of the principal charms of the English garden' (1850: 148) and Reginald Blomfield writes, 'The turf of an English garden is probably the most perfect in the world' (1892: 143). Two further examples: 'the English brought across the sea the memory of the green lawns of England and did their best to make memory a reality' (Fairbridge

1924: 41) and 'a fine green swathe is the epitome of the English Garden' (King & Oudolf 1998: 22).

Buchan not only imagined an English sense to the landscape, he also imagined an English sense of ownership. As W. J. T. Mitchell has emphasised, the '"prospect" that opens up is not just a spatial scene but a projected future of "development" and exploitation' (1994a: 17). Buchan's reference to the 'demesne' suggests that he 'was imagining a quasi-feudal, pre-capitalist ownership of the land, with the implication that local people would be allowed little more status than rural serfs' (Wittenberg 2004: 131). The *Oxford English Dictionary* describes a demesne as 'land immediately attached to a mansion, and held along with it for use or pleasure'. By referring to the landscape as a demesne, Buchan attaches the land to a grand home, presuming an owner, of both home and lands. For Buchan, the landscape he finds is still '*waiting* for a human life worthy' of it and *The African Colony* should be read as a kind of advertisement intended to attract white English immigration as part of Milner's plan to ensure imperial domination.

Lawn trouble

The second passage from Buchan is something of a Victorian temper tantrum, dated August 1903. Taken from the beginning of Chapter 10, 'The Great Road North' (Buchan 1903: 146), the extract describes his trip in the Transvaal, from the Repatriation Depot at Pietersburg. He spends some time on the topic of 'The Road', the imagined highway from the Cape to Egypt, on which he is travelling. The road, he writes, is 'insufficiently provided with water', has no signposts, no inns, no 'white habitations' and at some points must be navigated by 'the eye of Faith'. To the frustrated writer, it is as if 'lions [did] the survey work and wild pigs the engineering' (148)!

The passage in question is one of Buchan's 'arrival scenes', a narrative type that is 'a convention of almost every variety of travel writing and serves as a particularly potent site for framing relations of contact and setting the terms of its representation' (Pratt 2007: 77). Buchan and his men are about to set up camp for the night. He describes the dusk; it is August, winter, and the veld is 'bleak, dusty ... a sombre grey':

> The great mountain walls were dim with twilight, but there was day enough left to see the immediate environs of the road. They had a comical suggestion of a dilapidated English park ... the coarse bush grass seemed like neglected turf. It is a resemblance which dogs one through the bush veld. You are always coming to the House and never arriving. At every turn you expect a lawn, a gleam of water, a grey wall; soon, surely, the edges will be clipped, the sand will cease, the dull green will give place to the tender green of watered grass. But the House remains to be found. (Buchan 1903: 151)

I want to draw attention to two grammatical elements in this passage: the lack of lawn care ('dilapidated', 'neglected') and softness ('coarse bush grass'/'tender green of watered grass'). J. M. Coetzee's analysis of the picturesque in *White Writing* addresses the likelihood of 'the European eye' being disappointed in Africa if it seeks in African landscapes European tones and shades (1988: 39). The 'white' eye is 'continually on the lookout for green', and thus the lack of deep greens, shade and subtle modulations of light, and the limited reflective surfaces of water frustrate the imposition of picturesque conventions (42).

In the scene above Buchan is writing the anti-lawn: a landscape evocation that stands in contrast to the lawn. The anti-lawn is not a repository of wilderness: this is the tension set up, in the previous scene, between a lawn (real or imagined, it does not matter) and the wilderness. In this case, the anti-lawn is the imagining of dilapidation and neglect – not as the opposite of the colony, but as a sign of its anxiety. Buchan's picture of the neglected and dilapidated 'lawn' draws on and inverts the archetype of the 'well-kept' lawn. Nominally, a well-kept space refers to one that is, according to the *Oxford English Dictionary*, 'maintained in good order or condition' and is 'clean, tidy and cared for' (*Cambridge Dictionary*). The disappointment of the passage is caused not only by the absence of lawn but also by the absence of 'the House'. The lawn implies habitation, permanence and care. It also marks the end of a journey, a return to the domestic, which the relentless African landscape never seems to provide. Buchan is dogged by a suggestion that the lawn is ultimately only a comic resemblance. He wishes to impose the orderliness of lawn onto the landscape but is defeated.

Experts advise that a lawn must not only be kept, but it must also be *well kept*. Keeping implies a keeper who owns, or is paid to care for, the lawn and the capacity, knowledge, competencies, capital, tools, materials and desires that make it possible to do the labour of keeping the lawn. The literature is full of advice on what to do to attain 'the restful delight of a well-kept lawn' (Jeffs 1964: 9), including trimming leading to a 'well-kept air' (Taylor 2008: 277) and mowing in 'stripes [to] emphasise the calm and orderliness of a well-kept lawn' (Johnson 1979: 154). On a secondary level, one encounters a question of capacity and evaluation: how to know if a lawn is well kept and to be able to take pleasure in it. A well-kept lawn 'is not only a joy to its owner but all those whose privilege it is to admire its gracious expanse of verdure' (Jeffs 1964: 9).

The reading of Buchan's passage can be augmented with that of another imperialist – James Froude, writing about his travels through the colonies a few years earlier. In *Oceana, or England and Her Colonies*, Froude describes his arrival at a homestead in Australia. In his account, the well-kept lawn is an important indicator of the family's accomplishment of Englishness and of their class position: 'A clean-mown and carefully-watered lawn, with tennis-ground and croquet-ground ... we had arrived, in fact, at an English aristocrat's country house reproduced in another hemisphere, and shone upon at night by other constellations. Inside, the illusion was even more complete ... We found a high-bred English family – English in everything except that they were Australian-born, and cultivated perhaps above the English average' (1886: 121). The lawn that Froude 'discovers' (for surely it is a discovery, a 'non-event') is, in Homi Bhabha's formulation, 'almost the same, but not quite' (1994: 86). The lawn *appears* to be a convincing 'reproduction' and completed 'illusion', except that, as Froude notes later in the passage, instead of 'our delicate grass there is buffalo-grass, whose coarse fibre no care in mow'ing [*sic*] can conceal' (quoted in Macinnis 2009: 93). Bhabha's conception of mimicry as resemblance containing 'both mockery and a certain menace' (1994: 86) can help to explain why Buchan would have described the landscape's imperfections as 'comical', and why Eliovson would worry that a badly kept lawn would be a 'mockery' (1968: 113). The lawn 'reproduced in another hemisphere' will be 'a "blurred copy" ... that can be quite threatening. This is because mimicry is never very far from mockery, since it can appear to parody whatever it mimics' (Ashcroft, Griffiths & Tiffin 2007: 125). This failure to fully approximate is unsettling because it 'locates a crack in the certainty of colonial dominance, an uncertainty in its control of the behaviour of the colonized'. The colonial lawn cannot be complete; it is a 'resemblance which dogs one', suggesting a 'house', suggesting a 'gleam of water', suggesting a 'grey wall' and enclosing a property to which you 'are always coming … and never arriving' (Buchan 1903: 151).

Unkind soil

'Botany at the point of political unification of South Africa was an activity for people who had plenty of leisure time and high-society connections' (Anker 2001: 54). Dorothea Fairbridge was one such well-connected Cape lady. The 'romantic and charismatic doyen of South African Englishness' (Dubow 2006: 187), she was one of the leading members of the so-called 'Closer Union' loyalists, 'a group of architects, artists, writers, historians, archivists and photographers, all of whom were dedicated to the idea of a united South Africa' (Merrington 1995: 653) and who 'would encourage imperial links, along with a conciliatory sense of national heritage' (Merrington 1999: 230). Fairbridge was closely connected to Lord Milner – with whom she is rumoured to have had an affair (Dick 2005: 6) – and Lady Florence Phillips, who was her friend and patron. Florence Phillips, the wife of Randlord Sir Lionel Phillips, a prominent social and cultural figure in the country, was a co-founder of the Johannesburg Art Gallery. As well as supporting Fairbridge's writing, Lady Phillips also commissioned and sponsored the lumbering and weighty *Flora of South Africa* by Rudolf Marloth (1913–32). She also, after 1910, funded *The State*, a pro-Union periodical, which was orientated towards the 'construction of a new ameliorative South African identity' (Merrington 1995: 654) and included articles on design by Fairbridge and Herbert Baker and other friends.

Fairbridge's coterie successfully lobbied for the founding of Kirstenbosch National Botanical Garden and the Botanical Society in the Cape, a major coup in the ongoing battle between the Cape botanists and the officially sanctioned Pretoria Herbarium (Carruthers 2011: 259; Dubow 2006). In addition to being a founding member of the Guild of Loyal Women of South Africa, whose subtitle 'Daughters of the Empire' left little doubt about their political allegiances (Dick 2005: 6), she also was a founder of the Commonwealth War Graves Commission and the Michaelis Art Collection (Merrington 1995). Fairbridge was a well-regarded writer. She penned five novels, the controversial *A History of South Africa* (published in 1918), a number of heritage-related and botanical publications, travelogues, essays, short stories and articles.

Gardens of South Africa was published in 1924 and emerged during what Foster calls the '"heyday of landscape", a time when the discursive use of landscape as a prop of imaginary identity was most intense in South Africa' (2005: 302). The book is a tangle of political philosophy, race theory, botany, name dropping, garden history and practical garden advice: *House & Leisure* magazine meets Thomas Malthus. There are many uncomfortable moments in the text, including a discussion on the virtues of kikuyu grass, which was then new in the Transvaal (Fairbridge 1924: 34), alongside zealous imperial, and racist, exhortations like '[the] gardens that grow peacefully on the lands that were once the Black Man's and may be the Black Man's again if the White Folk of South Africa let themselves forget the necessity for standing together, shoulder to shoulder, to hold the land for Civilisation' (37). It is unfortunate, according to some (Merrington 1995; Wylie 2011), though not at all surprising, that Fairbridge's writing has remained unfashionable after apartheid and also under-theorised. The passage below is taken from an anecdote on 'mine gardens' of the Reef, which for Fairbridge 'present a different problem':

> They are set in surroundings which are sometimes frankly ugly and always bare and uncompromising. Yet, note what love can do. In a locality that seems made of mining gear, dust ... you may open a gate and pass into little gardens with emerald lawns ... little gardens upon which some woman has spent herself in the passionate love of loveliness and a craving for beauty in a world of unredeemed utilitarianism ... Think of the courage of it and the rare quality of soul ... content to feel that she has redeemed thirteen corners of the Reef from ugliness ... but the soil of the mines is poor and thin, this must first be supplemented by good earth brought from a more kindly area. (1924: 34)

The Reef is 'frankly ugly' for two reasons. The first is Fairbridge's dislike of the industrial aesthetic of the Reef and the scars upon the landscape. The criticism of capitalist aesthetics is in keeping with the ideals of the Arts and Crafts movement exemplified in John Ruskin's 1862 opposition to industrialisation and capitalism in *Unto This Last*. The second is because the Reef environment *itself*, apart from being scarred and damaged, was at odds with Cape-based Fairbridge's national landscape and garden picture. For her New-Imperial eyes, the lawn trope offered hope for articulating one possible commonality of landscape across the nation, but also great frustration. Because of the Reef's geographic and climatic conditions, especially the lack of winter rainfall and winter frost, the 'vivid green lawns ... turn golden and the gardens compose themselves to sleep' (Fairbridge 1924: 34). It was in this context that Fairbridge was involved with Pole Evans, the head of Botany and Plant Pathology in the Department of Agriculture, who managed the planting of kikuyu grass for the lawns at the Union Buildings (Fairbridge 1924: 36; Stapf 1921: 88).

The Reef is depicted as ugly, bare, uncompromising, thin-soiled and the woman's little garden (or more correctly her gardening) is presented as beautiful, the redemption of this dusty utilitarian life. In Fairbridge, goodness and beauty are knotted together in notions like 'good earth', gardening as an act of 'redemption', and the idea that *good* soil and *good* grass can, and should, be brought from somewhere else. The prayerful acts of gardening, even the subtle mirroring of 'soil' and 'soul', have their origins in the primogenial gardening texts of medieval Dominican bishop Albertus Magnus. In his forty-volume encyclopaedic account of the *vita occulta* or the 'hidden life' of plants, Magnus argues:

> Nothing refreshes the sight so much as fine short grass. One must clear the space destined for a pleasure garden of all roots, and this can hardly be achieved unless the roots are dug out, the surface levelled, as much as possible, and boiling water is poured over the surface, so that the remaining roots and seeds which lie in the ground are destroyed and cannot germinate ... The ground must then be covered with turves cut from good [meadow] grass, and beaten down with wooden mallets, and stamped down well with the feet until they are hardly able to be seen. Then little by little the

> grass pushes through like fine hair, and covers the surface like a fine cloth. (quoted in Thacker 1985: 84)

The notion that the lawn refreshes the 'sight', or the 'eye' in Petrus de Crescentiis's later transcription (1305), or the 'eyes' in the earlier *De claustro animae* (of 1172) by Hugues de Fouilloy – 'the green lawn of the cloister garden refreshes the eyes of the beholder and recalls to their minds ... the future life' (quoted in MacDougall 1986: 51) – recurs in a number of other places. Speaking about the Kirstenbosch Botanical Garden, John Merriman, former premier of the Cape Colony, said: 'God Almighty first planted a garden. And, indeed, it is the purest of human pleasures. It is the greatest refreshment to the spirit of man' (quoted in Carruthers 2011: 264).

The goodness and beauty of the lawn is not, however, value free. In *The Theory of Leisure Class*, Thorstein Veblen writes that while lawn has 'sensuous beauty ... to the eye of nearly all races and classes ... it is, perhaps, unquestionably more beautiful to the eye of the dolicho-blond than to most other varieties of men' (2007: 90). There seem to me four things to say about the beauty of the lawn here. First, its beauty is seemingly 'undeniable', 'unquestionable'. According to *Gardening with Grasses*, 'The beauty of a well-maintained lawn is undeniable' (King & Oudolf 1998: 23). Second, to be more accurate, it is really the *well-maintained* lawn that is unquestionably beautiful. The badly kept lawn, or in Buchan's earlier example, the 'neglected turf', *can* be ugly or *is* ugly: 'In order to get out of grass-work its full possibility of beauty, it is necessary that decent order and restraint, that fine sobriety of taste that once reigned paramount over all the arts of design in England' be maintained (Blomfield 1892: 143). Third, it seems that it is 'grass-work', the gardening activities and labour in Fairbridge's example of 'spending' oneself on the lawn, and not necessarily *the* lawn itself, that is beautiful and virtuous. Lastly, the beauty of the lawn tends to be more readily discerned by those of the correct race or class, those with 'fine sobriety of taste', those with the predisposition to observe how beautiful the lawn is.

It is important to stress the gendered dimensions of lawn work that Fairbridge's texts bring up. It has been argued that historically Western women of a certain class tended to focus on flowers (Hoyles 1991; Munroe 2006; Taylor 2008). Nevertheless, even as early as 1707, Charles Evelyn wrote in *Lady's Recreation* to 'encourage women to lay out orangeries, lawns' (quoted in Bell 1990: 476). The invention of new lighter, easier-to-use lawnmowers from the nineteenth century onwards encouraged the idea that woman *could* mow. As a 1952 editorial in *House and Gardens* claimed, 'it was no more difficult than running your vacuum cleaner'. Notwithstanding the appeals of futuristic advertisements, the reality is that in South Africa at least, a 'garden boy' would likely have done most of the mowing.

There were exceptions to this argument. For instance, Marion Cran writes in *The Gardens of Good Hope* (1927: 166–168) of a Mr and Mrs Webber who lived in a Herbert Baker home in Johannesburg. He collected succulents for his 'kopie garden' and below this were his wife's green lawns and coloured borders. 'She leaves all the rock gardening to him, being absorbed in the lawns, borders and pergolas of her part of their domain' (166). In addition, Cran had the opportunity to meet the 'jobbing gardener of Johannesburg', Mrs Soames, 'a delightful little laughing lady whose old two-cylinder Renault is a familiar sight, jogging along the streets of the city, loaded with trays of plants for sale' (169). The peculiarity of this female jobber, who worked with 'a heart full of sweetness', foreshadows later lady landscapers, such as Joane Pim, who experienced pronounced gender-based discrimination (Foster 2015; Murray 2010). Mrs Soames also had in her employment that 'precious possession', 'a well-trained and devoted native servant; he is called Solomon, and grinned with wide appreciation when my hostess presented me as the "big Missis who writes books". Solomon has been eight years in her service, and he loves flowers. He was pricking out stocks, godetias and granadillas with fastidious care when we came round, his black face bent with deep attention over the delicate task.'

The ugly/beautiful binary is one articulation of the dialectical relationship in which lawn is constituted. The relational grammar of Fairbridge's passage sets up oppositions between the mine authorities and the gardener in her garden. The binary system here is obviously gendered: Fairbridge tells us it is 'her garden', 'her lawn', on which 'she spent herself', her pursuit. The 'craving for beauty and a passionate love of loveliness' is figured as feminine, in antagonism to the utilitarian masculinism that surrounds her. Commerce is set against domesticity, the public realm against private space, utilitarianism against beauty, and usefulness, productivity and efficiency against the lawn. The rampant industrialisation of the highveld would no doubt have sharpened these contrasts. The Arts and Crafts movement tended to depict lawn as a romantic foil for capitalism, as is the case in Ruskin's comparison of underappreciated and underpaid gardening labour compared with better-paid factory labour: the comparison of 'green velvet' worked with seed and a scythe compared to 'red velvet' worked with silk and scissors (1862: n.p.).

The gate – which can open and close – is the marker of a boundary and implies the crossing of a threshold to enter an inside. The gate marks the entry into the private space of the domestic realm. The garden is figured as a retreat, with the lawn providing a kind of domestic protection and safety. This stands in opposition to Harris and Buchan, whose manly lawns exemplify the conceptual and physical expansion of colonial power. Fairbridge's lawn is delicate, vulnerable actually. David Bunn has argued that closer attention ought to be paid to '*the role played by landscape in the reproduction of a gendered distinction between domestic interiors and a male public sphere*' (1994: 147; emphasis in original). This passage brings into particular focus the notion of the lawn as gendered and as the ground for gender-specific activity.

Fairbridge continues her narrative with reference to the obliteration of the lawn, and presumably the entire home: 'Many blows have been rained upon her garden; in one instance the mine authorities decreed that a shaft should be sunk in the middle of her lawn, just when it had attained the perfection of velvet smoothness' (1924: 35). A crude action indeed; sinking a shaft into an unwilling, perfect, velvety smooth lawn seems very ungentlemanly. The intrusion into the female domestic space is figured both as a muscular masculinity and as aligned with nature, for the blows 'rain' down. The metaphor of rape is difficult to avoid. In this instance the boundary is defined by two kinds of permeability: both horizontally, by a visitor or the narrator who could walk inside, and vertically, by the rain (of blows) of the mining shaft coming down into the garden and the earth.

Lawn labour

Sima Eliovson was an amateur gardener-turned-author of popular gardening books in apartheid-era South Africa. She was a contemporary of Una van der Spuy, author of *Wild Flowers of South Africa for the Garden* (1971), and Joane Pim, landscaper of Welkom and the gardens of Oppenheimer's Brenthurst, and author of the landscape polemic *Beauty is Necessary* (1971).

Eliovson published twelve books on mid-century suburban gardening, including books on wildflowers, Japanese gardening, Namaqualand flowers, proteas and Brazilian modernist gardening. The books are typical of their genre and include advice and guidance, Latin names of plants, historical explanations and case studies, illustrations and photographs (which she took herself, with her husband's help). Her most popular book was her first, *South African Flowers for the Garden* (published in 1955), which was inspired by the challenges of taking up residence in a new home with a 'wattle plantation as a garden' and the dearth of literature to help her confront this problem.[3] She notes in the introduction the exhaustive research she conducted, consulting all available sources – Curtis's *Botanical Magazine*, the *Royal Horticultural Society at Kew Register*, *Flowering Plants of South Africa*, Rudolf Marloth's *Flora of South Africa* – complemented by experience in her own garden.

It is worth noting that, like Eliovson, both Una van der Spuy in the 1970s and Ruby Boddam-Whetham, writing in the 1930s, were writing from and about their own gardens. Their experiences in their private gardens and the (sometimes) intimate relationships with their black labourers form a seam that runs through their work.

For instance, 'Old Nectar', Van der Spuy's historic Cape Dutch homestead, was the backdrop for many a rose photograph and was, in the end, the focus of her last book, *Old Nectar: A Garden for All Seasons* (published in 2010). Her gardener was John Mashati, whom she thanked in the introduction to *Wild Flowers of South Africa for the Garden*.

Boddam-Whetham's book *A Garden in the Veld* (1933) is, among other things, a record of her and her 'garden boy' Blesbok's battles with the veld around her new home Kirklington. Bought in 1911 by her husband, the farm near Ficksburg in the Orange Free State was named directly after his family's English home Kirklington (Gardiner 1991: 56–61). Cran describes him as one of a scattering of British 'gentleman farmers' who have 'taken their expensive educations and their traditions of honour' and have 'reinvested the name of their calling with romance': 'They work in the bush and on the veld in shirts and shorts, use their hands, talk and act like gentle-people, and are altogether a most attractive type. They come back to the old world now and again, sunburned men and women, bringing with them whilst they visit us something of the magic of the spacious lands beyond' (Cran 1927: 244–245). She met his wife while doing the research for *The Gardens of Good Hope* (1927). She describes her as 'a slim, dark-eyed brooding woman, who moves like a priestess among her torch lilies and roses; she is, above all, an observer and a dreamer who sees the possibilities of hybridisation in a land where the hybridist's patience and vision are hardly yet surmised' (178–179).

Ruby was not enamoured of the harsh surroundings, so she set about building a romantic garden with lawns, 'long, wide terraces, high walls and steps of dressed stone' (Gardiner 1991: 56). The gardens were planted with a hybrid of 'indigenous plants, and many flowers of the veld [which] took the place of less hardy species, though some of these showed reluctance at being "caged"'. Ruby was a frail woman and spent most of her days in the shade barking orders at her gardeners, writing about their exploits and enjoying the garden at night. In addition to Blesbok, she gardened with 'two-and-a-half kaffir boys' her husband had 'given' her from the farm (Boddam-Whetham 1933: 111).

Writing *from* one's own garden and with immense physical assistance could account for the staggering first line of the introductory paragraph of Chapter 24, 'The Lawn', in Eliovson's *The Complete Gardening Book for Southern Africa*: 'It is probably true to say that every garden in Southern Africa has a lawn ... The lawn, therefore, is one of the most important features to every homeowner, who realises that it enhances the value of his property, prevents dust from entering the house, provides a pleasant playground for his children and last, not least, gives his ground a cool, green, cultivated look that implies peace' (1968: 113).

Eliovson concludes with a stern warning: without sufficient care 'the lawn will deteriorate and be a mockery of what it should be' (1968: 113). It is safe to say that not every garden in South Africa had a lawn in 1968. But then Eliovson was not really writing about *every* garden: she was writing about *white* people's gardens, white people who were legally able to buy their own homes, could afford her books, the water bills, the lawn food, compost, ant-killer, sprinkler systems and the black labour to work the garden. Indeed, in her *Garden Design for Southern Africa* Eliovson goes so far as to say:

'If you do not have labour at hand ... then it is better to think along the lines ... of lawn substitute' (1983: 30). A sensible recommendation, but would a 'lawn substitute' still enhance property values, prevent dust, provide a pleasant playground for children and give the garden a cool, green, cultivated look that implies peace? Perhaps somewhat, but what it would not achieve is the display of the means to create and maintain a lawn. The 'lawn substitute' is laid out like a stage for those who did not have labour, a kind of second prize of garden surface treatments, for those white folks of the wrong class position. What Eliovson is saying is that it is preferable to have no lawn at all, rather than a badly kept one. No lawn means that the location – the terrain – on which white, patriarchal, middle-class, heterosexual, healthy, capitalist family life is lived, is barer, but still intact. An insufficiently cared-for lawn, however, is an incitement, a 'mockery'; it is dangerous. *Merriam-Webster Dictionary*'s definition of mockery as an 'insincere, contemptible, or impertinent imitation' and 'a subject of laughter' points towards some of the postcolonial conceptions of mimicry addressed in Buchan's Great Road narrative. Lawn substitutes like the tiled or paved-over gardens of Portuguese immigrants to the highveld (Vladislavić 2009: 20), or obviously synthetic artificial turf, such as in the film *Triomf* (Raeburn 2008), are, from a class perspective, also a kind of mockery.

Having 'labour at hand' was not a general concern for many white homeowners during apartheid. David Harrison in his critique *The White Tribe of Africa* writes: 'A hard day's work in the garden for many white[s] starts off in the car. He will drive to one of the many unmarked yet well-known pick-up points in the suburbs where he will find black mine workers ... Thus he can sit back and enjoy his Sunday lunch, give the "garden boy" his bread and jam and tea, take a nap till the digging is done' (1983: 78).

The invisibility of labour in the landscape is echoed in Coetzee's study of the pastoral in South African writing. 'Blindness to the colour black is built into South African pastoral,' writes Coetzee in *White Writing*. 'What inevitably follows is the occlusion of black labour from the scene: the black man becomes a shadowy presence flitting across the stage now and then' (1988: 5).

Coetzee's notion of 'blindness' is poignantly evident in Angela Read Lloyd's writing about gardener and artist Moses Tladi (1897–1959), who worked for her grandfather Herbert Read at his home

Lokshoek on the Parktown Ridge. Tladi tended a garden designed by Harry Clayton (Read Lloyd 2009: 18), which included a tennis court, pergola, croquet lawn, herbaceous borders and a lawn of fine grass (kikuyu and other coarse grasses had not yet come into use) (2–3). The house also had a 'staff lawn with granadilla creepers' (11). Tladi depicted the Lokshoek garden (at Read's suggestion) in a number of his paintings as well as his own garden of the home in Kensington B, from which he and his family were removed under the Group Areas Act (see Plate 2). He is often considered South Africa's first black landscape painter (Caccia 1993). In *The Artist in the Garden: The Quest for Moses Tladi*, Read Lloyd writes that she remembers Tladi as 'a dark man blending in as part of the company: tending the ferns, wheeling a barrow along the grass, tying and trimming. He seems serene, and is certainly a benign presence. I cannot see this man's face' (2009: 19). She wonders why she cannot remember Tladi. There are obviously many possible reasons, one of which was that she was just a little girl at the time. The hard truth is that for many white South Africans black domestic labourers were (and indeed remain) anonymous, nameless, faceless, history-less. The workers are a part of the background.

Read Lloyd's history of Tladi has a tendency to bathe his existence in her childhood garden with warm sunshine, softening and sentimentalising his presence: 'Images of childhood would forever belong in that garden, suffused with some magical light. In memory, that early, beautiful time remained the same, always. But many years went by before I realized that my paradise-garden was a place created and tended by Moses Tladi; a place where he had first begun to paint, and to explore the techniques of his art. That "artist's garden" had truly been his' (Read Lloyd 2009: 13).

A thing so familiar to the eye

The discourse of lawns is characterised by an overwhelming sense of agreement about the lawn – how it works, who it is for and what one should do with it. The norm is presented as a flat, green, soft, cool surface, which is understood to be an English colonial import, bringing with it transferred and transformed notions of class, race, gender and sexuality. It is also a discursive imposition on the landscape, in many cases one that has not (yet) been made. Where the lawn is imagined or read into the landscape, the discourse becomes indicative of the desire for belonging, for Englishness, and also an expression of melancholy. As a pursuit of an idea of order and civility over and against the perceived wilderness, the lawn is 'kept' in a dialectical relationship with wilderness and always bounded. Sometimes it is literally bounded; at other times and places that boundedness is repeated discursively when the landscape is perceived as resisting domestication. The lawn is always confronted by all that is NOT lawn. The making and keeping of the lawn, both discursively and corporeally, is characterised by anxiety. The lawn seems to be located on the borderline between desire and anxiety. This is all the more so as, by its very nature and as I have argued, the lawn is always a provisional accomplishment, always prone to decay, never final; impermanent, and thus imposing a regime of order as it requires and wants constant attention. The peculiarity of the lawn is that more than any other thing in the garden, it requires being kept; its visual comforts remain elusive, particularly on the highveld, which became the heart of South African industrialisation and modernisation. Because of this, the availability of labour was an essential condition, particularly for large lawns. From this, one could argue that the history of the South African lawn cannot be separated from its social and labour histories.

In conclusion I want to touch on an exemplary statement by famous garden designer Gertrude Jekyll (1843–1932). She was a garden designer and prolific garden writer influenced by Arts and Crafts principles and the work of John Ruskin and William Morris. She is known for her ideas about the cottage garden and for her association with the architect Edwin Lutyens. (It is rumoured that she was the inspiration behind Lutyens's designs for Joubert Park.) This is from her treatise *Some English Gardens*:

> That close, fine turf of the gardens of Britain is a thing so familiar to the eye that we scarcely think what a wonderful thing it really is. When we consider our flower and kitchen gardens, and remember how much labour of renewal they need – renewal not only of the plants themselves, but of the soil, in the way of manurial and other dressings; and when we consider all the digging and delving, raking and hoeing that must be done as ground preparation, constantly repeated; and then when we think again of an ancient lawn of turf, perhaps three hundred years old, that, except for mowing and

> rolling, has, for all those long years, taken care of itself; it seems, indeed, that the little closely interwoven plants of grass are things of wonderful endurance and longevity. (Jekyll & Elgood 1904: 104)

For Jekyll it is a pleasure to see the lawn anew, to defamiliarise it, because she then notices its 'wonderful endurance and longevity'. It is a concern that by presenting so vast a historical span of the lawn in this chapter (which is, of course, necessary) I might contribute to the notion of the lawn's terrible permanence. For while it is certainly old, an 'ancient' thing, what I am hoping to point towards are its limits – and even more strongly how it is philosophically constituted by its limits and its limitations. I want to, not so subtly, move towards the argument that the lawn is a temporary accomplishment, or what Ms Hirsh in the novel *Another Country* refers to as a 'provisional victory' (Schoeman 1991: 33). I hope to foreground the notion that the lawn is not permanent; it can die, it turns brown; it needs constant, vigilant, 'dictatorial' attention. It causes anxiety because it is never *fully* accomplished, it is always about to fall (is always already falling) into disrepair. Contrary to Jekyll's observation that the lawn 'needs very little attention' and takes 'care of itself', it appears instead that what a lawn *wants* is our constant attention.

Chapter 2
Keeping the Lawn

and still we smile and
beg to mow your lawns
beg to clean your toilets
while you look past us

— Mike Alfred, *Poetic Licence*[1]

The domestic lawn is directly attached to or surrounding the house, it is privately owned, kept (well or badly) by someone, and is totally, partly, or not at all visible to the public. It always ends somewhere, bounded by a wall, a pavement, a fence, a hedge, a herbaceous border, in some more or less conscious relationship with adjacent lawns, veld, roads, parks and the larger landscape. Does the domestic really end at the kitchen door? Is the lawn simply a 'view' through the bedroom window, a backdrop to the battles within? The lawn is sometimes considered the outside of the house but, as I argue in this chapter, it can also be seen as fundamentally part of and within the domestic sphere.

In this chapter I aim to explain how the domestic lawn as a working landscape is implicated in issues of belonging, ownership, success and failure, gender and race. It describes the 'garden boy' via an analysis of various gardening texts, literary passages and historical records, and then locates the 'boy' in relation to the master/madam/gardener. It also analyses white post-apartheid literary, artistic and archival representations of lawn mowing. Last, orientated around David Goldblatt's photograph *Saturday Afternoon in Sunward Park. 1979*, the chapter offers a critical reading of whiteness and respectability in relation to the lawn. The photographs informing this reading are related to geographical spaces – Boksburg, Orania, Epping Garden Village, Sasolburg and Zamdela.

Domesticating

Two ideas frame this chapter. The first is that lawn maintenance, keeping the lawn – the flurry of activity that includes mowing, fertilising, watering, composting, weeding and edging – is surely the most acute example of landscape as verb. Without effort, time, money, knowledge and equipment the lawn cannot grow. Work – paid or unpaid, fun or fearful, for leisure or labour – is the foundation of the lawn. It is also worth reflecting on the synecdochical quality of mowing, the way in which lawn mowing tends to end up standing for lawn keeping in general.[2] What activities does it eclipse, what silences does it produce? I return to this question at the end of the chapter by examining *watering*, an obviously necessary input that is not always possible all year round, to many gardeners' frustration. Not to put too fine a point on it, the lawn *is* work.

Secondly, I want to propose that the idea of the domestic, of domestication as a process, and of domesticity as both *space* and '*social relation to power*' (McClintock 1995: 34) is central to understanding human relationships to the lawn. What the notion of the domestic does – as opposed to 'civilising', for instance (although until the 1960s the verb 'domesticate', as Anne McClintock points out [1995: 35], was also used to mean 'to civilise') – is to bring the biological, zoological and botanical into the landscape along with the processes of human interpellation. The *beast*, as Achille Mbembe argues in *On the Postcolony* (2001), has been the sign under which the native, under which Africa has been read. Frantz Fanon made this point too. As he argues in *The Wretched of the Earth*, colonial vocabulary constantly deployed 'zoological terms' for natives: 'breeding swarms', 'spawn' and 'vegetative' rhythms of life (1963: 41–42). Jean Comaroff and John Comaroff concur that 'the idea of domesticity was saturated with natural imagery', in the imperial centre as well as in the periphery (1992: 39). In fact, according to Kay Anderson, before the seventeenth century the term 'savage' was applied not only to primitive peoples, but to plants, too (1997: 474).

For Mbembe, domestication is the process whereby the *beast*, close to being human, can (1) come 'to where he or she can enjoy a fully human life' (2001: 2) and (2) come to be known as familiar, that is to say, made familiar and understood to be familiar. According to Mbembe, domestication is not only a process of making humans (or at least approximating humanity) but is also a mode of knowing, empathising, giving an account of the *beast*. Provocatively, Mbembe's definition insists on what he terms the 'logic of conviviality' (110): a mode of familiarity expressed and experienced as intimacy, affection, even love. In contrast to the conception of the native as property – a 'thing of power ... [that] ... could be destroyed, as one may kill an animal', cut up, cooked and, if need be, eaten – Mbembe posits an interpretation of coloniality that rests on the idea that 'one could, as with an animal, sympathize with the colonized, even "love" him or her; thus, one was sad when he/she died because he/she belonged, up to a point, to the familiar world'. He writes:

> Affection for the colonized could also be externalized in gestures; the colonized would have to, in return, render the master or mistress the same affection the master/mistress gave. But, beyond gesture, the master's/mistress's affection for the animal presented itself as an inner force that should govern the animal. In the Bergsonian tradition of colonialism, familiarity and domestication thus became the dominant tropes of servitude. Through the relation of domestication, the master or mistress led the beast to an experience such that, at the end of the day, the animal, while remaining what he/she was – that is, something other than a human being – nevertheless actually entered into the world for his/her master/mistress.
>
> This entry was, however, only possible after a process of grooming. The colonizer might inculcate habits in the colonized, treat him/her violently if need be, speak to him/her as a child, reprimand or congratulate him/her. But, above all, the colonized, like the animal, was an object of experimentation in a game that the colonizer played with himself/herself, conscious that between him/her and the colonized there hardly existed a community of essence. (Mbembe 2001: 26–27)

What are the implications of Mbembe's concept of conviviality, of co-living (from the Latin *con* 'with' + *vivere* 'live'), which inscribes 'the dominant and the dominated within the same episteme' (2001: 110)?

The domestic space is 'fraught by the fact of ... its "subjects" having to share the same living space' (104). Sarah Nuttall proposes that 'while race has been a vector of segregation, especially in terms of macro spatial arrangements and judicial dispositions, it is also clear that in everyday life there have been spaces – some public, others private, domestic – in which if not intimacy, at least a close proximity of "oppressor" and "oppressed" developed' (2001: 119). And, according to Deborah Posel, it was in the 'sites of routinised interracial contact and dependency', sites like domestic service, that whites and blacks experienced each other (2011: 329). 'Precisely this logic – the necessary familiarity and domesticity in the relationship – explains why there has not been (as might be expected from those so dominated) the resistance to the accommodation, the disengagement or the "refusal to be captured"' (Mbembe 2001: 104).

Comaroff and Comaroff's postcolonial study of nineteenth-century Tswana life, which outlines the acceptance, rejection and contestation of British missionary civilisation, especially regarding domestic rituals, gender roles and architecture, argues that imperial domesticity was dialectical: 'the poor of Britain were as "strange," as much "other" as any African aborigine, and as urgently in need of improvement. The bourgeois burden in Britain, it followed, was no less pressing than the white man's burden abroad' (Comaroff & Comaroff 1992: 61). Both the savage and street urchin required reformation and the 'cult of domesticity' (McClintock 1995: 34) had the following principles:

> (1) to create the conditions for – and an attitude of – 'cleanliness,' thereby to achieve a world in which all matter, beings, and bodies were in their proper place; (2) to reform sexuality by encouraging legal, Christian marriage and the creation of nuclear households, thus putting an end to 'drunken indulgence' in 'child-breeding'; (3) to spread the ideal of private property, beginning with the family home; and (4) to reconstruct gender relations and the social division of labor. (Comaroff & Comaroff 1992: 64)

Comaroff and Comaroff observe how native women's agricultural and botanical work struck white missionaries as 'profoundly unnatural' because their farming and gathering drew them away from the home. However, they point out, 'Rather than the bounded British "home," then, it was a matricentric group, with a radiating network of ties through females, that was the focus of material subsistence, reproduction, and nurture among contemporary Tswana' (1992: 42).

The nineteenth-century Methodist evangelist Samuel Broadbent recorded his attempts at civilising in *A Narrative of the First Introduction of Christianity amongst the Barolong Tribe of Bechuanas, South Africa*: 'I and my colleague had each enclosed a plot of ground, which we had, of course, in English fashion, broken up and cleared of the roots of weeds,' he writes. What became the 'subject of wonder and remark was the notorious fact that these and other vegetables grew much more luxuriantly, and were more productive, in our grounds than in the natives' (1865: 105). Broadbent recounts how a 'number of respectable natives came to ask the reason of this difference'. His answer was to become one of the exemplary statements of British colonial discourse:

> My first answer was, 'Your idleness.' 'How so?' they inquired. I said, 'You have seen that we have dug the ground ourselves; you leave it to your women. We dig deep into the soil; they only scratch the surface. You have observed there is moisture in the earth, and even water is obtained at a certain depth. Our seed, therefore, is protected from the sun and nourished by the moisture in the ground; but yours is parched with the heat of the sun, and, therefore, not so productive as ours.' I added, 'Work yourselves, as you see we do, and dig the ground properly, and your seed will flourish as well as ours.' They readily assented to all that I said, except to the part about digging themselves, instead of leaving that to their women, as such a practice would be so much opposed to their ideas and habits. (1865: 104–105)

Comaroff and Comaroff rightly argue that Broadbent's fable presents foundational 'lessons of the sacred garden' (1997: 135). Firstly, the lessons recommend themselves as seemingly technical – for greater yields and increased productivity, dig deeper, enclose after the 'English fashion'. That technical advice, with modernising intentions, is never only (or indeed actually) non-political, is a point made forcefully by James Ferguson in *The Anti-politics Machine: 'Development' and Bureaucratic Power in Lesotho* (1990). Ferguson proposes the concept of the 'anti-politics machine' to explain what the development apparatus in Lesotho did, which was to fail on its own terms, and to simultaneously expand and entrench bureaucratic state power, 'side by side with the projection of a representation of economic and social life which denies "politics"' (1990: xv).

The lessons are a theological 'celebration of labor' (Comaroff & Comaroff 1997: 135). On the one hand, Broadbent's preaching is a critique of black idleness – he 'demanded mastery over field and furrow, not scratchings on the soil' (136) – and, on the other hand, his sermon is a clarification that 'not all toil was the same'. The gendered division of labour that Broadbent and his colleagues observed fitted neatly into a historically entrenched discourse on the 'lazy African man' (Rönnbäck 2014) and was precisely the opposite of the colonial domesticity they hoped to foster (see Comaroff & Comaroff 1992; McClintock 1995).

Working

The following passage from Charles Smith's *Home Gardening in South Africa* (1940) might sound astonishing to a contemporary reader. The description is disconcerting because of its casual racism, the lack of drama in the way that rather cruel and dehumanising notions are floated so nonchalantly. Also, bookended as it is by botanical information on the pages that precede and follow it, this passage evokes a long history of so-called non-white humans embedded in a biological *mise en scène*, whether as biomedical specimens, museum objects in dioramas, live casts, living exhibits, ethnographic photographs, measurements or in nature videos. Between 'soil' and 'seasons for sowing', we find the 'native boy':

> Having a native boy to work in your garden is much like getting a sort of labour-saving machine to perform the different gardening tasks. This is one of his excellent qualities, he does not prevent you from setting your own mark on the garden and giving it the stamp of your own individuality. Even when we cannot be our own gardeners in the right sense, we still rule the destinies of our gardens. For the native garden boy, unlike jobbing gardeners in other countries, seldom intrudes his ideas, or takes things on himself. If you are not there to direct his labour and tell him what to do next, he will probably do nothing at all. In spite of his faults, I think our native garden

> boy is usually underrated. He has his faults, but what would our big gardens be without him? It is true that if he is not watched he will only sprinkle the top of the ground instead of watering the roots of the plants, he may only break up the top inch or so of soil when he has been set to dig, instead of pushing the blade right down, the full length of the blade. He will as often as not pull up the seedlings instead of the weeds in the garden beds. By shirking his work, by taking hours over his meals, by doing everything wrong that could possibly be done in the wrong way, a garden boy appears to be the most annoying pest the long-suffering gardener has to put up with. But if he is a pest, unlike any other pest, he has his uses, and as I say, is often indispensable to busy people, who are also garden lovers. Unlike the Indian or Chinaman, the native gardener is not a hereditary gardener. Up to quite recently, his womenfolk did all the digging and planting, sowing and weeding there was to do. A man's place was with the cattle, the women did the gardening, such as it was. Fortunately for us and for themselves also, the natives, like the Athenians, love any 'new thing'. They are the most imitative race on earth. And if you show them how to do a simple gardening task they are able to do it with very little practice, no matter how unfamiliar it may be. The garden boy is only a failure when his master or mistress does not know enough about gardening to put him right when he goes wrong. (1940: 81–82)

Smith's characterisation of the garden boy can be located within a dense historical discourse, which, as Mahmood Mamdani argues in *Citizen and Subject* (1996), pre-dates Hegel. Mamdani quotes a speech that Jan Smuts delivered at the Oxford Rhodes Memorial Lecture of 1929 about the African: the special type with 'some wonderful characteristics', who has 'largely remained a child type, with a child psychology and outlook':

> 'A child-like human cannot be a bad human, for are we not in spiritual matters bidden to be like unto little children? Perhaps as a direct result of this temperament the African is the only happy human I have come across.' Even if the racism in the language is blinding we should be wary of dismissing Smuts as some South African oddity. Smuts spoke from within an honourable Western tradition. Had not Hegel's *Philosophy of History* mythologized 'Africa proper' as 'the

> land of childhood'? Did not settlers in British colonies call every African male, regardless of age, a 'boy' – houseboy, shamba-boy, office-boy, ton-boy, mine-boy ... In the colonial mind, however, Africans were no ordinary children, they were destined to be so perpetually – in the words of Christopher Fyfe, 'Peter Pan children who can never grow up, a child race'. (Mamdani 1996: 3–4)

Smuts was a keen botanist and South Africa's leading specialist on grass in his time. Piet Beukes, in *Smuts the Botanist*, argues that grass was Smuts's 'second great love' (1996: 83).[3] No doubt the bluntness of Smith's language would have offended Smuts the diplomat, but he would likely have been acquainted with Rudyard Kipling's influential poem 'The White Man's Burden' (published in 1899) and may have appreciated the more genteel characterisation of the 'new-caught, sullen peoples, / Half devil and half child'.[4]

Smith's description of the garden boy is an example of the way in which race, gender and class were woven into botanical literature, which at face value is purely technical. His characterisation comes from the chapter 'Digging and the Garden Boy', where Smith constructs labour, and its management, as a technocratic system of tasks, inputs, actions: a modern approach to gardening in South Africa in 1940. In this system, the garden boy is dealt with in much the same way as topics like digging, composting and the planning of a herbaceous border.

In his luminous history *New Babylon New Nineveh: Everyday Life on the Witwatersrand 1886–1914* Charles van Onselen argues that one of the key features of the masters and mistresses of the time, the '*nouveau riche* middle classes', was that they 'lacked the domestic managerial experience of the English ruling class' (1982: 234). Van Onselen's study is a rich resource for scholars interested in the complex relationships between white homeowners and staff on the Rand. The gap in 'managerial' experience in Johannesburg was acutely felt in the colonies because of dramatic class mobility but was not an uncommon concern in London. From the mid-nineteenth century, a slew of guidebooks and magazines, exemplified by periodicals and *Mrs Isabella Beeton's Book of Household Management* (published in 1861), were aimed at assisting women with the challenge of managing a large home, which included cooking, parties, maintaining etiquette and knowledge of the exact duties of each kind of servant.

That the Johannesburg 'new money' was in need of such assistance is clear from the nickname given by their servants to the 'veld aristocracy' (Van Onselen 1982: 234).

If, however, we read Smith as simply a guide to managing a garden boy, we miss the more interesting idea that garden boys are *made*, not managed – or made by management, at any rate. In *A Garden in the Veld* R. E. Boddam-Whetham explains that when the physical labour of transforming the 'raw' veld into her garden exceeded her capacity she petitioned her husband for help: 'The digging and stone-carrying were too much for me, so I was given one of the farm-boys to make into a gardener. I knew little enough; but the boy knew nothing at all; he was not even good at growing mealies in his own mealie land. I had him for years, and under my direct supervision, he eventually became quite a valuable under-gardener' (1933: 15).

Both Smith and Boddam-Whetham present a kind of primitive anthropology of the garden boy. His emergence is based on a displacement from what is assumed to be a natural state (not unlike the raw veld) and occurring in relation to the Gardener, the master/mistress.

There have been no thorough studies of the particular southern African colonial notion of the 'boy', although a handful of scholarly publications touch on the subject. Robert Morrell's article 'Of Boys and Men' (1998), for instance, provides valuable context by sketching out a history of South African masculinities and locating the boy within that schema. D. F. Janssen (2007, 2008) offers extensive and detailed linguistic and historical studies of the term 'boy' that are useful but really only gesture towards colonial usage.[5]

To advance a precise description of the boy, it is necessary to outline four of the subject's main features: (1) gender, (2) temporality, (3) labour and (4) race.

Can a boy become a man?

The boy is a fundamentally gendered concept, related to concepts of masculinity insofar as boys are (almost) always biological men, although never quite fully actualised men. The boy is also related to the female in such a way that boys are often emasculated by their work (both inside and outside the house, above ground and below) and by their relationship with both white and black women. That each of these relations is arranged in terms of race, class and sexuality will become clear.

Morrell argues that the character of the 'relationship between white coloniser and black colonised involved emasculation' (1998: 616). He stresses the problematic relationship between black men who have been 'boy-ed' or subjected to the status of boyhood and the women they relate to:

> In the earliest days, [black men] undertook women's work. While this was a wage-earning activity which was in a sense empowering and part of a process of developing the job as a key feature of being a man, it was also demeaning. The kinds of jobs were menial, brutal or unmanly. When black men launched sexual attacks on white women in early twentieth century Johannesburg, thus setting off swart gevaar scares amongst white residents, they may have been giving Fanonesque expression to the emasculation they felt. (Morrell 1998: 623)

The *swart gevaar* (black peril) was 'the perceived sexual threat that black males posed to white females ... the rape or attempted rape of white women by black men. The rape or attempted rape of black women by white men was not considered a peril' (Jackson 2005: 210). The anxieties that coalesced around the notion of the black peril reveal how fraught the relationship between white and black men was. The fear, as Fanon expressed it in *Black Skin, White Masks*, is that white 'women are at the mercy of the Negroes': 'All of them endowed the Negro with powers that other men (husbands, transient lovers) did not have. And besides there was also an element of perversion, the persistence of infantile formations: God knows how they make love! It must be terrifying ... when a white man hates black men, is he not yielding to a feeling of impotence or of sexual inferiority?' (2008: 122).

Kobena Mercer writes that the 'deepest mythological fears in the supremacist imagination' is the belief that all black men have 'monstrously huge willies' (1991: 188). According to Mercer, the big black dick is perceived as threatening not only to the white master 'who shrinks in impotence from the thought that the subordinate black male is more sexually powerful than he' but to civilisation itself since the 'bad object' represents a danger to white womanhood and therefore the threat of miscegenation, eugenic pollution and racial degeneration. His analysis is animated by the Fanonian realisation regarding the black phallus: 'One is no longer aware of the Negro but only of a penis; the Negro is eclipsed. He is turned into a penis. He *is* a penis … The white man is convinced the Negro is a beast; if it is not the length of the penis, then it is the sexual potency that impresses him' (Fanon 2008: 130).

In *The Grass is Singing* the narrator agrees about the 'jealousy of the white man for the superior sexual potency of the native' (Lessing 1994: 186). The novel describes how the madam, Mary Turner, 'used to sit quite still' watching her houseboy Moses work. 'The powerful, broad-built body fascinated her,' writes Doris Lessing. Mary 'had given him white shorts to wear in the house, that had been used by her former servants. They were too small for him … his muscles bulged and filled out the thin material' (142).

In the novel *The Black Peril* (1912) by George Webb Hardy another Mary, this time Mary Roseberry, describes the houseboy Jim: 'His bull-like neck and chest and splendid limbs were visible for all to see ... Mary could not conceal her admiration of his magnificent manhood, although she treated him as a boy and could not get it out of her head that so he was. He had a chest as wide and deep as that of a champion bull-dog, a neck like an Ayrshire Bull, a loosely built frame as erect as a soldier in uniform' (1912: 65).

And in Nadine Gordimer's novel *Occasion for Loving* Jessie Stillwell talks to the artist Gideon Shibalo about her recollections of the man mowing the lawn:

> I remember the young black man with a bare chest, mowing the lawn. The bare legs and the strong arms that carried things for us, moved furniture. The black man that I must never be left alone with in the house. No one explained why, but it didn't matter. I used to feel, at night, when I turned my back to the dark passage and bent to wash my face in the bathroom, that someone was coming up behind me. Who was it, do you think? And how many more little white girls are there for whom the very first man was a black man? The very first man, the man of the sex fantasies. (1994: 253)

Like the two Marys in the novels above, Jessie remembers a man who is all body and body parts: bare chest, bare legs, strong arms. Like

Angela Read Lloyd's accounts of Moses Tladi (2009), discussed in Chapter 1, Jessie's young black man does not have a face; he does not have a name – he is just a body, labouring. The illicit pleasure in the passage above is in large part derived from the fact that the man is (1) black, (2) a labourer, (3) her family's labourer, *her* black man and (4) in the end, forbidden territory. He is, fundamentally, the man she 'must never be left alone with in the house'.

In terms of the sexual fear of black men in the domestic realm, we can discern in Gordimer's dialogue a precise architectural boundary, one that splits the home into the residence on the one hand and the garden on the other. Observing this division is essential if we are to understand how the black peril functioned both to subjectify black men as rapists and, as Van Onselen (1982) argues, to push houseboys out of the house and into the mines and inadvertently into the garden also. A 1920 editorial on 'The Houseboy' in the November issue of *The South African Woman* argues that houseboys are a 'malodorous' problem and that housewives, as 'domestic government', must be aware of the 'very real dangers' they pose, for 'there is not a corner of the house he does not penetrate' (Anon. 1920: 1). While the problem of the houseboys' health and cleanliness could be seen to and the spread of venereal diseases controlled, the best solution was, in fact, to 'eliminate them altogether': 'At present we employ "boys" in the house because we can get no other service, but the principle is wrong. Natives are wanted on the farms, mines, and many other avenues of labour more suitable for them than domestic service, and if they are not employed as houseboys hundreds would be released for heavier work.'

In his rich history of the houseboy on the Witwatersrand, Van Onselen connects black peril scares to economic patterns and household economies (1982: 257–268). He proposes that the major black peril scares in the Witwatersrand between 1890 and 1914 occurred during recessions when incomes of white families were generally decreasing. Thus, he argues, the scares 'were firmly rooted' in periods when the domestic servant's wages were also falling. Economic pressure in some cases manifested in black peril conflicts between mistresses and houseboys. Pointing to the findings of the 1913 Commission on Assaults on Women, Van Onselen shows that a number of cases of black peril were trumped up to defraud houseboys of their wages (1982: 265).

Jeremy Martens suggests that Jonathan Hyslop's 'White Working-Class Women and the Invention of Apartheid' (1995), read in tandem with Van Onselen's *New Babylon New Nineveh*, 'underline[s] the importance of probing the social and economic context in which white panics took place' (2002: 386). However, Martens points out in his study of the Natal rape scares of 1886 that 'Natal's agrarian settler society and economy of the nineteenth century bears scant resemblance to that of the industrialising Witwatersrand'. Rather, he argues, 'economic difficulties threatened to undermine the position of white men within the colonial hierarchy, and increased concerns about the implications of black male domestic servants performing what was considered "women's work" in settler homes, as well as white women's "inappropriate" behaviour towards them'. This created a context for reasserting the dominance of white men over black men and women.

The anxiety about black men doing 'women's' work inside the home is evident in Jock McCulloch's *Black Peril, White Virtue: Sexual Crime in Southern Rhodesia, 1902–1935* (2000). He shows how rape scares were used politically by white elites to entrench more deeply their racial supremacy and points out an intriguing paradox: for white Rhodesians, domestic labour simultaneously 'made black men both sexually threatening and effeminate' (2000: 120). As the 1930 *Report on Domestic Service* by the Women's Institute argued at the time, domestic labour 'tends to render [houseboys] effeminate and to sap their physical and mental energy. It has been noted that on their return to their kraals they refuse to assist in the lands or any other physical work' (quoted in McCulloch 2000: 120). In effect, the presence of the houseboy violated a gender economy of labour. This sentiment was echoed in a questionnaire on the black peril circulated by the General Missionary Conference of 1911. Two black male respondents in the Witwatersrand, G. Kakaza and G. Tyamzashe, were emphatic about what 'proper' work for men was: 'Let no men be employed as domestic servants: in the kitchen, to mind babies, to wash clothes. Let these works be done by Native women ... Let Native men work outside and where other men are; men should be employed in their proper sphere' (quoted in Gaitskell 1979: 49).

Scholars like Morrell (1998) prefer the line of reasoning that foregrounds violence: emasculation as a kind of violence, experienced by black labourers, led to the real and symbolic violence of the rape perils. In contrast to other economic arguments, Morrell presents a narrative of revenge: subjected to 'demeaning … menial, brutal or unmanly' work, black men express their emasculation in Fanonian terms (1998: 623).

The overall result was that black men became progressively banished from the white household, relegated to the garden. It is not that houseboys in single-servant homes did not often (probably generally) already do 'such routine garden work as weeding and watering' (Van Onselen 1982: 240). We know that grand households kept five servants, one of whom was preferred to be a desirable white 'cook-general' and another three to five black male servants (houseboy, garden boy, kitchen boy, and so on) who would be supervised by the white female servant (264). In these households, dedicated garden labourers would have tended the grounds. The boundary between home and garden was in some ways profoundly inaugurated by and reliant upon fears of interracial sex, with inside and outside separated into their properly gendered spheres. The isolation of the garden boy from normal social (and sexual) intercourse was a structural part of the pattern of household management and employment.

The time of the boy

In *Time Binds: Queer Temporalities, Queer Histories* (2010) Elizabeth Freeman proposes the concept of 'chrononormativity' to explain capitalist heteropatriarchal temporal regulation. What Freeman argues, following Michel Foucault – along with other queer writing interested in temporality, such as Lee Edelman's *No Future* (2004) and Jack Halberstam's *In a Queer Time and Place* (2005) – is that time organises bodies towards productivity and that to queer time would be to develop chronologies according to 'other logics of location, movement, and identification' (Halberstam 2005: 1).

It is worth considering the fundamentally chronological aspect of the boy in two senses. First, in the most general sense, the boy is situated somewhere within a heterosexual telos, which is implicitly unidirectional. To put it another way: the boy is understood as part of, or a stage in, the natural journey *towards* manhood. In his rigorous linguistic anthropology of the term 'boy', Janssen argues that 'boy/hood, in what we may call the term's orthodox "deployment", is part of a narrative (whether despised, allowed, or subverted) of male progress, more specifically of male "departure", itinerary and "arrival"' (2007: 49). Second, in the South African case, the subject of the boy is arrested in that trajectory, unable ever to graduate to the stage of manhood. Morrell (1998: 616) calls the boy in South Africa the 'denial of adulthood', the 'refusal to acknowledge the possibility of growth and the achievement of manhood amongst African men'. To be sure, the use of the diminutive appellation for a 'black man of any age, whether he is in the white man's employ or not', is deeply humiliating. As Chantal Zabus points out: 'When the Afrikaner policeman asks in the presence of that [black] man's girlfriend – "Hey boy, where's your pass?" – the man reasons: "Am I a man to my girl or a boy? How do you think I feel?" To the "African man" as a generic heterosexual, "boy" is contracted with "man", and suggests a phase of arrested development before accessing a hypothetical full-fledged, heterosexual masculinity' (2013: 189).

A short homily on the dignity of work

As Zabus points out above, even when a black man is not in the employ of a particular white person (or employed at all), he is still seen as a boy. Even though 'boy' is essentially labour terminology, denoting certain kinds of work within a specific capitalist system that emerged under British colonialism, its use has transcended the original meaning. For example, in *Reeftown Elite* Mia Brandel-Syrier develops an interesting notion of 'attachment' with regard to the 'boy' (1971: 184–187). She explains that the notion indicates a 'personal relationship rather than a category of work; a "boy" was attached to someone whom he addressed as "master" or "baas"' (184). Brandel-Syrier argues that the notion of the 'boy' is related to the distinction between manual and non-manual, skilled and unskilled labour, where the boy represents the manual part of the master's skilled work. In fact, she argues, often the boy did most of the master's skilled work, too, and so functioned as a kind of apprentice. Her study also shows how the terms of attachment evolved to describe black-on-black relationships: 'Thus, Africans were now using the term to designate all those who stood in a relationship of personal dependence toward a fellow African; they used it to describe the same derogatory meaning [*sic*] the one who does all the work while the other gets the honour and the pay' (187)!

Mamdani points out that 'boy' often comes with a linguistic qualifier or prefix – houseboy, shamba-boy, mine-boy, garden boy (1996: 3). This qualifier (1) denotes the type of work to be done, (2) in almost all cases it specifies a *space* where the work is done, but (3) it also specifies the place where that boy belongs and had to be under apartheid passbook laws. He is the boy who does housework but is also the boy in/of the house; the boy who does garden work, in the garden – the boy in/of the garden.

As we have seen in Smith's anthropology, the garden boy is a 'labouring machine', an animal that does *tasks* or a 'unit of menial labor' (Lelyveld 1967: 13). This is not the conception of a gardener who is in touch with the seasons, connected to nature; this is a mechanistic notion of brute strength. The boy offers only physical labour, what Boddam-Whetham calls 'kaffir-boy-power' (1933: 53). He is given no credit for creativity and leaves no 'stamp' on the owner's garden. If the 'native' was, in fact, not a 'hereditary gardener', as Smith supposed, and 'womenfolk did all the digging and planting, sowing and weeding' (1940: 81), the exclusion of black female gardeners illustrates the imposition of gendered norms of labour. The black gardener is, despite his assumed total lack of botanical knowledge or skill, admired for his strong muscles – and his willingness to be corrected when wrong.

In her essay 'Sudden Life, Never Seen or Expected Before' on Goldblatt's photograph *Boss Boy* from *On the Mines* (Goldblatt & Gordimer 1973), Gordimer asks: is the copper bracelet punched with stars a medal of status, distinction or servitude? It is indicative of the boss boy's position within the discriminatory job reservation system and in relation to white men. Gordimer stresses that under the industrial laws of the time, 'he will never be SHIFT BOSS like the white man whose BOY he is' (2001: 437).[6] To be a boy is also to be placed on a continuum of employment opportunities in terms of which black men were officially restricted to certain jobs and proletarianised. Their work was limited to physical labour. Even among the occupations available to black men, domestic jobs were not well regarded. While we have no equivalent study for South Africa, a very telling 1954 social survey from Northern Rhodesia designed to form an 'occupational prestige ranking' found that 'garden boy' was the second-lowest ranked job out of thirty-one occupations, only just above 'scavenger' and below 'wood cutter', 'petrol pump boy' and 'station boy'; 'houseboy' did not fare much better, ranking seventh from last, not far above garden boy (Mitchell & Epstein 1959: 24).

If the boy is a subject of labour, he is also a subject of its opposite: idleness. J. M. Coetzee's foundational work on idleness (1988) is deployed by McClintock in *Imperial Leather* where she quotes Lady Barker: 'It is a new and revolutionary idea to a Kaffir that he should do any work at all' (1995: 253). James Bryce, also cited by McClintock, agreed: 'The male Kaffir is a lazy fellow who likes talking and sleeping better than continuous physical exertion.' The discourse on idleness is more properly speaking a discourse on work that is used to distinguish between desirable and undesirable labour. Elsewhere McClintock comments: 'Pressure to work was, more accurately, pressure to alter traditional habits of work … At the same time, the discourse on idleness is also a register of labor resistance, a resistance then lambasted as torpor and sloth. Colonists borrowed and patched from British discourses and couched their complaints in the same images of degeneracy, massing animal menace and irrationality familiar to European descriptions of the dangerous urban underclasses' (2009: 365).

I would like to bring under the rubric of *failure* the discourse of idleness and a particular anxiety also about white labour. We have already seen how Smith characterised the garden boy as a pest who shirks his work, takes hours over his meals and does 'everything wrong that could possibly be done in the wrong way' (1940: 81). As this book progresses we will see a number of other examples where boys are described as idle, lazy, slow and also as sly, devious, threatening. If we read these white worries only as concerns about productivity, or even of failure at domestication, we will miss the fear of *white* idleness. Indeed, Coetzee, the great theorist of work in South Africa, argues that as a 'remedy' for white degeneration in the face of 'Africa's insidious corruptions', 'cheerful toil' was prescribed (1988: 3).

In *The Grass is Singing* Mary Turner discusses the labourer's 'attitude towards work': 'Whenever two or three farmers are gathered together, it is decreed that they should discuss nothing but the shortcomings and deficiencies of their natives … They never cease complaining about their unhappy lot, having to deal with natives who are so exasperatingly indifferent to the welfare of the white man, working only to please themselves. They had no idea of the dignity of labour, no idea of improving themselves by hard work' (Lessing 1994: 76). In another scene Mary echoes past evangelical attempts at conversion like Broadbent's pastoral gardening exhortations:

> She ended with a short homily on the dignity of work, which is a doctrine bred into the bones of every white South African. They would not be any good, she said (speaking in kitchen kaffir which some of them did not understand, being fresh from their kraals) until they learned to work without supervision, for the love of it, to do as they were told, to do a job for its own sake, not thinking of the money they would be paid for it. It was this attitude towards work that had made the white man what he was: the white man worked because it was good to work, because working without reward was what proved a man's worth. (Lessing 1994: 114)

The boy's blackness

The final aspect to consider is the garden boy's obvious blackness. To remark that 'boy' is a racial and racist concept seems absurdly self-evident. However, the blackness of the boy is not value free. Just as South African whiteness became actively invested, to a greater and lesser degree, with unearned privilege, wealth, goodness, modernity – especially in relation to the figure of the black man – so blackness became further burdened with gendered, chronological and sexual judgements. The term 'boy' functions linguistically as a racial enunciator – 'Hey boy, where's your pass?' The South African policemen 'hailing' the black man functions similarly to Louis Althusser's notion of ideology in that he '"acts" or "functions" in such a way that he "recruits" subjects among the individuals'. As Althusser argues, ideology '"transforms" the individuals into subjects (it transforms them all) by the very precise operation which I have called *interpellation* or hailing, and which can be imagined along the lines of the most commonplace everyday police (or other) hailing: "Hey, you there!"' (1971: 163).

To be recruited as a boy was to be located within a matrix of spatial, temporal, gender, sexual and productive coordinates and to have one's race as a mark of this location. The boy's blackness becomes the sign of this position.

Mowing

In the index of John Loudon's authoritative nineteenth-century *Encyclopaedia of Gardening* the 'lawn' is defined as necessarily 'kept short by frequent mowing' (1825: 1417). Much of the literature is preoccupied with the importance of mowing and especially offering advice on techniques, novel technologies of mowing and so on. For example, the well-known American landscaper Andrew Jackson Downing (1849: 526) insists that the lawn should be frequently mowed, whereas Petrus de Crescentiis suggests (in a minority opinion) that grass should be mowed only twice a year so that it will remain beautiful and permanent (in MacDougall 1986: 165). Walter Thwing suggests that mowing *properly* 'requires some thought' (1948: 26); Hugh Johnson believes mowing can be a 'pleasure in itself' (1979: 154); Wilfrid Jeffs enjoys the 'exciting fragrance of newly-mown grass' (1964: 9); and Thomas Meehan admonishes that mowing is one of 'the heaviest expenses' in gardening (1868: 354). The burden or pleasure of keeping grass short has a logical connection to the levelling of surface: 'Lawns that are relatively level and have straight sides are easier to maintain' (DeWerth 1961: 26). It follows, therefore, as *The Gardeners' Magazine* instructs, that 'if your lawn is uneven, take the turf up, and have the ground made perfectly level' (1850: 148).

Mowing is fun and easy

The caption in Anton Kannemeyer's painting *Splendid Dwelling* (see Plate 3) asks the rhetorical question, 'How can anyone be unhappy who lives in such a splendid dwelling?' Yet the black man mowing the lawn in the starkly rendered suburban garden does not look very happy; he looks determined, even angry, and he still has lots of mowing to do, with only a solitary strip of emerald green carpet having been completed. The image is not a cheerful one; the clichéd house and the cartoon-like flowers in the tree highlight the fact that this bleak image has what one reviewer called 'an unnerving sense of the depressing, suicidal atmosphere of life in the 'burbs that carries no hint of nostalgia or escape' (Smith 2012).

There are at least two interpretations of this artwork. The first is that the man mowing does not dwell in the 'splendid' dwelling; he is the poorly paid gardener. *Splendid Dwelling* is part of the series 'Paintings for Doctors and Dentists', the companion painting depicting a cleaner with a feather duster in a clichéd domestic worker's uniform. Seen together, the presumption of the black mower's status as a boy rather than owner seems to be supported. In this case, mowing is but one of the disconnected 'tasks' the boy attends to, an activity that is ultimately thankless, an entirely unrewarding experience of labour.

The general absence of labouring bodies in the landscape makes Kannemeyer's work unusual. In *The Politics of Landscape* (1979) James Turner argues that poets, too, have generally excluded from their work any reference to the labours of the countryside and 'it takes some effort to appreciate what has been censored from the ideal landscape'. He continues: 'There is virtually no mention of land-clearance, tree-felling, pruning, chopping, digging, hoeing, weeding, branding, gelding, slaughtering, salting, tanning, brewing, boiling, smelting, forging, milling, thatching, fencing and hurdle-making, hedging, road-mending and haulage. Almost everything which anybody does in the countryside is taboo' (1979: 165).

Coetzee suggests that the injunction against representing certain kinds of labour in the pastoral and georgic mode takes on an added racial significance in the colonial landscape. For if 'the work of hands on a particular patch of earth, digging, ploughing, planting, building, is what inscribes it as the property of its occupiers *by right*,' writes Coetzee, 'then the hands of black serfs doing the work had better not be seen' (1988: 5). In South Africa, white colonists were in a difficult position in which the incorporation of the black man was 'embarrassing'. The difficulty entailed the following tangle: the black man's presence on the farm testifies to his original ownership of the land; therefore it is necessary that his improving condition be demonstrated by his labour. Yet in order to demonstrate the right to dominate the land white settlers must show the land being put to use and improved by *their* hands. The demonstration of the black man's productivity challenges this requirement: the problem of the pastoral genre makes 'silence about the black man the easiest of an uneasy set of options'. The weed-eating landowner with powdered wig and blackface of Brett Murray's self-portrait *The Renaissance Man Tending His Land* (2008; see Plate 4) dramatises this anxiety. The fact that he is shirtless conforms to the standard leisurely presentation of white gardening and also reveals his 'tan-line', thereby calling attention to the performance of the blackface. Is there also a 'farmer's tan' joke here, drawing on the evidence of working-class whites who labour outdoors?

A second reading of Kannemeyer's *Splendid Dwelling* suggests that the mower is in fact the owner of the home. He is, however, still not happy. This presumption of ownership opens up an opportunity for critical reflection on post-apartheid black middle-class suburban practices and to consider the postcolonial notion of mimicry as it relates to the expression of ownership though the landscape.

Generally the lawn is described as 'the joy and delight of every homebuilder' (Kellaway 1907: 55), 'a joy to its owner [and for] all those whose privilege it is to admire its gracious expanse of verdure' (Jeffs 1964: 9). Writing about nineteenth-century trade cards for lawnmowers, Jenkins notes that the message was: mowing is fun, easy, not labour (1994b). Mowing is described as an overwhelmingly positive, rewarding and healthy exercise: 'To a lawn fanatic the process of mowing is a pleasure in itself' (Johnson 1979: 154). This pleasure is a dividend that accrues to the owner, not (generally) to the labourer.

That the dividend of pleasure in Kannemeyer's image seems not to accrue to the possible owner is extremely provocative. It suggests that the lawn may operate as what Lauren Berlant calls a form of 'cruel optimism' (2011), a desire that actually functions as an obstacle to flourishing. As will be seen in Chapter 3, the apartheid state was actively involved in an ideological and political programme that equated gardening with respectable middle-class subjectivity, including the attendant promises of happiness.

Clothing is one of the key visual markers that establish the distinction between gardener and garden boy. The legal concept of the 'reasonable man' has also been known as the 'man in his shirtsleeves' or the man who 'takes the magazines at home and in the evening pushes the lawn mower' (Dean 1996: 115). In Richard Yates's novel *Revolutionary Road* (2008) a domestic interaction between his characters Frank and April places lawn care and clothing to be worn while mowing at the centre of their suburban disease:

> Awakening from a late night solo-drinking binge, Frank rises at eleven o'clock on a Saturday morning to the sound of April mowing the lawn. Decked out in Frank's old clothing, April assumes the

> role of suburban lawn-keeper, which is traditionally a masculine duty; however, she does this more out of a feeling of disgust for her husband's laxity than out of a desire to compromise her husband's position in the family. Frank, of course, does not interpret her actions this way. As such, he has forfeited more than his function as the man of the house – however implicating and emasculating that title might be in the topography of suburbia. (Moreno 2003: 90)

In Goldblatt's *Saturday Afternoon in Sunward Park. 1979* (see Plate 5) the white mower is shirtless and in shorts, as is Murray's *Renaissance Man*. Both white men gesture towards an informality, an affected casualness, which points to a leisure activity rather than paid work.

In contrast, Kannemeyer's 'unhappy' mower wears something like suit pants, formal shoes and a long-sleeved shirt. It is not possible to establish the happiness of Goldblatt's mower as his back is to us and I would not describe Murray as happy per se, rather as smug. And, even with his back to the camera, Mr Boksburg strikes a heroic pose, assured of his right to take ownership of his space and to take pleasure in not only his 'work' but also the future appreciation of others who have the 'privilege' to admire his 'gracious verdure'. The black man seems to accrue none of these joys, neither the pleasure of the act nor the future appreciation of the lawn's perfection.

Masters and men

Kannemeyer's technical treatment of the lawn is striking. It recurs throughout his work and creates the ambiguous possibility of the lawn being green and at the same time not-quite-green. The deliberate choice of red grass blades on lime green is abrasive. His visual treatment of the mown and not-yet-mown grass sets up a visual tension. The lime green strip of lawn runs along orderly straight lines. Note that Goldblatt's white mower has expertly managed this task and created visible lines in the grass, parallel to the driveway and perpendicular to the road. This mowing technique speaks of an obsession with rationality, order and control.

The mathematically precise lines, the aspiration of the suburban gardener, echo the large flat historical lawns of the great estates of England and, closer to home, the early twentieth-century croquet lawns of suburban white settlers, and later the bowls, rugby, cricket and soccer fields. If perfect, the lawn is a series of parallel straight lines on an entirely flat surface – a rational equation of sorts. While the central bulk of the lawn can be rationalised in this way, the borders of the 'garden picture' cause more consternation. The lawn adjacent to the walls and fences and the irrational edges of an 'informal garden' including serpentine flower beds present challenges for a mower. In *Standard Garden Practice for Southern Africa* W. G. Sheat points out that the garden boy is not equipped to manage such challenges because while he may enjoy mindless exercise he is overtaken by technology: 'There is nothing that appeals to the garden boy more than to spend the day armed with a pair of cutting shears, at ease in his favourite position, slowly edging his way along the border, earnestly contemplating each blade of grass as it falls. The mechanical edger has taken all the romance out of this congenial pastime for it will cut the edges, and efficiently too, as fast as the operator can walk' (1956: 19). The sarcastic jokes shared with the (presumed white) reader function on a level of shared disdain for the garden boy – his laziness, lack of modernity, slowness, stupidity, inefficiency. That Sheat was the general manager of the Parks and Community Services Department for Johannesburg at the time of writing his book, and that the foreword by D. F. Malan praised him for addressing unique South African conditions, make the legitimacy of the semantic assault on black labourers even more forceful.

However, this attitude towards gardeners was not unique to South Africa and had its precedent in Britain. Martin Hoyles (2002) shows that the job of gardening was so poorly paid at the beginning of the nineteenth century that gardeners often had to advertise for charity in the gardening press. The Benevolent Institution for the Relief of Aged and Indigent Gardeners and Their Widows was formed in 1839 to deal with such cases. In his *Gardener's Magazine* John Loudon 'constantly campaigned for better wages, working hours and lodgings for the hired gardener. He compared an illiterate bricklayer, with wages of between five and seven shillings a day, to a journeyman gardener who, despite having studied geometry, land surveying and botany, received only two shillings and sixpence a day. In 1841 even head gardeners were paid only about a tenth of a cook's salary and half that of a footman' (Hoyles 2002: n.p.). In his *Encyclopaedia of Gardening* Loudon describes how gardeners lived: 'In one ill-ventilated apartment, with an earthen or brick floor, the whole routine of cooking, cleaning, eating, and sleeping is performed, and young men are rendered familiar with the filth and vermin, and lay the foundation of future diseases, by breathing unwholesome air. How masters can expect any good service from men treated worse than horses, it is difficult to imagine' (1825: 336–337). In 'Masters and Men', from her book *Wood and Garden*, Gertrude Jekyll expresses an attitude more typical of her time, warning readers about the 'ignorance and obstructiveness of gardeners' (1899: 271). She explains:

> Various degrees of ignorance and narrow-mindedness must no doubt be expected among the class that produces private gardeners. Their general education is not very wide to begin with, and their training is usually all in one groove, and the many who possess a full share of vanity get to think that, because they have exhausted the obvious sources of experience that have occurred within their reach, there is nothing more to learn, or to know, or to see, or to feel, or to enjoy. (Jekyll 1899: 272)

Jekyll later uses the metaphor of an artist to clarify the difference between master and gardener: 'The servant may set up the canvas and grind the colours, and even set the palette, but the master alone can paint the picture' (1899: 279).

True gardeners

The gardener's treatment of the garden boy is pernicious, if sometimes only semantically, and structured by a more or less violent opposition of owner/gardener with garden boy. It is worth reading, in comparison, what Boddam-Whetham suggests a 'true' gardener is like. Her saccharine description sounds like a kitsch watercolour illustration from a children's Bible: 'Every true gardener is fundamentally a loveable person. If the plants under his care grow healthily and happily, it is because their guardian is that kindly soul who is compassionate to all weak creatures that need protection and care. He is tender hearted to shy children and wild birds and stray kittens. He is gentle and considerate to plants and flowers' (1933: 106).

A pointed opposition emerges between, on the one hand, the 'courage' and 'rare quality of soul' (Fairbridge 1924: 34) of a 'fundamentally loveable' true gardener and, on the other hand, the garden boy who leaves the tap running. The boy is a lazy, pestilential child-demon who, by 'shirking his work, by taking hours over his meals, by doing everything wrong that could possibly be done in the wrong way … appears to be the most annoying pest the long-suffering gardener has to put up with' (Smith 1940: 81).

The notion that garden labourers are deceitful, negligent and ignorant is not a recent one. Writing in *The Female Spectator* the magazine's editor Eliza Haywood, also a major novelist and an advocate of cross-dressing, asks: 'Why should our gardeners be wiser than ourselves? … Why should we put it in their power to deceive us, and not be able to detect either their negligence or want of skill in the cultivation of a produce we are so proud of when brought to perfection?' (Haywood 1745: 58–59). In fact, one of the qualities most valued in a servant is being 'very stupid' because, as the 1910 novel *Jill's Rhodesian Philosophy or The Dam Farm* by Gertrude Page argues, the stupid boy 'will often end up making a good servant' because, his head empty of ideas, he will, like a parrot, perform whatever he is taught (quoted in McCulloch 2000: 114).

The garden boy is not always described in such overtly pejorative racist terms. As noted in Chapter 1, garden writer Una van der Spuy named and thanked her gardener John Mashati in the introduction to *Wild Flowers of South Africa for the Garden* (1971). In the *Artist in the Garden* Read Lloyd is invested in framing the partnership between her grandfather H. A. Read and his Parktown gardener-artist Moses Tladi in a kind of retrospective warm sunshine of kindly collaboration between two equals. She opines that their relationship seemed 'something very subtly *other*' and that 'imagination as well as perspiration' led to the establishment of a garden that reflected both the personalities involved (2009: 16). The more cynical reader would interpret the 'imagination' belonging to Mr Read and the 'perspiration' to Mr Tladi; this is how Smith's text structures the relationship between gardener and garden boy. We can assume, however, that Read Lloyd, who was exceedingly fond of both her grandfather and Moses Tladi, meant that *both* men's imaginations and perspiration were mixed into making the garden of her memories. However good-hearted Mr Read was towards Tladi, there can be no doubt about the degree to which their relationship must have been profoundly organised by the paternalism that characterised the treatment of black men by white men in South Africa at the beginning of the twentieth century.

The distinction between kindness and equality is illustrated in a bizarre but also poignant interview that apartheid-era Minister of Law and Order Adriaan Vlok gave to *The New Republic* about his foot-washing 'repentance'. When asked what he believed was his greatest wrong, he answered, 'I hurt my gardener ... I regarded myself as better. Many [white] people still believe, "I treat my [black] gardener nice!" But I did not treat him as an equal' (Fairbanks 2014).

In *Portrait with Keys: Joburg & What-What* (2009) Ivan Vladislavić captures the structural asymmetry in a record of an encounter along a green belt on the Braamfontein Spruit – a liminal landscape, a no-man's-land – between a gardener and white resident.[7] The record of the exchange is shot through with fear, a desire for recognition and the sad realisation of the impossibility of such recognition:

> As he's running along the Braamfontein Spruit early one morning, Mike sees a man lounging on a scrap of wasteland beneath a pylon, right beside the footpath. Mike is visiting the country. He's heard the stories of people getting mugged for nothing more than their shoes, and so he's wary. He slows down, considers turning back. But now he's close enough to recognize the man: it's the gardener of the townhouse complex where he's staying, apparently relaxing before he reports for duty, smoking the first cigarette of the day. The man recognizes him at the same moment and calls a greeting, Mike stops to chat. Their paths have crossed half a dozen times in the past week around the complex, and Mike was struck by his surly submissiveness, but now he seems forthright and approachable. Meeting here on no-man's-land has freed him to be a different person. Or rather, has freed them to stand in a different relation to one another, because Mike realizes that he must be a different person, here. When the gardener lights his second cigarette, Mike takes one too, although he's trying to cut down, although he's in the middle of a run. They talk for twenty minutes about work and soccer and politics, and then it's time to go back to the past, where their old selves are waiting. (2009: 170)

On the other hand, in his short story 'The Tuba' Vladislavić writes about an encounter between a white character called Cliffie, 'always a trouble maker', and a nameless black pieceworker who shows up on a typical Saturday morning 'asking to weed the flower-beds and mow the lawn' (2010: 118). If Cliffie had been a 'respectable' white like Goldblatt's mower in Sunward Park, perhaps he may have spent his Saturday morning diligently mowing his own lawn. Instead, Vladislavić describes how Cliffie would spend the weekends performing typical white male leisure activities with his 'boys', drinking beer and brandy, braaing ('Cliffie piled his sosaties on the edge of the grill, put down the tongs and bent to wipe his hands on the lawn'), watching cricket, joking about politics ('It's the same, wherever you go, some black face laughing at you. They'll be toyi-toying in your front garden just now'), swearing and playing darts. It is worth noting that their dartboard is decorated with the face of Saddam Hussein and that they appear to relish throwing darts 'like assegais' at his eyes and nose. The dartboard is an ironic indication of the political nature of leisure in the story and also a pointer towards the manner in which humour (for it is obviously a joke dartboard?) is wrapped up in violence.

On the particular Saturday the narrator describes, the pieceworker asks for 'twenty rand for the morning's work, but Cliffie offers him a bonus if he washes the car'. When the man is finished mowing Cliffie breaks their agreement and, in front of his 'boys', hands over an oversized, kitsch wooden Krugerrand as big as a 'dinner plate': a prank they had played many times before. The narrator explains that this worker 'saw the joke immediately and began to weep, resolutely, in a language we did not understand' and walked out of the yard (Vladislavić 2010: 119).

The gardening scene is an interlude that occupies only three paragraphs of the story: a parenthetical, bracketed digression or supplement, with an emotional and ethical impact far out of proportion to its word count. It could be suggested that it was written in the margin to the *proper* account of the Salvation Army band and the racist drama involved, from which the short story takes its title. A lawn serves as background to the action, just as the story describes the bright green, flat cricket pitch of the Wanderers on the TV screen in the background.

The narrative is essentially (about) a bad joke. 'The Tuba' is full of references to jokes, laughter, being laughed at and paranoia about being laughed at. The poor mower is the butt of this specific joke and just as we are told that Cliffie had played this prank before – 'the memory of these transactions made him laugh until the tears ran down his cheeks' – from the black man's response, we can guess he may have experienced this punchline before. This story does not end with anyone laughing. Cliffie notes: it just goes to show that blacks just do not 'have a sense of humour, it [is] the funny thing about them' (Vladislavić 2010: 119). The tragic quality derives, in part, from this (as well as the narrative to which we now turn) being *public* humiliation, in front of white people – Cliffie's boys who 'were summoned as an audience' (118). This story ends with a terrible sadness, a sadness that is unintelligible to 'us' – for the garden boy's suffering was 'in a language we did not understand'.

Vladislavić's narrative is not aberrant. In *The Number* (2004) Jonny Steinberg recounts an event with remarkable similarities. Magadien – convict, Number 28 and protagonist of Steinberg's history – was serving parole entrusted into the service of a white farmer, Sterfontein, as free labour. After he had undermined the authority of the farmer on Saturday, on Sunday he was

> summoned to the farmhouse. There were several men standing around the braai. There were women seated around a table on the verandah. There was the smell of meat being cooked, and of beer. Afterwards, Magadien would remember the setting as a makeshift amphitheatre, an audience assembled around a stage. Sterfontein motioned Magadien to come to him. 'Closer,' he said. 'Stand right next to me.' Magadien felt a blow to his stomach, he felt himself fall. '*Kom ons wys wat maak ons met hierdie hotnot*,' he heard Serfontein say. (Let's show you what we do with this *hotnot*). A pair of strong hands grabbed the back of his neck; the farmer pulled a rubber tyre tube over his head. 'He suffocated me until I thought I was going to die. Then he pulled the tube off my head, let me breathe a bit, then put it back over my face. When he was finished, I vomited on his lawn. He laughed, and I heard the others laugh too. I couldn't get up. I lay there in front of them for a long time, and they laughed until they got bored.' (2004: 192)

Not working

The previous section developed an argument that sees the master and garden boy emerge dialectically. The gardeners in these ecosystems are, as Smith notes, not their 'own' gardeners in 'the right sense'; they manage black labour and 'rule the destinies' of their gardens without getting their hands dirty (1940: 81). There is, however, another tradition of garden work, one in which white (male) hands are directly involved – and seen to be directly involved – in the keeping of gardens as part of a 'search for respectability' (Sparks 2012: 96). I now turn to an examination of the problem of respectability in relation to whiteness in the work of Goldblatt and the town plan of Sasolburg and resultant civic attitudes towards garden maintenance and good citizenship.

The work of leisure

I begin by focusing on Goldblatt's iconic black-and-white photograph *Saturday Afternoon in Sunward Park. 1979* (Plate 5) from the series 'In Boksburg', which was published as a book of the same name in 1982. In the photograph, a shirtless white man mows his lawn with an electric lawnmower; the serpentine power cord lies across the lawn that has been mowed in stripes, parallel to the brick driveway and perpendicular to the tar road that edges a veld; there is no boundary wall. Across the road is an apartheid-era suburban house with a low-pitched roof, sheltered eaves and north-facing orientation. On the lawn are two solitary plants. *Saturday Afternoon* is an arresting image that captures a strange monumentality, a kind of white heroism and eroticism.[8]

The photograph was taken in the winter of 1979 (Goldblatt 1982: ii), so the lawn may have begun to turn golden, burnt by frost and dormant from the lack of rainfall. Mike Nicol wrote about the 'brittle lawns' of the winter suburbs in his poem 'Returning' (1984: 6) as did Vladislavić in *Portrait with Keys* (2009: 86). Those who have lived on the Rand through the dry winters, which batter the lawns, can testify to the bleakness of the season: an intractable time for lawn keeping.

The 'land' being worked in this image belongs to the white mower. We cannot be sure that he owns it legally but assume that he does because he is white and because of that hard-to-define quality about the way that he occupies the space, physically owns it, which reflects his (presumed) ability to own it correctly and convincingly. The predisposition to inhabit space in such a convincing way has something to do with the notion of whiteness. Far from the garden activities examined below being easy expressions of pre-earned whiteness, they exemplify an uneasy attempt to secure an elusive respectable white subjectivity.

The white gardener's body is styled in the 'heroic mould', which is characterised by the 'inflection of work with nobility' (Wolkowitz 2006: 44).[9] He is muscular, frozen like a statue; if not an Olympian nude in marble then perhaps a Grecian plaster garden statue like that captured in Santu Mofokeng's photograph *Diepkloof Ext 2 Soweto* (1991), or Goldblatt's *Garden and house, Sixth Street, Orange Grove, 16 May 1968* (1968).[10] The mower in Goldblatt's *Saturday Afternoon* exudes the sense of being a sportsman, healthy, productive; no doubt heterosexual. It is a Saturday afternoon (as Goldblatt has told us by way of his careful and specific titling style) and instead of employing a black worker to mow his lawn, or spending the day watching sport or drinking, he is keeping his *own* lawn. This man is an archetype of a particular white subjectivity that connects viable whiteness to a form of respectable modernity. While this white man is being productive, it is important to emphasise that he is not 'working'; what he is involved in is broadly conceived of as leisure. Garden maintenance, of one's own garden, as leisure, is a proper activity for respectable whites.

Perhaps the most extreme example of this kind of thinking is to be found 'outside' South Africa's borders in the Afrikaner *volkstaat* (people's state) of Orania. Founded by apartheid ideologue and South African Bureau of Racial Affairs intellectual Carel Boshoff III, Orania was conceived of as the embryonic point for an independent, ambitious Afrikaner geopolitical entity. Built in a wretched, unwanted corner of the Northern Cape, the barren little town is explicitly (though not legally) intended only for whites and founded on the ideology of *selfwerksaamheid*, or self-reliance. 'There were to be no Blacks in Orania,' writes Goldblatt, 'there was to be none of the culture of dependence of Whites on Blacks for physical work' (Goldblatt 1998: 255). The ideology of 'self-work' operates on a number of practical levels, the most basic of which is that whites perform all labour, including domestic and garden work. '*Ons werk self!*' reads the caption below an image of garden tools hanging against a face-brick wall on the official website. The muscular diligence of this kind of whiteness is epitomised by the semi-official mascot of Orania, Kleinreus (Small Giant), a little boy rolling up his sleeves, bracing for good physical work. Still, one would be hard-pressed to find young shirtless whites in rugby shorts mowing lawns in Orania.

Boshoff IV, the son of Orania's founder, current president of the Orania Beweging (Movement) and self-styled philosopher, got fed up with his home's lawn, tearing it up and planting vegetables instead, fertilised by rotating chicken coops (Cane 2010). His rejection of the lawn relates to its uselessness and its non-sustainability, and is part of a subscription to ultra-modern ideas like bicycle-sharing schemes, off-the-grid electricity strategies, digital and web-based teaching methodologies and curriculum development, extensive recycling systems, research into sustainable building technologies and town-wide wireless Internet coverage in Orania.

The melodramatic performance of white work and the self-conscious concern with modernity evident in Orania is germane to the respectability in *Saturday Afternoon*. The garden as an important site of white subjectification, of becoming white, is highlighted in two ethnographic studies. The first, *The Making of a Good White* by Annika Teppo (2004), a study of the 'rehabilitation of poor whites' in Epping Garden Village, Cape Town, argues that 'gardens were central semi-public spaces where [respectable poor whites or *armblankes*] could demonstrate their commitment to rehabilitation' (2004: 161). The second, 'Apartheid Modern: South Africa's Oil from Coal Project and the History of a South African Company Town' by Stephen Sparks (2012), is an investigation of Sasol, the apartheid state's oil-from-coal project, and its accompanying built environment, Sasolburg and the township of Zamdela. Sparks argues that 'respectability was a synonym for whiteness inflected with particular class and gender emphasis ... Respectability's key external markers in Sasolburg were properly tended gardens, houses and yards' (2012: 97).

At the core of both studies is a certain observation about whiteness, or rather a particularly South African whiteness, which resists some of the more universal definitions of racial privilege. A number of other authors – Nuttall (2001); Powell (2002); Ratele (2009); Ratele & Laubscher (2010); Stevens (2007) and Wicomb (1998) – have proposed a reworking of 'traditional' whiteness theory in the context of South Africa. Whiteness, we are generally told, is the 'norm that is invisible, working in the background as a standard, not of one particular way of being in the world, but as normalcy, as universalizability, of just being "the way things are"' (Vice 2010: 324). Further, we are told that whiteness operates as 'taken-for-granted privilege, allowing white people to be unconscious of their own racialisation and the unearned advantages they take as simple entitlement' (Steyn 2007: 421).

In their precis of orthodox whiteness Samantha Vice and Melissa Steyn point to two things against which I would like to put question marks. The first concept that seems questionable is the un-markedness, the invisibility, even the unconsciousness of whiteness. The argument is that white people are just white, that white is not a race; it just is 'the way things are'. The reality is that whiteness was marked in South Africa, legislated for in a number of Acts, and very much visible. The second is the idea of entitlement, or 'unearned' privilege, the argument being that benefits (economic, cultural capital) just accrue to whites by virtue of their race. The key word here is 'just'. In South Africa, where earning credentials by correct living as a white was necessarily a process, whiteness was not something one could just presume to benefit from, always, for all 'white' people. This line of argument implies, among other things, that whiteness always needed to be affirmed, even created. This makes whiteness very similar to the lawn, which also need to be constantly worked at.

The line of argument I am pursuing requires two cautionary notes: (1) one should be wary of claiming South African exceptionalism (as has so often been the case elsewhere) and yet confront the unavoidable specificity of apartheid whiteness; and (2) one should avoid even the slightest sense that pointing out the unfinishedness of some white people's racialisation lends any sympathy to the notion of whiteness in crisis during or after apartheid.

Whiteness and modernity

Posel's work is a more compelling way of approaching race in South Africa. Her histories of apartheid (1999, 2000, 2001, 2011) stress the self-conscious modernity of the apartheid project (2000: 125). In the influential article 'Race as Common Sense: Racial Classification in Twentieth-Century South Africa' Posel addresses the epistemological underpinnings of race, tracing how in South Africa both the 'semiotics of blood' (2001: 100) and genetic descent became officially supplanted by 'common-sense' judgements based on appearance and lifestyle (102). This eclipse can be seen pointedly in the racial classification matrix of the Population Registration Act of 1950:

> A white person is one who in appearance is, or who is generally accepted as, a white person, but does not include a person who, although in appearance obviously a white person, is generally accepted as a coloured person. (Section 1 [xv])
>
> A 'native' is a person who is in fact or is generally accepted as a member of any aboriginal race or tribe of Africa. (Section 1 [x])
>
> A coloured person is a person who is not a white person nor a native. (Section 1 [iii]) (Union of South Africa 1950)

According to the Act, whiteness was a matter of *appearance* and *acceptance*, not essentially of blood or ancestry. This is a fundamental observation, because what the definition does is to locate race somewhere more or less outside of the inside of the body, between bodies, on the surfaces of bodies. Rather, race is a seen as a matter of how bodies appear to be, move and locate themselves. The question of *appearance* suggests both the idea of (1) emergence (as a subject), the process of becoming visible, of coming into existence; and (2) the way something looks, how it seems to someone *else*. This double sense of *appearance* helps to illuminate the circumstance that even though apartheid classification did not hinge on ancestry or blood politics, there was nothing superficial or shallow about what it meant to appear. The Act's definition is also profoundly relational or intersubjective – one needed not only to appear to someone *else* but also to be accepted by them too. It is worth clarifying the composition and qualifications of those who accept. An earlier, pre-apartheid piece of legislation – the Mixed Marriages Commission (1938) – may help to qualify the 'whom'. According to the Act the concept of a 'European' or 'white person' is 'sufficiently well understood … for the purpose of distinguishing in most cases between a European and a non-European'. The Act continues to clarify that 'where a person is not manifestly white, or manifestly coloured, his true classification is generally determined, at any rate, in his own community, by his associations and general mode of life' (Union of South Africa 1938: para. 141).

In this instance of ambiguity, it was one's 'own community' that determined one's 'true classification'. 'As the Minister of the Interior put it, the test of race was "the judgment of society ... the classification of a person should be made according to the views held by members of that community"' (Posel 2011: 333). If we were permitted to play with the word 'accept', we could layer the notion of *general belief or recognition of trueness* with acceptance as *welcome and favourable regard.* To be accepted (*welcomed*) is what is required to be accepted (*recognised as true*).

What the 1938 Act can help us understand is how the notion of race as a *generality* was consolidated and then extended, for by 1950 the term 'generally' had become very important, probably central to racial classification. This terminology of *generality* and its place in the operationalisation of racism is what Posel calls the bureaucratisation of 'common sense' (2001: 87). She argues that in order to operationalise the Act, what was required 'was a process of mass racial classification, encompassing millions of people, to be undertaken as efficiently and inexpensively as possible. Hence the need for a definition of racial categories that was minimally controversial and maximally practical' (101).

The very 'looseness' of the Act's definitions was what made it (appear) possible to actually administer apartheid. Saul Dubow also stresses the workability of the Act: 'For all its pretensions to scientific rigour and taxonomical precision, the Act could not be made workable without making allowances for criteria like "appearance", "descent", and general social "acceptance"' (2014: 38). But whereas Dubow sees the non-biological criteria as 'allowances', supplements as it were, to the real core of the Act, Posel points to the more provocative idea that those allowances *were* the fundamentally modern elements of race. The general mode of life was what made race mean. It is worth underlining the fact that 'appearance' is only mentioned in relation to white people. One could be white by appearing to be white, or being generally accepted as white. But one could appear white and be accepted as coloured, in which case you would be classified as coloured. You did not have to appear black to be a native, only to be accepted as part of an aboriginal race or tribe.

The final point to be stressed is the ridiculous, comedic quality of the state's linguistic usage of 'obviously'. Even when a person was *obviously* white but was not accepted as white, their race was called into question. As Kopano Ratele and Leswin Laubscher argue: 'What is obvious to one person may not be obvious to another. Policing the borders, then, to root out suspicious whiteness, indications of abnormal White-types, forgeries, borderline cases, and the like, may well mean or imply usage of a criterion or decision rule beyond that of the legal and intuitive sense of the obvious, especially when natural appearance and the fundamental scientific tools are unavailable or itself suspect in rendering a definitive verdict' (2010: 84).

The respectable garden

We can now begin to see how South African whiteness required convincing performances of certain norms, especially regarding class anxieties, and particularly within white Afrikaans communities. Drawing up whiteness's boundaries had everything to do with the notion of 'respectability' and even more with being seen to be respectable. Indeed, just as missionary Samuel Broadbent stressed the fundamentality of the 'external arrangements' of the nineteenth-century evangelised and domesticated natives, so within whiteness itself, domestication was required to be outwardly demonstrated.

Sparks argues in 'Apartheid Modern' that gardens and yards (in Sasolburg, in this case) were especially important visible sites where evidence could be offered to the community about one's acceptable white ways. The 'search for respectability,' Sparks claims, 'has proven to be one of the key aspirational motors of identity-making in modern South African history' (2012: 96). Sasolburg was designed by the Wits-affiliated architect Max Kirchhofer who, just like his peers, was much in thrall to modernist and modernising notions. That architectural and urban modernity mapped neatly onto racial preoccupations of the time has not gone unnoticed by historians, most insightfully by Derek Japha in 'The Social Programme of the South African Modern Movement' (1998). Detailed analysis of seminal thinkers like the *Native Housing* collective thesis group of students Paul Harold Connell, Charles Irvine-Smith, Kurt Jonas, Roy Kantorowich and Frans J. Wepener and fellow Wits alumnus Douglas McGavin Calderwood must be bracketed until Chapter 3. Here, the important thing I wish to underline is the profound affinity that existed between modernism and apartheid.

Kirchhofer's plans were shot through with the kind of optimism to be expected from a modernist planner. Buoyed by Sasol's success at transforming an arid landscape into a tree-filled city and, indeed, the ability to transform coal into oil, Kirchhofer resisted advice from both the Orange Free State Townships Board and the National Housing Commission to distance the civic centre from poor white areas, to reduce plot size for 'low-income' whites, as they were 'more likely to be nicely kept than a bigger one', and to alter the plans that had south-facing plots onto the new town's main streets (Sparks 2012: 114–115). At stake was the visibility of *backvelders* (country bumpkins). Kirchhofer stubbornly held on to the belief that *backvelders* would 'remake themselves in the image of the dominant local culture linking respectability to everyday aesthetic practices including the management of gardens' (17). He was to be very disappointed. Six years later he noted his concern in a 1962 internal memo that in Precinct 1 a majority of stands occupied by 'the lower income groups ... remained unused, lying fallow, overgrown' (quoted in Sparks 2012: 117). 'Kirchhofer's plans [had been] inserted into a fractious class politics where officials and self-consciously respectable residents were preoccupied with the conspicuous presence of purportedly unrespectable "lower-income" white residents in the town' (96).

What Kirchhofer and Sasol managers envisioned, and what David de Villiers, the Sasol company secretary, claimed, was that they could and would take a 'bunch of *kombuis kaffirs*' (literally, kitchen kaffirs) and transform them into 'completely sophisticated people' (quoted in Sparks 2012: 95). As Sparks notes in commentary about De Villiers's statement, the salvation they offered was both racial and gendered: 'SASOL made Afrikaners modern and saved them from their subjugation, emasculation and, above all, from racial transgression' (90). The home was considered a prime site for the salvation of Afrikaners, for modernising backward rural people, but the domesticated Afrikaner is in an ambivalent position where the newly urbanised are expected to demonstrate a kind of correctly gendered relation to the house and garden.

Respectability as a concept is founded on a dichotomy – rough/respectable (where 'rough', of course, has multiple permutations: *kaffir, kombuis kaffir*) – and is, as Robert Ross proposes in *Status and Respectability in the Cape Colony, 1750–1870*, 'the outward manifestation of a specific class ideology' (1999: 5). Indeed, in the nineteenth century Friedrich Engels described the ideal of respectability as 'a most repulsive thing', 'a false consciousness bred into the bones of workers' (quoted in Skeggs 1997: 3). As Mike Huggins argues: 'Notions of class and class relationships have often been empirically linked by historians to the concept of respectability. Indeed, some historians have preferred to use respectability rather than class as a way of explaining the nature of social and political divisions and modes of social integration in Victorian Britain. Respectability, many have argued, was a sharp line of social division, consolidating bonds between middle- and working-class respectables, in order to reform now distanced working-class roughs' (2000: 585).

If the Victorian 'rise of respectable society' was a predominantly metropolitan phenomenon as the middle class sought respectability 'to maintain their status and self-respect against the lower-classes, and the aristocracy', in the colonies 'respectability was a defense against the colonized' (Mosse 1985: 5). Hence, the fundamentally dual meaning of 'going native': a descent into lethargy and sexual partnerships with the natives. As Anne Stoler points out: 'Good colonial living now meant hard work, no sloth, and physical exercise rather than sexual release' (1989: 649).

Coetzee makes a similar point about idleness and the work of white hands; he famously argues that whites 'must not only perform but, more important, be seen to perform' (1988: 5) the work on the land. 'Respectability was the means by which morality was made public and seen to be an object of knowledge' (Skeggs 1997: 3).

Indeed, respectability is an outward-facing, communal concept. Writing about early Cape society Ross stresses that 'respectability and gentility were manifested most clearly in material things. After all, the distinction between them was largely a question of income, although a gentleman, assured of and recognised in his status, might be permitted transgressions of behaviour which would condemn to the ranks of the disreputable someone who was struggling to be recognised as respectable. It was thus the outward signs that truly mattered' (1999: 78). What mattered, as 'outward signs' – forms of behaviour, possessions and associations – were different for men and women. Among other things, men were scrutinised for their leisure pursuits (Huggins 2000: 588) and women for cleanliness – of their children and home – and their sexual restraint (McClintock 1995; Ross 1985; Ross 1999; Stoler 1989).

The male injunction was not only *against* uncouth activities like gambling, drinking, whoring but also *for* manly, productive, healthy unpaid work. The burden on women was even more onerous, as their 'respectability was under perpetual suspicion' (Ross 1985: 49). Cleanliness was the sign under which women were policed and under which they policed themselves, a way of distancing themselves from 'women who were positioned as pathological, polluting and poisonous' (Skeggs 1997: 13). Cleanliness was, as McClintock (1995) argues, profoundly implicated in modern imperial capitalism and embodied in the mass marketing of soap and the reciprocal exchange of imperial imagery.

The fear of contagion, especially for those not quite assured of their respectability, leads to a state of perpetual surveillance, where the behaviour of suspect individuals and families is under scrutiny. This fear is founded in the essential characteristic of respectability as 'always a process, a dialogue with oneself and with one's fellows, never a fixed position' (Harrison 1982: 161). In fact, it was, if anything, an aspiration, 'a marker and a burden of class, a standard to which to aspire' (Skeggs 1997: 3).

In the geopolitics of Sasolburg, the insecurities and aspirations of the not-quite-securely respectable middle class, who happened to live in close proximity to the poor, recently urbanised whites, found expression in a culture of 'epistolary performances' (Sparks 2012: 127), letters of complaint to local newspapers and civic representatives, in which the writers decried the failure (or refusal!) of *backvelders* to keep their gardens correctly.

One such letter from Sparks's study, by a Mr Turner to the town clerk in 1969, complains that 'a few people … have no pride whatsoever' and 'we who keep our yards clean have to put up with the mess from yards of those who are too lazy to keep the place clean'. Mr Turner continues:

> I am sure it must be a pleasure for any member of the municipality when passing a house with a nice green and tidy lawn. The house directly behind me ... well a lion could lay there without being seen. No. 75–74 lawns are both the same ... Sir, I feel that the sooner you are able to take steps against such people the sooner Sasolburg will be rid of weeds and be a pleasure to live in ... I am sure something could be done to keep the lawn clear of such messy sights. (quoted in Sparks 2012: 126)

Images of 'uncut lawns, dirt, improperly tended gardens, messy back yards, ferocious dogs that bark incessantly', 'dismantled motor cars', weeds, 'odd bits of fencing', 'propped up motor cars, miscellaneous litter and undisciplined children' (Sparks 2012: 122) were the context in which community members attempted to perform their precarious respectable selves.

A letter from 'Clean Stand Lover and Lawn Proud Lady' to the municipal health department asked the municipality to come and inspect her street: 'You will find No. 2, 4, 6, 8, 12, and 14, a pleasure to see how nice the people keep their stands', but No. 10 was 'a disgrace … there the weeds are coming into seed already and will of course blow into other stands and create a lot of extra work for people round about' (quoted in Sparks 2012: 125).

The consternation 'tenuous' respectables experienced depended largely on the question of whether or not the roughs were willing or in fact able to be transformed. This distinction between ability and willingness is germane to later chapters, which concentrate on lawn projects that have failed. I want to present a fascinating observation made by Susan Schweik in her book *The Ugly Laws: Disability in Public* (2009) about a map made by an anarchist doctor called Ben Reitman in early twentieth-century Chicago. Schweik's use of disability theory to critique the notion of respectability is pertinent here. According to Schweik, Dr Reitman was the founder of the radical 'Hobo College' and an 'advocate for and ally with people (particularly women) with venereal diseases' (2009: 71). At a lecture called 'Reitman's Social Geography', the doctor presented a map drawn on a bed sheet where he had creatively schematised the 'ugly laws' that were in effect in the city at the time. These laws were motivated to remove the disabled from the public view. Reitman's map schematised this spatial injustice in a conceptual cartography: he drew an island called Vagrant Isle, which included towns like Hoboville, Bumtown, Sea of Isolation; Vagrant Isle was separated from the lands of Respect/Ability, Race Prejudice Isle, Prostitute Isle, Criminal Island and Radical Island, with its towns Freethinkville, Freeloveville, Tolstoy (Schweik 2009: 71).

What occurred to Schweik in her analysis of the map was that Reitman's annotation for the 'Land of Respect/Ability' was broken in his drawing – it reads 'Land of Respect', with 'Ability' directly below it. 'Perhaps Reitman enjambed the word simply because he ran out of space,' muses Schweik, 'but the separation out of "ability" opens up the possibility of a political pun that calls attention to the "ability/disability" axis in the dynamics of the respectable' (2009: 310). The linguistic gap opened in this conception of respectability is useful for assessing the modalities of failure I address in Chapter 4.

Watering

David Lynch's 1986 thriller *Blue Velvet* opens with a shot of a white picket fence, cheerful blue sky, gay red roses, then an American fire engine in slow motion, flower beds of yellow tulips bobbing in the breeze and children crossing the road under the protection of an elderly crossing guard. An old white man with rolled-up sleeves and a trilby hat is watering a dried-up, diseased section of his green front lawn; meanwhile, his wife inside the house drinks tea and watches television. Their garden has a herbaceous border, an angelic white fountain, a statuette. As the man tries to jerk free the hosepipe, which is twisted and has compromised flow, he has a stroke and falls to the ground. Slavoj Žižek notes that 'when he collapses, the jet of water uncannily recalls surreal, heavy urination', after which the camera approaches 'the grass surface and depicts the bursting life, the crawling of insects and beetles, their rattling and devouring of grass' (1995: 206).

We are wont to think of the lawn as a unified, thin and flat surface; that is to say, as a horizontality. Recall Dorothea Fairbridge's description of the noble lady gardener with the 'passionate love of loveliness' whose garden was destroyed when a mining shaft was sunk 'in the middle of her lawn, just when it had attained the perfection of velvet smoothness' (1924: 35). The quiet horizontality of the domestic garden is rudely interrupted by the vertical. The tension in this little garden is not only between masculine and feminine, beauty and ugliness, but is also related to a certain conceptualisation of the horizontality of the lawn. What kind of readings would a vertical inquiry yield? Do lawns really just cover the soil? And what is their connective logic? What happens to our analysis of the lawn if we do not view it as a unified, flat surface? The poor Benades' lawn in Marlene van Niekerk's *Triomf* (1999) invites such questions. Literally built on the ruins of Sophiatown, it fails to grow, poisoned by rubbish and rubble, which perpetually rises to the surface thwarting the family's best efforts – the verticality of the lawn resists their attempts at horizontal gardening.

The depth of the lawn

The complaints of white gardeners have often centred on the issue of lawn watering. Boddam-Whetham grumbled: 'Nearly all native boys seem quite incapable of even learning about [watering]; if the ground looks wet, all the ground is wet ... the depth of the soil, since they cannot see it, is beyond their mental grasp' (1933: 55). Smith concurred that garden boys only water the ground but not the roots; apparently the abstract notion that plants draw water through the roots seems lost on them. The explanation for this and other difficulties is that the 'the native gardener is not a hereditary gardener' (Smith 1940: 82). Van der Spuy moaned that in 'southern Africa more failures in gardening are due to inadequate watering than any other single cause. So often a garden boy or some member of the family opens the tap, sprinkles the surface of the ground for a short period, and when it is wet decides that the task of watering is done. The surface-splattering, although it may make the gardener feel cool, often does more harm than good' (1953: 13).

Beyond the general claim that garden boys are failures at everything, including watering, what can we discern from this very specific accusation regarding watering? On one level these claims are the familiar claims of idleness: garden boys do not water for long enough, they shirk work. What, however, if they actually have been seduced by the flatness of the lawn's discourse? If they do indeed believe that the lawn is flat and thin, it is because that is what the lawn wants them to think.

Water must surely be foregrounded in any account of the lawn in South Africa, especially in places like the highveld or the Free State or the Western Cape, with its recent extreme drought. And yet, not only does mowing, as a practice, dominate the discourse field but also the central question of water availability is deprioritised.[11] Water, of course, is essential to the lawn, a requirement that British gardening may take for granted but is certainly a source of stress for South African gardeners. There are very few gardeners for whom water is not a proportionally expensive primary input, along with other expensive things like grass seed or turf squares and rolls, or mowers. Additional costs relate to secondary inputs like fertiliser, specialised mowing equipment, weed-eaters, compost and sprinkler systems, and tertiary inputs like lawn decorations, birdbaths, storage sheds.

Tamar Garb, in *Home Lands – Land Marks*, writes of Goldblatt's *Miriam Mazibuko* (2006; see Plate 6) that she is 'watering the garden of her hard-won, but minute house ... The stream of water gushing forth from the owner's hose provides a sign of her relative wealth in this dry, impoverished landscape' (2008: 18). The water here is a sign of respectability, of ability, but also profoundly a sign of ownership. Watering is the act of possession, the act of owning, of keeping. Lawn keeping always also invokes the idea of keeping away (the lawn, leisure, private space) from someone else, keeping it for oneself.

Water(ing) can be read against this grain, as it is in Ernest Cole's untitled photograph of five ebullient black children frolicking in the sprinkler on a lawn.[12] It is neither their lawn nor are they designated legal users of the water. In *Lost and Found in Johannesburg* Mark Gevisser describes the photograph as a 'kind of baptism', depicting 'a group of small boys [that] have stripped naked and are running through the municipal sprinklers irrigating a sun-scorched park in Cole's Mamelodi township. The boys are arrested in motion as if they were Greek athletes.' In contrast to Cole's 'signature' violent images of naked Africans, Gevisser suggests 'there is redemption to the sprinkler image: even in the house of bondage that was Cole's South Africa, these joyous children are free, abandoned to the waters' (2014: 230).

Other interesting watering images include Goldblatt's *The garden of the Dutch Reformed Church with the tomb of Dominee Pieter du Toit. Edenburg, Orange Free State. 26 August 1986* (in Goldblatt 1998), with a coiled hosepipe laid across the church lawns; *Malebogo Informal Settlement. Hertzogville, Free State. 27 December 2007*, which shows a hosepipe snaking across a dirt driveway;[13] *Jan Boland Coetzee*, a press image with a sprinkler in the background of the portrait; and *Ephraim Zulu of the Salvation Army 179 Central Western Jabavu Soweto, South Africa 1972*, which shows a seated man spraying water into the garden.[14]

Miriam Mazibuko is a unique image because of its unusual gravitas. Goldblatt's photograph segues into the argument of the next chapter, where the scale is not of the individual home but rather the discourses and processes by which towns and townships are established and the place the garden takes in these imaginary places. The larger scope includes public lawns – sports grounds, parks and green belts – and an interest in professional planners and landscapers. Black labour, imagined as a pool of affordable faceless power, is ignored in favour of white pioneer discourses of heroic modernists and technocrats.

Chapter 3 Planning the Modern Lawn

The earth should never be too kind: it spoiled people.

— Ivan Vladislavić, *Flashback Hotel: Early Stories*

A montage from a 1935 *Architectural Review* article by W. A. Eden (see Plate 7) shows the design for a high-rise apartment block superimposed on top of Blenheim Palace, with its eighteenth-century landscape gardens.[1] The resulting image provocatively envisages not only the replacement of a national monument with functionalist mixed-class dwellings but also that those modern dwellings could sit comfortably within the iconic gardens of the palace. The image's rhetoric was part of an energetic international debate about public housing and the role that high-rise developments could play in the provision of modern accommodation.

This chapter includes a number of geographical locations, physical spaces like KwaThema and Welkom, in addition to a collection of plans, models, notes, lectures, collages of landscapes, many of which remain unbuilt. These sites and strategies dialectically relate to a third space, what Henri Lefebvre (1991) calls 'representational space'. The architect's plans are what Lefebvre refers to as 'representations of space'. The attempted applications, successful building schemes, in the dust and mud, as it were, are the domain of 'spatial practice', 'the material reality in which the body is situated and nature is transformed' (Warf 2006: 445). These spatial practices result in the everyday spaces that people produce, inhabit and act within, 'the artistic views of geographic reality that allow room for the imagination and unrealized possibilities' (445). Inherent in this chapter is a kind of tension between the full realisation of professional landscapes and lived realities. The questions worth asking here are: How were the plans eventually executed? What lapses, slips, amendments, changes, rebellions, exist between the paper place and proper place? What is the relationship between the plans, images and records and the actual buildings and their dissemination, reception, repetition, rejection, valorisation? How did these spatial practices circulate during apartheid and after?

Premeditated lawns

The chapter focuses on three key actors. The first was a collective of radical architecture students at the University of the Witwatersrand (Wits) in the late 1930s. Paul Harold Connell, Charles Irvine-Smith, Kurt Jonas, Roy Kantorowich and Frans J. Wepener produced a collective publication in 1939 for a high-rise 'native township' set in verdant parklands, which they also presented at the 1938 Wits Town Planning Congress and Exhibition (which they organised). Their 'model native township for 20 000 inhabitants' signified the incursion of politics and the planning concept into the architectural discourse of South Africa, and the introduction to and incorporation of international modernities for many local architects. While their polemical proposal was never adopted, most of these young men graduated and moved on to occupy powerful and influential academic and bureaucratic positions in the country. For example, Connell (1915–1997) was appointed professor of Architecture at the University of Natal in Durban in 1949 and was a founding member and first head of the architectural division of the National Building Research Institute (NBRI). The NBRI was set up in 1946 as a branch of the South African Council for Scientific and Industrial Research and was 'charged with drawing up national standards for state-funded housing while minimising cost' (Haarhoff 2011: 190).

The Institute recruited many idealistic and talented architects and planners and its aims and principles were, from 1948 onwards, sometimes at odds with government policy. Ivan Evans (1997) argues that researchers consciously sought to foster a 'modernizing spirit' through research and public discourse. Kantorowich (1917–1996) was on the team that prepared the winning design for the civic centre in Welkom, and was involved in the foreshore development in Cape Town and the planning for Vanderbijl Park (Mabin & Parnell 1995). He was one of the 'socialist radicals' (Evans 1997), the 'radicalised white architects, whose early formation overlaps with the emergence of the Transvaal Group. These architects, including Rusty Bernstein, Ozzy Israel, Alan Lipman and Clive Chipkin, studied at Wits University in the late 1930s, or in the immediate post-war period' (Le Roux 2007: 72). Both Connell and Kantorowich served on the NBRI's influential Building Research Committee from 1950 to 1955 (Evans 1997).

The second key figure was Douglas McGavin Calderwood, a Wits student in the 1950s, who became head of the architectural division of the NBRI and then chair of Building Science at Wits. His master's dissertation, 'An Investigation into the Functional and Aesthetic Aspects of Garden Architecture' (1952), and doctoral thesis, 'Native Housing in South Africa' (1953), formed the basis for the extensive application of the now ubiquitous 'matchbox' house. His work served as the official death notice for high-rise discourse and the victory of the house-with-private-lawn model for native housing for the next half a century.

The final key figure in this chapter, Joane Pim, was a landscape planner with strong connections to Wits and a favoured gardener to the English-speaking Johannesburg elite. Her book *Beauty is Necessary* (1971) is partly a record of her landscape designs for the town of Welkom and partly a collation of her lectures, research and historical analyses. Pim had all the right social connections: she grew up as the neighbour of Read Lloyd and the Oppenheimers (from whom she obtained many of her commissions). She argued that landscapes could have positive effects for labourers, increasing productivity and decreasing staff turnover.

Each of the three actors produced an important text, with pedagogic intentions and pretensions, which were directly connected to Wits as theses or teaching material. Each of these include (1) rhetoric, a written *argument* that draws on a number of theories; (2) a *plan*, a proposed real-life solution/intervention flowing from the rhetorical proposition; and (3) a number of visual devices: illustrations, drawings, models, photographs of models, photographs of places, paintings. All the people in this chapter were empowered by the state or semi-state institutions of learning that allowed them to produce, if not always built structures, at least plans with institutional legitimacy. Because the producers of these plans were academically engaged and wrote texts to accompany and explain the designs, we have a carefully worked-out set of arguments to read in conjunction with the designs. While the gardeners in the previous chapter were professional, the owners were not; in this case, both the gardeners and the planners are professionals.

While excellent research exists on the planned South African township, thus far no research has dwelt at any length on 'native' gardens. This is the focus of the current chapter: to explore how, from Connell and his colleagues onwards, every major plan proposed lawn, either explicitly or implicitly, as the outdoor context of the native dwelling. This is a remarkable fact.

Highveld modern

Theoretically, the chapter is concerned with the question of modernity. What does it mean to argue that the lawn on the highveld is modern? If we take the lawn less as a place that can be visited or located in space and rather as a bundle of processes, norms, expectations, techniques and interactions between human and non-human actors, can we claim this bundle to be modern?

Thinking through modernity requires some care. As James Ferguson points out in his ethnography of modernity's failure on the Zambian Copperbelt, the concept is 'notoriously vague, analytically slippery, and susceptible to multiple and sometimes contradictory sorts of invocation' (1999: 17). Part of the concept's slipperiness derives from the profusion of anti/post/plural modernities, such as 'multiple modernities' (Eisenstadt 2000), 'entangled modernities' (Randeria 2002) and 'alternative modernities' (Gaonkar 2001), which have emerged in contemporary scholarship. It is a hotly contested term. I endorse Frederick Cooper's (2005) pointed critique that overdiagnosing modernism, finding modernity everywhere, claiming everything as modern (even, or perhaps especially, as an anti/post/decolonial manoeuvre) means that modernity potentially loses whatever conceptual purchase it might still have.

The 'explicit modernity' of the apartheid project – and the modernisation of governance from the time of Union in 1910 onwards – has been most convincingly demonstrated by Deborah Posel (2000, 2011). Most memorably, Posel's 'A Mania for Measurement' examines the 'blustering grandiosity' and 'mundane, at times farcical' governmentality of the apartheid bureaucracy, as it dedicated itself to counting, classifying and controlling the population (2000: 116). That mania, she argues, 'illustrates the ways in which the apartheid project was understood and represented as a "modernising" one, invoking many of the assumptions, expectations and norms typical of modern states elsewhere in the world'. To avoid essentialising, Posel recommends that we view modernity as a set of processes that are always situated in specific times and places and so do not unfold uniformly.

Paul Rabinow's research on French modernism in Morocco has yielded the notion of 'archaeological moments' in modernist planning (1989, 1992), which has been taken up by Derek Japha (1998) and Jeremy Foster (2012). Rabinow's proposition is that 'under the twin imperatives of industrialization and welfare' (1992: 53) one can discern at least two archaeological moments: *technocosmopolitanism* and *middling modernism*. The former is characterised by an 'attempt to regulate history, society, and culture by working over existent institutions and spaces – cultural, social, and aesthetic – that were seen to embody a healthy sedimentation of historical practices' (53). According to Japha, technocosmopolitanism is a kind of regional modernism that blends 'universal technical imperatives of modern planning with the particularities of local sites, customs and social and cultural institutions ... modernism tailored to the local context' (1998: 437). In his influential essay 'The Social Programme of the South African Modern Movement', Japha argues that the South African Modern Movement began as a middling modernist project and eventually, as the influence of Le Corbusier was supplanted by Lewis Mumford, tended towards technocosmopolitanism.

Middling modernism 'shares the norms of industrialization, health, and sociality as well as the technological processes aimed at regulating social practices' but without the attention to 'cosmopolitan' culture or 'sedimented historical practices' (Rabinow 1992: 54). Instead, the latter's project was to create 'New Men', 'purified and liberated to pursue new forms of sociality that, it was believed, would inevitably arise from healthy spaces and forms. Science, particularly social science, would define humanity's needs, which technical planners would meet' (54). Foster's reading, in line with Japha's, is sensitive to the 'overlapping' and coexistence of the two strands of 'urban planning during the 1930s, when there was a growing sense that the rationalism of early modernism needed to be tempered by greater attunement to regional difference – a vaguely defined amalgam of local cultural traditions and the natural environment' (2012: 46).

I want to point out two critical aspects of the metanarrative of modernity, which offer a counterpoint to the 'tropes of development and progress, emergence and advance' (Ferguson 1999: 15). The first concerns the 'ubiquity of violence' (Posel 2011: 345) and the second concerns failure, 'the inevitable and critical counterpoint to modernity's empty promises of progress and betterment' (O'Gorman & Werry 2012: 1). That violence is 'behind, or rather in the neighbourhood of, the official rationality and rule of law to which the modern state is committed' (Das et al. 2000: 6) comes as no surprise to those un-moderns who have been coerced into modernity. Or to those who are set as its foil, or set upon its path of progress already understanding that, as Jean Comaroff and John Comaroff argue, 'accomplishment of anything like the real thing, the Euro-original, is presumed, at worst, to be flatly impossible, at best to be deferred into a dim, distant, almost unimaginable future' (2012: 2), a Fanonian future where it is always already 'too late. Everything is anticipated, thought out, demonstrated, made the most of' (Fanon 2008: 91). What happens, Ferguson asks, to the 'modernization myth' – where *myth* refers to both the 'factually inaccurate version of things that has come to be widely believed' and, in the anthropological sense, 'a cosmological blueprint that lays down fundamental categories and meanings for the organization and interpretation of experience' – when it is 'turned upside down, shaken, and shattered' (1999: 13)?

Before engaging with South African case studies, it is worth discussing the eighteenth-century landscape garden in order to appreciate its counterintuitive, persistent legacy in modernist planning.

Improving the landscape

To think about the English landscape garden requires, as Ann Bermingham points out, engaging with the political and economic context of the 'accelerated enclosures' between 1740 and 1860. During these enclosures, the old commons and wastelands of Britain were taken up by landowners and enclosed by quick-growing shrubs, thus forming larger, more productive farms and dispossessing the peasantry and radically altering their rights to access the land. Bermingham notes that in the first half of the eighteenth century only 74 000 acres of land were expropriated, but in the next fifty years a massive 750 000 acres were enclosed by Acts of Parliament (1986: 10).

The expropriated lands were integrated, depoliticised and naturalised by the ideology of the landscape garden. In *The Englishness of English Art* (1955), Nikolaus Pevsner writes of the eighteenth-century English landscape garden that it is

> asymmetrical, informal, varied … and made of such parts as the serpentine lake, the winding drive and winding path, the trees grouped in clumps, and smooth lawn (mown or cropped by sheep) reaching right up to the French windows of the house. The English garden is English in a number of profoundly significant ways not yet touched upon. First the simplest way: formally the winding path and the serpentine lake are the equivalent of Hogarth's Line of Beauty, that long, gentle, double curve … It introduces such elements as surprise in the composition of the English garden, and surprise was indeed one of the elements consciously aimed at … But surprise or, as Pope said more comprehensively in another place, 'the contrasts, the management of surprises, and the concealment of the bounds' is not all that he demanded of a garden. There is also 'the amiable simplicity of unadorned nature'. (1955: 163–164)

Pevsner itemises not only the elements of the landscape garden but also the principles underlying these aesthetic choices. Underpinning the predilection for the serpentine is 'Hogarth's Line of Beauty': the particularly eighteenth-century attribution of life to the curve and death to the right angle, vitality to the S-shape and stasis to the straight line: the preference for the natural over the artificial, the affected informality of the curve over the formal line. It is also worth noting here, once again, the interrelation and intersection of painting and gardening (Hoyles 1991: 39). Among other things, the serpentine lends itself to surprise. Bermingham notes that the management of surprises, a 'series of multiple oblique views to be experienced while one walked through it' (1986: 12), was essential to the garden. For its preponderant size, with the landscape gardens swallowing up or displacing whole villages, and the necessity to reduce the cost of maintenance of formal gardens but making for a large initial outlay, a significant amount of land was the prerequisite, both as 'raw material to be worked but as its own ornament' as well (13). The ha-ha, a concept derived from the element of surprise – *haha!* – conceals the boundaries, thereby emphasising the size and also managing the contrast between inner and outer. Contrast, Pevsner continues, is central in 'the formal house and the informal, picturesque garden surrounding it. These are polarities evident at one and the same moment' (1955: 17).

During the accelerated enclosures, Bermingham (1986: 14) argues, garden and 'common nature' were no longer seen in opposition but in 'symbiosis':

> The dialectic between *art* (the formal garden) and *common nature* (the real landscape) achieved in the gardens of the first half of the century ... foreshadowed the conflation of the two terms. Whereas the formal garden had stood between art and nature, the landscape garden tended to collapse the distinction altogether. In this sense, it became a *tromp l'oeil.* By conflating nature with the fashionable tastes of a new social order, it redefined the natural in terms of this order, and vice versa.

Martin Hoyles reminds us that the construction of private deer parks occurred in that period and that they were known as 'lawns' (1991: 33). He explains how the importance of the vista as an 'expression of power and authority' (39) was articulated in a subtler manner than the radiating avenues, which by now had become negatively associated with formality, monarchy and Frenchness. Instead of the mastery of nature, it was mastery through nature.

The works of Lancelot 'Capability' Brown (1716–1783) and his successor Humphry Repton (1752–1818) came to exemplify the 'improvement' of nature. The landscape garden sought improvement through (1) the replacement of pre-existing formal gardens, gardens of earlier styles, of aesthetically unpleasing people, villages and industry and 'disagreeable objects' (Mavor 1806: 7); (2) the correction of, tinkering with and incorporation of existing *improvable* ('natural' or built) landscape and architectural elements; (3) the integration of elements into an ideal Arcadian landscape, which blurred the distinction between the garden and uncontrived nature outside (by way of the ha-ha, for instance), which resolved the contradictions between non-productive pleasure grounds and productive (farmed) land (in the *ferme ornée*, 'ornamented farm', for example); and (4) the reorganisation of elements into pictorial compositions, treatment in painterly terms like Nicolas Poussin and Claude Lorrain (Hoyles 1991: 39), or scenic constructions contrived to arrange views.

Le Corbusier's lawn

I want to spend some time considering Le Corbusier's approach to the lawn and his broader approach to the landscape because his ideas are fundamental to understanding the modern lawn in South Africa. Writing about Le Corbusier's iconic early project, Villa Savoye (1931), landscape historian Dorothée Imbert describes the villa as 'placed unobtrusively on a soft crowned pasture and orchard, [conveying] the image of a modernist fabrique set in a Virgilian landscape' (1993: 163). Similarly, she argues that the earlier, unbuilt Villa Meyer (1925) was 'set within, or against, a naturalistic landscape of the eighteenth century' (151). Le Corbusier explains his thinking about the setting of Villa Savoye: 'The view is very beautiful, grass is a beautiful thing, and so is the forest – to be barely touched. The house will be placed on grass, like an object, disturbing nothing' (quoted in Imbert 1993: 163). According to Imbert, such statements of non-intervention echo the 'improvements' of Brown, whom Uvedale Price praised not for 'what *had*, but [for] what had *not*, been done' (quoted in Imbert 1993: 163).[2]

The romantic idyll in which Le Corbusier's buildings were to be set were 'reminiscent of overgrown landscape parks; mature trees irregularly spaced in grass and sinuous walks'; the 'home life of the inhabitants would be set in a Virgilian dream, providing all the stylistic references in his design of the early landscape style, with serpentine drives and irregular clumps' (Woudstra 2000: 137–138).

Brenda Colvin critiqued Le Corbusier's lack of intervention, which resulted in landscapes that were 'incomplete and immature' (quoted in Woudstra 2000: 136). Christopher Tunnard, who had observed some of Le Corbusier's garden layouts, argued that they were 'adaptations rather than pure creative works' (quoted in Woudstra 2000: 136). Le Corbusier's natural landscape backgrounds and settings were underpinned by a foundational paradox: the 'interpretation of nature as both original condition and an emblem of rational order' (Constant 2012: 149). By reducing the landscape to context or setting, to a 'mute ground plane, lacking in topographic character or scale', Le Corbusier failed 'to invest such collective zones with formal or programmatic content to activate their social potential'. The outcome was a flat sea of grass, a green abstract horizontality that functioned as setting: both as the ground plane and as background view. The 'timeless' and abstract quality of Le Corbusier's landscape is in 'contrast to the temporal aspect of landscape'.

His design for the Pavillon de l'Esprit Nouveau (1925) was an architectural prototype of the single cell imagined as a modular component of a larger housing structure. It was designed with a generous double-volume patio with an internal 'hanging garden', planted with 'vegetation that provided texture or touch of color, [conceptualised] as if plantings were another standardized component of the housing system' (Imbert 1993: 150). Le Corbusier was scathing of the idea that citizens should spend time maintaining private gardens. He criticised the 'vegetal camouflage of garden cities for simply perpetuating an illusion. He argued that garden maintenance not only burdened the worker with an additional chore but also required "bad movements" that "deformed" and "wore down" the body. Claiming that it caused only "illusions and rheumatism," he denounced the campaign to "cultivate one's garden"' (180). Le Corbusier ranted that this kind of garden was a 'stupid, ineffective and sometimes dangerous thing':

> The present-day solution, which exists all over the world and is looked on as ideal; it consists of a plot of roughly 400 square yards with a little house in the middle. Part of the plot is a flower garden, and there are a few fruit trees and a tiny vegetable garden. It is complicated and difficult to keep up, and involves endless pains (call it the romantic simple life if you like) for the householder and his wife to keep things tidy, to weed it, water it, kill the slugs and the rest; long after twilight the watering-can is still on the go. Some people may call all this a form of healthy exercise ... The children

> cannot play there, for they have no room to run about in, nor can the parents indulge in games or sports there. And the result of all this is a few pears and apples, a few carrots, a little parsley and so on. The whole thing is ridiculous. (Le Corbusier 1987: 202–203)

One is struck by Le Corbusier's contempt for the 'ridiculous' private garden. His polemic takes aim at the ineffectiveness of this parochial spatial practice: not only is a private garden too small to actually grow a meaningful amount of crops or to provide sufficient space for recreation. The notion that people should valorise garden labour is, according to Le Corbusier, at best quaint and at worst dangerous.

In contrast to 'stupid' un-modern gardens, Le Corbusier's hanging gardens and roof terraces functioned hygienically, for rooftop exercise, sun tanning in the solarium, fresh air, sunlight; and architecturally, as compositional devices, textural elements, and to serve theoretical notions like liberating the ground plane. The gardens and their maintenance were, however, not expressive of the moral character of the inhabitant per se. If there was insufficient sun, air, vegetation, opportunity for healthy activity, the planner was responsible. Total planning of the environment was the mechanism whereby the architect could effect radical changes to social conditions.

Writing about the total plan in *The Modernist City*, his excellent anthropology of Brasília, James Holston explains that in terms of social transformation, the discourse of the influential Congrès Internationaux d'Architecture Moderne (CIAM) proposed 'that modern architecture and planning [were] the means to create new forms of collective association, personal habit, and daily life' (1989: 31). According to Holston, whether in Brazil or Germany, the 'linking of a plan for urban design with a program for social change is a fundamental feature of master planning in modern architecture' (60). Holston argues that this link is forged in two ways:

> First, the architecture of the plan consciously embodies new and desired forms of social life ... Second, the modernist link between architecture and society is conceived instrumentally. Modernists propose that people inhabiting their architecture will be forced to adopt the new forms of collective association and personal habit the architecture represents. In this way, architecture is considered an

> instrument not only of social change, but also of good government, rational order, and the renovation of life through art. (1989: 60)

Total planning found its expression in the study and rearrangement of the functions of the city. CIAM's study of the city's functions was never purely technical because, indeed, they set out to systematically redefine the 'social basis of each function' (Holston 1989: 51). The ideology does not simply aim to 'redesign apartment buildings; it proposes to restructure domestic organization and the family as an economic unit ... In planning a city in a park ... it does not simply "green" the city; more significantly, it proposes a new focus on sports for the displaced public activity of streets' (51–52).

The unbuilt township for 20 000 'urban natives'

In South Africa the landscape garden formed the implicit basis for the debates in favour of the vertical, which were taken up by the left-leaning architects associated with Wits and found their form in *Native Housing: A Collective Thesis* (Connell et al. 1939),[3] the 1938 Town Planning Congress and Exhibition convened by the Wits Architectural Students Society and the ensuing publication of articles and conference proceedings in the *South African Architectural Record* (hereafter the *Record*).[4] The 1938 moment represents a remarkable stage of buoyancy, political energy and creative inquiry in South African urban planning.

The design proposed by the students was a township for 20 000 'urban natives', married men and women and their families (see Plate 8). The primary structures were ten residential apartment blocks, each housing 2 000 people. The ten blocks were arranged in a way that, as Japha points out, owed much to the 'redent blocks of the Ville Radieuse' designed by Le Corbusier in 1924 (1998: 425). The symmetrically placed high-rises are grouped 'about a central axis in the one direction, and juxtaposed against the low buildings and open spaces of the recreation centre and vegetable gardens' (Kantorowich 1939: 119). Among the 'low-rise' civic buildings were primary schools, a cultural centre, a shopping centre, a technical college and library, a hotel and the pass office, post office and administration block. The civic buildings are bold and generous but it is not their design that is most significant; the inclusion of all the administrative, cultural, educational, recreational functions that people would require was because the contemporary discourse of segregation insisted on a self-contained township, which residents would have to leave only in order to work in the European city. On the southern periphery of the township, a single railway line with two stops (one for every five blocks) provides an exit to employment. The students' pragmatic acquiescence to the prevailing segregationist notions is balanced by their utopian idealism, which is evident in the generous proportions of the structures and the expansive landscaping that connects them. According to Kantorowich's painterly description, a 'textural background of greenery and earthy browns run throughout the entire scheme like an under-current of episodes in a Bach fugue'. With a flourish, Kantorowich explains that the landscape is designed in 'great sweeps of surface, modulated with light and shade, set back balconies, heightened in definition by the liberal use of big areas of strong colour to offset the general pure white facades. In the strong sunlight, with a deep blue bowl of sky above and the play of terra-cotta and greens below, the buildings will sparkle and glow' (1939: 119–120).

The optimism in Kantorowich's description was partly an effect of the promise of modernism – as a programme of rationality, aesthetic sensibility, technical problem solving – that could re-engineer the social lives of its inhabitants for the better and, in retrospect, partly the naïvety of young students. The local excitement was linked to a broader international flourishing of pre-Second World War architectural and planning utopianism evident in the CIAM and the Garden City movement, Ebenezer Howard's idea of self-contained communities surrounded by green belts, with its presence felt locally via Le Corbusier's anointed Le Groupe Transvaal. Posel has pointed out how important it is to situate South African modernisms and their relation to race (before, during and after apartheid) within an international context, thereby making visible the 'resonances between the political logic of apartheid and more global adventures in modernity' (2000: 126).

Alan Mabin and Mark Oranje suggest that *Native Housing* was informed by the 1934 Drancy scheme in France (2014: 103). The students were also undoubtedly aware of Ernst May's Frankfurt *Siedlungen* (settlement) built from 1925 onwards in Germany and much publicised through CIAM II 1929 held in Frankfurt. In addition to the students' voices, Leonard Thornton-White, professor of Architecture at the University of Cape Town, delivered a lecture at the 1938 Town Planning Congress and Exhibition in which he added his voice to the growing sense of agreement that *up* was the best way to build. In the vertical development, he argued, the earth 'is almost entirely liberated. Houses stand feet to head, instead of side by side or chest to behind. Man enjoys a large area of parkland, his vision is almost unlimited over his own balcony fence, and no neighbours' houses are seen' (1938: 329). He continues in line with Corbusian orthodoxy:

> In the vertical solution, with its park-like appearance, its openness, its airiness, the majority of the population can with little or no effort see their own town as a complete organism – will be aware of the cultural centre; will see an all-important focus for the community ... A great criticism of this town solution was the absence of private gardens, the absence of a patch of ground which the individual himself can tend and enjoy privately. It was thought for some time beyond the wit of man to overcome this difficulty, to answer this criticism. The problem is now solved. The wit of man, concentrating on man's real needs, concentrating upon the individual within the community, has risen to the occasion. The superimposed site, as distinct from the superimposed house – the flat – has evolved. The vertical town need not be a town of flats, but of houses on superimposed sites, each with a garden as necessary to different individuals and with adequate sun and air space between the sites. The gardens, of course, will be a synthetic rock, on concrete, instead of natural rock foundations. (1938: 329–330)

The opposition between the vertical and the horizontal is evident also in Kantorowich's thesis chapter: 'The vertical face, on the one side, of the building is opposed on the other by the horizontal expanse of garden, a simple contrast ... There is always space around the individual, and when large masses of building are seen they are across an intermediate expanse of garden greenery' (1939: 120). Within the scheme, green is conceptualised as the horizontal, as a park-like surface, integrating and offsetting the strong vertical elements. This vision of expansive horizontality is contrasted rhetorically with the small-mindedness of desiring a house with one's own little piece of earth. Thornton-White continued that when one focuses on *real* needs, 'concentrating upon the individual within the community', humans will rise to the occasion. The private garden is parochial compared to the sweeping 'unlimited vision', which would provide context, a view of the plan from above.

High-rise housing and the private garden

That the utopian South African high-rise proposals were not built, when such plans were executed globally, requires explanation. Thus far, no research directly deals with the profound shift from high-rise to single-family homes between 1938 and 1951. Japha, as pointed out earlier, argues that this shift in the South African Modern Movement was from middling modernism towards technocosmopolitanism with middling modernist tendencies. This is a useful contextualisation, one taken up by Foster, who argues that after the Second World War the 'CIAM-type proposals offered as alternatives by the Wits modernists were dismissed as Fascist, anti-democratic, and less locally relevant (i.e., regional)' (2012: 58). I aim to offer some detail on how the optimistic sweeping (paper) lawns of the middling modernists shifted to a discourse that favoured small, lawn-based private gardens belonging to a family home.

After the initial stir caused by *Native Housing*, a slow but consistent debate can be distinguished among academics, professionals and politicians in, among other places, the *Record*, at university conferences and within the NBRI. At the centre of the debate was the problem of the so-called 'urban native',[5] an ambiguous and 'shadowy' subject (Foster 2012: 53) whose position somewhere between urbanised and detribalised caused much consternation. The anxieties planners felt towards the urban native found form in the pastoral trope that permeated even the most modern planning. The landscape proposed by the middling modernists precipitated the 'great criticism' of the high-rise typology – the absence of a private garden, which was felt to be acutely at odds with the 'African way of life' (Vestbro 2012: 354). Whether or not Africans actually wanted a garden – or would use and care for their garden in the ways intended and expected – was difficult to ascertain. Some scholars argued that largely, but not wholly, while 'we like gardens … they do not appeal to the Bantu' (Silberman 1943: 218); however, in an informative empirical study, *Urban Bantu Housing* (1969), H. L. Watts and H. J. Sibisi argued that even

> though not every Bantu householder makes good use of a garden, they nonetheless generally prize a piece of land which they can use, and the loss of a garden of their own is likely to cause frustration ... if individual families are to lose their gardens, some serious attempt must be made to provide an outdoor living area where they can sit – we have shown how important a feature of the way of life of the urban Bantu the outdoor living area is. (1969: 105–106)

Kantorowich's position in *Native Housing* was that even if it were possible to establish a house and garden scheme, the plot size to be allocated would have been too small to render the benefits of privacy, fresh air and direct sunlight, or to provide a safe place for children to play off the road (1939: 92). In any case, Jonas argued, Africans would not legally be able to own their own piece of land and so while houses are 'conducive to such civic virtues as cleanliness, sobriety, dignity ... obviously, there is no incentive to the exercise of any of the civic virtues in a system stripped of its very basis: private ownership' (1939: 45). Communal 'ownership', argued Wepener, and the shared responsibilities for a cooperative landscape could re-energise the 'old democratic ways of the Bantu people' (1939: 84). This solidarity is potentially just what those in power might have feared. As Foster argues, the individual plot typology 'spatially discouraged forms of political solidarity (like the syndicalism envisaged by Le Corbusier) from developing among residents whom the government preferred to see in terms of ethnic origins' (2012: 58). I have no historical data to confirm Foster's supposition, but I think it is sensible to imagine that a communally managed, well-kept park would be threatening to those in power.

One aspect of the ongoing conversation that was entirely incontestable was the belief that the family was the primary unit of planning. That the foundational unit of home and garden planning was nuclear and heterosexual was also not up for debate. It was acknowledged, of course, that there were single people for whom, as W. D. Howie argued in the *Record*, the flat, as 'the counterpart of urban concentration, developed by technics and functionalism', 'has emerged as an eminently suitable setting for urban living. It is a compact dwelling with a high standard of communal services, it relieves the tenant of the added responsibilities met with in the house, and it provides an environment adequately proportioned to the needs of the single person, the elderly couple, and the young married couple without children' (1943: 240).

Families, however, would never willingly choose to live in a flat, Howie contended. If there was one thing families needed it was privacy – from each other and their neighbours. Within the home, it was understood to be immoral for boys and girls, and parents and children, to be too close. It was also argued that close proximity could lead to 'quarrels and immorality' (Wepener 1939: 82) and, more strangely, Watts and Sibisi alleged the fear of a 'higher incidence of accusations of witchcraft and sorcery. People will not only be afraid of being bewitched, but will be afraid of being harmed by medicines which other families are using to protect and strengthen themselves against both physical and spiritual dangers' (1969: 105).

I want to point out here that Calderwood, to whom we turn shortly, was *the* believer in the family. As we will see, his conception of the family was naïve and profoundly flawed, based as it was on Western ideals and no small amount of sickly moralism. For now, however, I want to highlight that in the same issue of the *Record* in which Howie presented the high-rise and the family as definitively incompatible, Norman Hanson insisted on the opposite. In his response to a lecture by Graham Ballenden, manager of the Non-European and Native Affairs Department, to the Wits Architectural Students' Society, Hanson politely advised the students that Mr Ballenden's 'aversion to flats for non-European people should not lead us to exclude proper experimentation in high-density construction, for under prevailing or probable conditions in our towns, it may be necessary to adopt such devices' (1943: 146). On the opposite pages of that issue of the *Record* are three unrelated but thoughtfully placed plans: apartment buildings for the Johannesburg Housing Utility Company in Mayfair and Fordsburg by Cowin & Elis Architects, part of a successful 'rehabilitation of slum dwellers' (147).

Notwithstanding the numerous objections, by the mid-to-late 1940s, high-rise housing for Africans had not been entirely ruled out. While the single-storey detached house dominated the native housing design competitions, published prototypes and, indeed, built projects,[6] the influential *Research Committee on Minimum Standards of Accommodation: Interim Report* recommended that research into 'increasing gross density in residential neighbourhoods' be 'vigorously pursued' (NBRI 1949: 37) and that a number of different types of combined dwellings be designed, constructed and tested (39). Even as late as July 1953 an innovative proposal for African high-rise building was floated in the *Record* (May 1953: 39–41). The prototype by May & Partners has barrel roofs and includes no windows – because 'in many cases windows are closed by the primitive inhabitants with newspaper' (1953: 40) – which are replaced with three rows of overhead cement cavity blocks, providing ventilation and light.

The reason that more such peculiar and innovative modern solutions to high-density housing were not suggested, never mind constructed, perhaps had less to do with the reasons suggested so far and more to do with two pragmatic questions: (1) who would bear the costs of construction and rental? and (2) who would build the dwellings?

The report *National Housing* by the National Housing and Planning Commission is helpful in understanding these two housing issues. The report argued that the extreme 'housing crisis' (Wilkinson 1998: 218) in the 1940s was to the result of (1) high building costs; (2) the shortage of skilled building artisans; (3) the acute shortage of building materials, particularly cement and steel; and (4) the unwillingness of local authorities to face the financial losses involved (Union of South Africa 1947: 10). Foster argues (most likely based on this same report) that 'the scarcity of skilled labor and materials such as concrete and steel required to construct multistory buildings (especially during the war), and the political nature of municipal financing' (2012: 58) contributed to the shift towards detached house schemes.

In the early part of the century the 1920 Housing Act and 1923 Natives (Urban Areas) Act 'imposed on local authorities the obligation to provide housing. But generally municipalities failed', displeased that they were effectively providing the capital and subsidising the wages of expensive white building labourers (Maylam 1990: 74–75).[7] Peter Wilkinson points out how in the 1950s the 'controversial and strongly contested' Native Building Workers Act (1951) and the Native Services Levy Act (1952) altered the housing landscape because of, on the one hand, 'the use of previously excluded African artisans on "Native housing schemes" …

and, on the other, levying of employers of African labour as a means of offsetting at least some of the costs of accommodating the African population in urban areas' (1998: 219). Tod Welch of the NBRI argued that 'single-storey development fitted well with the extent to which the building industry had developed at that period, and it allowed for the introduction of self-help schemes and on-the-site training of the Bantu themselves' (quoted in Vestbro 2012: 354). KwaThema, to which we turn next, was the first township to be built exclusively by African labour (Nieftagodien 1996: 1).[8] In addition to the debate between local government, employers and the central state over who would foot the bill for native housing, the institution of site-and-service schemes further skewed the argument in favour of small-scale housing.

Finally, Watts and Sibisi found that speaking about – indeed, even imagining – urban natives in high-rises was almost impossible to do:

> During the pilot survey, questions relating to the development of flats were put to housewives. However, the responses obtained made us decide to remove these questions from the main fieldwork interviews. The reason was that either the housewife had had no experience of flats whatsoever, and therefore would not conceive of the type of design she was being questioned about, or on the other hand she had had experience of White flats when working as a domestic servant. This type of flat development is far more expensive than the average Bantu household in the immediate future can afford, and therefore if the housewife framed her responses in terms of this type of design and finish her replies would be completely misleading. Essentially the problem was that there was no way of communicating adequately to the housewives an impression of the type of high-rise development which would be likely in urban Bantu townships during the next decade – and therefore it was not possible to obtain responses to something which they could not visualise accurately. Any replies we received would have been invalid, and hence the questions were dropped, as no solution to the problem could be found. (1969: 105)

The pull away from low-income high-rise housing set South Africa on a remarkably different trajectory from contemporaneous modernising programmes around the world. The movement towards an individual ground-level family house can be attributed to a number of factors: the cost involved; the lack of available expertise both in the building sector and in African labour; ideas about the African dweller wanting his own piece of land; fears of the results of communal living; lack of familiarity among the users about the kind of 'flat' that was envisaged. The shift was partly economic, partly pragmatic and partly ideological. As a result, the township house is an oddity, something that has the trappings of an individual home in circumstances where apartheid ideology was destroying the possibility of African family life in the cities. This evidence points towards saying, cautiously perhaps, that this is another example where apartheid lacked a grand scheme.

KwaThema

> *There Shall be Houses, Security and Comfort!*
> *All people shall have the right to live where they choose, be decently housed, and to bring up their families in comfort and security;*
> *Unused housing space to be made available to the people;*
> *Rent and prices shall be lowered, food plentiful and no-one shall go hungry; ...*
> *Slums shall be demolished, and new suburbs built where all have transport, roads, lighting, playing fields, crèches and social centres; ...*
> *Fenced locations and ghettoes shall be abolished, and laws which break up families shall be repealed.*
>
> — South African Congress Alliance, 'The Freedom Charter'

In 1950 the town council of Springs requested the NBRI's assistance in planning a 'new and separate' township to 'relieve the existing grossly overcrowded area of Payneville' (Calderwood 1954: 313). The 'relief' directed towards the Springs 'blackspot' (Nieftagodien 1996: 7) – which meant forced removals in Payneville – did not, as writer and photographer Muzi Kuzwayo put it, make 'it into the history books, not even as a footnote ... If Sophiatown was an African prince, then Payneville would be its quieter distant cousin' (2007: 23–24). The forced removals were authorised by the recently promulgated Group Areas Act.

The new Springs township was to be called Kwa-Thema, after an undefined 'prominent African figure' as Calderwood put it (1954: 314). The Department of Native Affairs and National

Housing Commission were brought into cooperation and construction in KwaThema commenced in 1952. In the first two years 2 226 municipal houses were built, and by 1958 there were over 6 000 completed (Nieftagodien 1996: 9).

The plans for KwaThema were a collaborative effort, drawing on previous research and the work of numerous planners within the NBRI; however, it is Calderwood whose name became associated with the project. Through his PhD thesis (1953) and a number of other publications (1954, 1955) Calderwood produced an argument so compelling that his ideas remain the model for low-cost housing in South Africa. Even in 1994 (forty-one years after publication) the national development plan of the African National Congress (ANC), the Reconstruction and Development Programme (RDP), applied Calderwood's principles to guide post-apartheid housing development.

The principal unit of the Calderwood plan was the family, who required certain minima to be provided by a small house surrounded by an economically determined amount of private space. These houses, devised through comprehensive studies of existing low-cost houses around South Africa, design explorations and scientific experimentation, were called the NE 51 houses (Non-European of 1951). These prototypes were presented by the NBRI as a demonstration of a 'rational design process' rather than a completed design per se, but the designs were taken up by local authorities across the country and built in their thousands (Haarhoff 2011: 191). Called 'matchbox houses', these designs were also built under the RDP, after apartheid (Shepherd & Robins 2008: 63).

According to Calderwood's vision (see Plates 9, 10 and 11), the individual 'units' with their own small gardens would be integrated into a park-like landscape, 'rather than in a maze of dusty, noisy streets' (1953: 19). Hannah le Roux, who has been involved for many years in a number of aspects of KwaThema life, explains the relationship between the detached homes and the neighbourhood units as arising from Garden City principles:

> Calderwood wanted KwaThema to be an ideal social microcosm for urban black living; he aspired to match household income with rental, to mix income levels, to construct appropriately sized neighbourhood units and to optimise the location and levels of social

> services in relation to housing. Garden City principles allowed each housing unit to reap the social benefits of land, in the form of a space for growing fresh produce, and by spacing houses from each other and giving children access to outdoor play space. However, Calderwood's designs for public space in KwaThema were never fully executed. While the township model had been conceived in a liberal, post-war period, it was implemented after the 1948 victory of the National Party ... The design for KwaThema was implemented, without Calderwood's final control, in a way that omitted many social proposals and that conflated the neighbourhood space with one of ethnic and racial segregation. His green belts became 'buffer zones' to enforce such separations. Nonetheless his scheme remains a powerful order in the township, the consequence of an era of modernist planning in which everything had a place and function, even if that function was simply separation. (2014: 121–123)

Le Roux points out how profoundly Calderwood's plan was organised along Garden City principles and how his idealism was frustrated by the nascent apartheid regime. Le Roux has suggested to me a more sympathetic treatment of Calderwood than I might have been disposed to give myself. For those who knew him, Calderwood is generally remembered fondly. Architect, historian and Calderwood contemporary Clive Chipkin remembers him as an 'architect of enormous organisational skill and personal integrity' and as someone who had a 'social mission' (1993: 215). Chipkin believes Calderwood regarded apartheid with 'disapproval'. Pragmatic, 'impatient with theories', Calderwood was the 'perfect technocrat'.

The minimum garden

Mark Wigley argues that in general architectural convention, the lawn is represented through its lack of representation. As a thoroughly naturalised trope, the lawn no longer needs to be explicitly specified; its absence (on the plan) is proof of its necessity:

> At most, the lawn is treated as a good surface for displaying the glories of the building; its own architecture is ignored. The lawn does not even appear on the architectural drawings in which it clearly plays a major role. While renderings for clients may show

> the lawn, and manuals of drawing techniques may describe the way in which it can be represented, the drawings with which architects communicate to themselves and other architects leave the lawn out. It is assumed that wherever there is nothing specified in the drawing this is grass. The lawn is treated like the paper on which the projects are drawn, a tabula rasa without any inherent interest, a background that merely clears the way for the main event … What is left out of the picture often rules the picture. (Wigley 1999: 164)

In the following analysis of Calderwood's KwaThema garden plans and garden studies, the problem of absence is central. While Calderwood explicitly specifies lawns in all his plans, there is a profound gap between the lawn's life on the plan (conceived space) and the manifestation of the lawn in the built environment and the various forms it takes (lived space). What we cannot know is the degree to which Calderwood's conceived lawns were entirely intentional, which is to ask: did he really imagine the lawns as lawns, knowing that this would be nearly impossible to achieve, or did they function as aesthetic shorthand, as a placeholder, as a kind of blank?

Calderwood was certainly aware of the profound paradox the lawns presented. Firstly, he understood that ownership, the fundamental precondition for the activity of gardening, was absent. Just as the collective thesis members had pointed out in the 1930s, Calderwood conceded that the 'European pattern of small plots' did not 'seem the most successful' for townships because Africans could not have more than, at best, an extended lease (1952: 17). Secondly, he understood that for a native family 'gardening in any form is an expense' (1953: 56). Writing in 1947 Connell published a report that describes the apparent lack of interest shown by natives in gardening:

> The degree to which gardening is carried out in the Native locations is generally low, and most of the plots remain more or less undeveloped, the best ones exhibiting rows of vegetables, the worst containing nothing but backyard debris, odd bits of wood, rusty corrugated iron and wire rigged up into rough fowl runs, or worst of all, a square of trodden earth, bare and lifeless, put to no use at all … the key to this state of affairs is that gardening costs money, even if the water required is available and laid on at convenient points, which is not usually the case. The Native's unbalanced

> budget cannot support such luxury, and the only allowable exception to this rule is the possibility that, under favourable conditions, vegetables may be grown to supplement the family food supply. (Connell 1947: 32)

The fact that the essential requirements for home gardening were absent, indeed were being actively undermined by the very system that denied ownership, a living wage and realistic possibilities for family development, did not lessen the fervour with which Calderwood pursued the ideal township garden and its requisite lawn.

The township garden, in Calderwood's estimation, was a technical problem to be solved through scientific research. In the same way that Rabinow anticipated the colonies to be 'laboratories for modernism' (1989: 26), Calderwood argued that township design offered a 'great field of experimentation' (1953: 20). His experiments (some of which are shown in Plates 9–11) had the objective, plainly informed by the international Modern Movement (see Le Corbusier 1987: 197–248), of deriving the 'minimum garden'.

The notion of minimum standards was a significant concept for early modern planners, one that, after much local research, was codified in 1949 by the Research Committee on Minimum Standards of Accommodation (NBRI 1949). The precedent had been set internationally in 1929, when CIAM II, hosted in Frankfurt, focused on *Existenzminimum* or 'the minimum subsistence dwelling' (Mumford 2000: 30). CIAM's 'main goal was to find rational patterns, which the new policies for habitation should follow' (Ferreira, Murtinho & Simões da Silva 2013: 1169). A particularly polarised debate took place between left- and right-leaning members. Czech Marxist Karel Teige argued in *The Minimum Dwelling*: 'Essentially, the housing question is a problem of statistics and technology, as is any question concerning the provision and satisfaction of human needs' (2002: 9). According to Le Corbusier, whom Teige situated on the far right, the minimum dwelling was '*the fundamental social instrument*' (Ferreira, Murtinho & Simões da Silva 2013: 1170; emphasis in original). Walter Gropius contributed an excellent definition of the minimum dwelling:

> The sociological facts must first be clarified in order that the ideal minimum of a life necessity, the dwelling, and the minimum cost of its production may be found; in view of the change in underlying

> principles, the program for a minimum dwelling can naturally not be solved by simply reducing the conventional, larger apartment in number of rooms and effective area. An entirely new formulation is required, based on a knowledge of the natural and sociological minimum requirements, unobscured by the veil of traditionally imagined historical needs. We must attempt to establish minimum standards for all countries, based on biological facts and geographic and climatic conditions. This approach is in the spirit of the impending equalization of life requirements under the influence of travel and world trade … The problem of the minimum dwelling is that of establishing the elementary minimum of space, air, light and heat required by man in order that he be able to fully develop his life functions without experiencing restrictions due to his dwelling, i.e., a minimum *modus vivendi* in place of a *modus non moriendi*. The actual minimum varies according to local conditions of city and country, landscape and climate; a given quantity of air space in the dwelling has different meanings in a narrow city street and in a sparsely settled suburb. (Gropius 1956: 112)

The South African Modern Movement had the question of minimum standards front and centre. In *Native Housing* Jonas argues that there was 'no sense in saying that the Bantu, because he is black, can be housed worse'. Indeed, he continued:

> To say that Native houses do not need floors because the Native huts in the reserves have no floors is like suggesting that the Native garage attendant should walk about in banana leaves. Once the Bantu has entered urban capitalist society, and our substantiated contention is that he has, he can only be treated as an integral part of that society. And the fact that he belongs to the exploited section makes him no less part of that system as a whole. Its standards must be his standards. (1939: 47–48)

On the basis of Catherine Bauer's *Modern Housing* (published in 1934), Kantorowich enumerated seventeen aspects to be considered in providing sufficient minimum housing for urban natives (1939: 97–101). In addition to these minimum requirements, he argued an 'attractive outlook' was necessary so that 'lawns and garden are visible from all windows' (100). This, he pointed out, was in stark contrast to Pimville, Alexandra or Orlando, which were 'plague spots' where the 'attractive outlook is onto a cabbage patch, watered with bath- and dish-water, and a dusty road separating a row of bleak identical houses' (102). In addition to the 'outlook', Kantorowich argued that it was imperative to provide off-street 'facilities for outdoor recreation life: play-spaces for small and large children. Walks, parks, athletic provisions, gardens conveniently located for adults' (99). The contrast between the minima he proposed and the lived reality in South African townships *circa* 1938 made Kantorowich wonder: 'In what respects are Natives treated as if they were more, in the white man's estimation, than "dumb animals", "beasts of burden"?' (102).

Calderwood's position was that while detailed and thorough investigation had been carried out in respect of low-cost housing, leading to the specification of minimum standards of accommodation, no such standards had been determined for outdoor areas (1953: 52). He argued that the

> demands of a private plot must be known in exactly the same manner as one accepts that facilities for eating, food preparation, seclusion, sleeping and entertainment are basically the requirements of a dwelling. The plot must accommodate the dwelling in such a manner that fresh air and sunlight are sufficient to ensure good health and the house must be positioned as to allow maximum use of the garden space. So often the house is merely dropped into the centre of the plot without any thought being given to the developed garden, which in the case of minimum gardens sets the owner an impossible task laying out a useful outdoor area. (1953: 53)

Calderwood established six minimum requirements for native residential plots: (1) privacy; (2) amenities – space for laundry, clothes drying, dustbins and storage area; (3) children's play space; (4) adult entertainment and leisure area; (5) area for cultivation; and (6) sufficient overall area to obtain fresh air and uninterrupted sunlight (1953: 53). These functions were expressed in Calderwood's plans for the NE 51 houses. The design of these dwellings has been subjected to thorough and penetrating study;[9] however, what has evaded scrutiny thus far are the ways in which the discourses of hygiene, patriarchy and respectability were articulated in the plot, its relationship to the house and its neighbours, the specification of plants and non-botanical elements and their arrangement in the garden. The minimum garden, therefore, requires explanation.

What the average family wants from its garden

A minimum garden is by intention and purpose a modern one; it, however, certainly does not *look* modern like the iconic work of modern landscapers Jean Canneel-Claes (Imbert 2009), Leberecht Migge (Haney 2010) or Christopher Tunnard. The native garden is explicitly small, rational and domestic. Japha argues that Calderwood's drawings are 'resonant with the nostalgic anti-urbanism of the Garden City movement. They include delicate free-hand drawings ... bizarre depictions of the NE 51 series houses as bucolic bungalows ... isolated in the countryside like part of a Robert Owen ideal village' (1986: 86).

If we examine the numerous plans and axonometric drawings done by Calderwood, we see that they all have a lawn specified; he recommended kikuyu, Bradley and Swaziland grasses (1952: 18). As already mentioned, to what degree Calderwood imagined that lawns would really be planted is not clear, but they certainly function rhetorically as a given surface treatment for the outside part of the houses. Watts and Sibisi found that of the gardens they surveyed 'just over half of the gardens had some form of lawn. In nearly all cases this was in front of the house, but six per cent of the gardens visited had some form of lawn both in front and at the back of the house' (1969: 66).

In the majority of Calderwood's gardens, the lawn is bounded by a fence or clipped hedge. All include at least one or more spherical topiaries, a little rough around the edges, not too neat. Surely, neither he or nor any other planner could seriously have imagined that topiary shrubs would indeed be viable or ever actually be planted in the townships? If they thought of the topiaries as indexical only, not literal, what does this tell us about how they pictured lawn? Were lawns generic gardening elements too?

No gardens depict large established trees (except NE 51/20A, where existing trees appear to be drawn inside the boundary of the property). The KwaThema gardens are all depicted as new and represented in a relatively early stage; just built, a year or two old perhaps. But all gardens are bordered by tall trees on both sides. These trees serve a compositional function, like picturesque Claudian framing devices. It is worth pointing out that almost without exception the plants Calderwood specified were alien: *Eucalyptus globulus*, *E. longifolia*, *E. rostrata* and *E. saligna*; *Acacia dealbata*, *A. decurrens* (green wattle) and 'local' acacia species; *Morus alba* (white mulberry), *Platanus x acerifolia* (planetree), *Robinia pseudoacacia* (locust acacia), *Schinus molle* (pepper tree), *Leptospermum* (myrtle), *Ligustrum* (privet) and *Ziziphus mucronata* (wag 'n bietjie bos) (Calderwood 1952: 18). When it came to flowers, he simply noted: 'Suggest local wild flowers.' I suppose it is clear that by 'suggest' Calderwood meant that he, Calderwood, would suggest local wild flowers. Would it not be interesting if he meant: local residents should suggest local flowers?

In his master's dissertation Calderwood argues, in line with orthodox modernist logic, that the garden should not be 'a decorative element, but rather a useful area' (1952: 19). Indeed, while the notion of the functional garden forms the basis of the argument for gardening in general, and while planners may not have conceived of the garden as decorative, much can be discerned from the aesthetic choices made in designing the so-called useful gardens.

The uses and functions Calderwood imagined, as outlined above, are aligned with the NBRI's minimum standards, which were set to promote 'conditions in which healthy, decent, family life may be enjoyed by the people of the Union, and [provide] conditions of good housing and community planning which will tend to make good citizens' (NBRI 1949: 19). The NBRI report continues:

> For *health*: Minimum standards of air space, ventilation, human comfort, lighting, quietness. For *decency*: Separation of children from parents in sleeping apartments; separation of sexes; privacy for bathing etc. For *family life*: Reasonable family privacy; provision of the needs of leisure, meals, study, entertainment and rest; these requirements should be met for every member of the family. For the promotion of *good citizenship*: Provision of all housing estates of the *minimum* communal facilities for this purpose. (NBRI 1949: 19)

Calderwood, drawing on Tunnard, argues that the garden is a 'useful area to assist the native in creating more private space beyond the walls of his dwelling' (1952: 19). Tunnard views the garden as 'an extension of the house: an out-of-door living room' (quoted in Calderwood 1953: 34), which provides room to foster decency by relieving family 'congestion' (Calderwood 1952: 17). Calderwood also suggests: 'The plot and the dwelling unit are not two separate units but one when considered from the point of view of living. The dwelling is roofed and the outdoor space unroofed but these spaces must be planned together so that human activities can flow from one to the other in a natural way' (19). That the lawn is often discursively constructed as an outdoor carpet has been noted already. This is important to emphasise because it brings specific domestic notions of hygiene and propriety to bear on the garden. The dialectical relationship between the garden and the house allows for the imagining of more room. In addition to the lawn, Calderwood argues for the importance of the stoep; the NBRI, however, formally considered a stoep non-essential for low-cost housing (NBRI 1949: 21).

The blurring of house and garden, such that gardens become the 'outdoor room', made the broader community, outside of the private nuclear family home, 'more and more important' (Calderwood 1952: 19). The private plot demands privacy from 'neighbouring gardens, and from passing vehicles and pedestrians on the street' (Calderwood 1953: 53). All NE 51 plans include small hedges or fences. It was important to Calderwood that these be professionally planned because, as Connell had reported, where no materials are provided, the residents 'almost invariably put up some sort of barrier with whatever material they can scratch together. The result of this is to intensify the air of shabbiness and squalor' (Connell 1947: 33). The fence has the function of both providing privacy (a presumed desire projected onto the urban native and for which no empirical evidence was shown) and of delimiting what was private and what was public space. It was repeatedly argued that children should not be playing outside on the dirty road: 'Children will not play in between fast moving vehicles, nor appear as dusty as the road they are compelled to play upon' (Calderwood 1952: 19). Instead of the public streets, they should be provided with 'a small grassed area where children can play' (17). The lawn functions to separate the home from the public street but also takes on hygienic functions by reducing dust and offering safety to children. The lawn provides both health and decency.

In a particularly (though not uncharacteristically) inappropriate passage Calderwood quotes British landscape architect Peter Shepheard to explain 'what the average family wants from its garden':

> a green setting, in which can be seen the seasons' change, and views of plants and trees, preferably with a view of something other than the neighbouring house or street. It may include a place for entertaining friends or strolling in the open air, a place for sitting in privacy out of doors such as an outdoor living room, a place where children can play in safety, a place to cultivate plants for recreation, or a place to keep pets. In addition, an area for hanging out washing may be required. This list can be interpreted in numerous ways – provision for entertainment can be in the form of a terrace where teas or sundowners are taken, a tennis court with tennis shelter, a swimming bath with its accompanying terrace or an open lawn with croquet, putting green or badminton laid out upon it. (quoted in Calderwood 1952: 10)

Wildly oblivious statements about the lawn, like the one above, mean that we are obliged to take Calderwood's utopian lawns and topiary trees with the proverbial pinch of salt. Further, talk of 'taking tea' and 'playing croquet' throws into sharp relief how seldom international and South African experts seemed aware of – or concerned about – how people actually lived or wanted to live. The lawn was a modernist imposition devised in accordance with theoretical, aesthetic, sometimes nostalgic and often political ideas, not as a response to realistic lived spaces.

Welkom

Joane Pim and the professionalisation of the landscape

In 1952 the little-known gardener Joane Pim was commissioned by Ernest Oppenheimer, her neighbour and chairman of Anglo American, to be his landscape consultant for the nascent mining town Welkom.[10] The urban planner William Backhouse, under instructions from Anglo American, had designed a garden city of 'wide boulevards, traffic circles … and expansive open spaces' (Foster 2015: 139). The Welkom commission transformed Pim, who had no formal training as a landscape architect or town planner (122), from a skilled amateur into a knowledgeable professional.

South Africa's 'landscape pioneer', as she is referred to by her doting biographer Esmé Moseley Wiesmeyer (2007), has received almost no scholarly attention. Foster's chapter in *Women, Modernity, and Landscape Architecture* (2015) is essentially the first sustained critical engagement with her work. Before that, Bettina Malcomess and Dorothee Kreutzfeldt briefly point to Pim's work in their fascinating and frustrating book *Not No Place: Johannesburg. Fragments of Spaces and Times* (2013: 110, 118), and Noëleen Murray, in her research on South African modernisms (2010), foregrounded Pim's landscaping of Welkom.

Pim grew up at Timewell, the Herbert Baker-designed Parktown home of her father, Howard. Their garden was designed by Baker himself, inspired by the work of Gertrude Jekyll, and its construction was strictly supervised by Mrs Rosamund Pim (Wiesmeyer 2007: 2). Opposite Joane's childhood home was Marienhof, now Brenthurst, the Oppenheimer residence from 1922 onwards. The Pim family was thoroughly British. They were Quakers and upstanding members of the anglophone community on the Ridge. Wiesmeyer describes how throughout Pim's life she adhered to the 'norms of her class': walking at Brenthurst, attending hunt balls and hunting, riding, watching ballet, adhering to propriety in all things, especially in terms of dress codes (2007: 6). In 1933, at the age of twenty-nine, while recuperating from an illness in England with Sir John and Lady Maud, Pim began working for the landscape architect Brenda Colvin (2007: 10). Colvin (1897–1981) was an influential British landscape planner and the author of *Land and Landscape* (1970). Her influence on Pim is quite evident if we examine her thinking about the relationship between beauty and function. The following passage could easily be a quote from Pim's *Beauty is Necessary*: 'Planning at the present time is actuated by motives of efficiency and the needs of the future. But does it allow sufficiently for landscape beauty among those needs? … We too readily discount as "sentimental nonsense" any argument based on the appearance of the landscape, still reacting to the idea of use versus beauty' (Colvin 1970: 178).

Throughout her career, Pim worked on many types of landscape – from desert farms to urban parks – but her oeuvre was dominated by mining properties (Foster 2015: 123). Much in demand for the rest of her career, she preferred projects on the grander scale. While she taught at a number of universities and often spoke publicly, she was not a gifted writer and published only one book. *Beauty is Necessary* (1971) elaborated Pim's position on the role of landscape in South Africa, which was, not to put too fine a point on it, that by 'improving' nature one could increase profits. Landscape, Pim believed, was good for business and good for people, too. To understand her position one must consider, as Foster makes clear, that in Pim's familial and social context of a 'liberal Anglocentric ethos of improvement', making a profit was seen as having to be balanced with 'a moral sense of trusteeship and the "natural" aesthetics of pragmatism' (2015: 132). Following this logic, Foster proposes that Pim had a 'far more engaged relationship with the Africans she employed than [did] most white South Africans', 'a significant fact given the then-common perception that white women "could not handle African labour" ... Following contemporary practice, she sometimes called them "boys", but she also used their individual full names and kept full records of their work ... She also negotiated on her workers' behalf with employers for medical leave. And with the [Department of Native Affairs] concerning the renewal of their passes. Unsurprisingly many of her workers remained loyal for years' (2015: 134).

According to Foster, this kind of paternalism was to be expected from the liberal, philanthropic elite. It would seem that Pim's concern for labour welfare was partly informed by her belief that the mines were broadly beneficial for black people, providing a significant source of employment and assisting in nurturing, as Foster puts it, 'a culture of interdependence and loyalty between white employers and black labor' (2015: 134). Pim even credited some transformation in the lives of workers because of her work. Ultimately, her belief was that beauty returned dividends: contented workers were more 'productive and orderly' and less likely to run off to the homelands or another mine (Pim 1971: 147). While Foster notes that, in retrospect, some of Pim's notions strike one as 'paternalistic and self-serving', he also suggests that Pim's landscape practice 'challenged dominant equations of race, labor and citizenship' (2015: 134–135). In order to advance this argument, Foster proposes that landscape labour may have provided a 'significant alternative to working underground, it developed transferrable skills', and that Pim's fondness for building with local materials and favouring artisanal techniques 'allowed laborers to retain agency in the making of the landscape and deploy their own experience about the region's stone, soils, water and plants into what was built' (135). Foster is perhaps attributing too much agency to Pim's intentions and not paying enough attention to the systemic violence of labour in this kind of landscape.

Beauty is necessary (and profitable)

Work is central to the landscape Pim created in Welkom. It had to be. It was, in the first instance, a town created to service six mines; its very existence (and current decline) is linked to gold-mining. The landscape that Pim designed and produced is explicitly concerned with making the environment of the mines habitable and productive. Making the town habitable required an enormous amount of heavy labour and it is the (non)representation of that labour that is of interest to me. How do the extensive fields, parks, green belts, private lawns, golf courses and the connecting fabric that holds them together work to obscure the relationships that went into their making? *Beauty is Necessary* is full of examples of barren wastes transformed into lush fields by what seems to be the mere passage of time. There are instances where a black garden labourer is presented; however, these are exceptions to the rule, which is 'to erase or neutralise images of work … to hide, in its insistent fetishisation … the relationships that go into its making' (Mitchell 1998: 103–104).

Work in the planned professional landscape is quite different from work in the unplanned domestic garden. In part, the difference has to do with intentionality, the premeditation with which the planner can deploy a number of professional tools (intellectual and physical) at her disposal to solve a set of problems, such as keeping mine workers contented: 'Who wants to fight when one can relax under shady trees on a pleasing lawn?' Pim asked (1971: 80). That intentions are often not fully accomplished or not permanently sustained provides scope for alternative interpretations. In addition to strategic intention, landscape planning on this scale requires, and sometimes comes with, the power and capital to attempt execution. In such a situation the means for botanical research, experimentation and plant propagation are available to the planner.

For the Welkom commission, Pim set up her own nursery called Klippan, which eventually became one of the largest in the country (Pim 1956: 28). She travelled extensively to investigate, collect and assess plants that would thrive in Welkom's 'climatically difficult district' (27). One of her 'experiments' involved the selection – 'against great initial local opposition' – of an indigenous grass for the lawns of Welkom's many parks. Writing in Anglo American's magazine *Optima* (1956: 29) Pim explains how she went against all recommendations of Kenyan and Cape grasses: 'It is not as fine of texture as some,' she writes, 'but gives a most pleasing effect for the minimum of attention, and, above all, it is hardy. There are no "Keep off the Grass" notices in Welkom.' In addition to the indigenous lawns in the parks, Pim points out that on the actual mines themselves every European staff member is entitled to (1) a lawn planted around their house, (2) an evergreen tree and (3) a hedge. To her bemusement, many white staff did not take up the offer. Pim describes the landscape gardens she designed on the mine properties as 'simple and straightforward in design and easy to maintain'. She continues: 'The miners coming up from underground, go through the change houses and out, in the summer, onto green lawns with trees and colourful beds of polyanthus, roses, dahlias, cannas and a blaze of annuals' (31).

Pim's treatment of the lawn on the mine properties suggests at least three important elements. First, for white staff, the domestic lawn is theirs by *right*; it is literally a given. That many refused what was freely given was incomprehensible to Pim. Who were those white miners, what position in the social hierarchy did they occupy and why did they reject their right? Second, the lawn is part of a landscape that is portrayed as 'straightforward'; in other words, a landscape that is 'honest' or 'sincere', with nothing to hide and about which no questions need be asked. Third, the lawn is structured as the threshold that marks the beginning and end of the working day for underground labourers. Emerging from underground, miners would be greeted by a blaze of colour and smiling lawns that would function as a counterpoint and antithesis to the dark, dirty and dangerous world of underground mine labour.

How did miners experience those green lawns? Perhaps, at the end of a shift, the lawn expressed a sense of cleanliness, order and safety, which their brutal work lacked. Or perhaps it seemed to them a terribly unjust and cruel articulation of their oppression. Probably they took no notice of that very straightforward surface. That the trope of the lawn, one of the key innovations of the English landscape garden, should seem the natural and politically unproblematic place for an ethnically diverse black proletariat and white working-class miners to begin and end their working day is a remarkable conceit. The power of beauty was to do away daily drudge (Pim 1971: 80) and to substitute it with the goodness of the garden; who indeed would want to fight when they could relax under shady trees on a pleasing lawn?

Parenthetically, recall how Dorothea Fairbridge's account (1924: 34) of the feminised domestic lawn was emphatically at odds with the masculinist mining industry. According to Fairbridge, the horizontality of the garden was at odds with the verticality of the capitalist desire for profit. In contrast, Pim's lawn is deployed on the mine in the service of profit – to be sure, as a counterpoint to the harshness of mining, but not antagonistic to its goals. The amenability of the lawn, its ambiguity and pliability, cannot be sufficiently underlined.

Pim's outlook on the landscape and conception of the lawn was profoundly influenced by the discourse of the eighteenth-century English landscape garden. The ideas of Brown and Repton – and, by the same logic, Colvin and early Tunnard (Jacques & Woudstra 2009) – underpin much of what she designed in Welkom and elsewhere. Ideologically, her work resonated with four key ideas: (1) a rhetorical system that emphasised improvement and the praise of capability; (2) an approach to planting and shaping that was serpentine and/or indigenous; (3) a concern with the prospect and as such a concomitant desire to camouflage the unsightly, the functional and the industrial; and (4) the possession of 'naturalness' as a domain that ambiguously denies its own made-ness while still marvelling in the evidence of its transformation, and also as a terrain that is anti-political.

Beauty is Necessary might equally have been titled *The Welkom Red Book*, taking as it did explicit inspiration from the well-known red leatherbound marketing pamphlets bequeathed by Repton. Pim includes a reproduction of Repton's delicately painted before-and-after designs for *The View from the Fort near Bristol* (Pim 1971: 53).[11] Repton's 'improvements' included a picturesque framing, achieved by the natural clumping of trees, the removal of silhouetted unsightly inhabitants, replacing them with a small and neat group of smartly dressed ladies, erasure of the town of Bristol by way of naturalistic planting, and the softening and integration of the ground plane into a single extensive lawn. In the images by Pim (Plates 12 and 13), we see the implementation of the idea that nature could be put to service to mask the unsightly objects such as the miner's change house, adding interest to a flat landscape through gardening and softening functional and hard-edged buildings. Pim used 'repeat photography', also called 'rephotography', a method for studying changes in the landscape, where a single site or vantage point is photographed with a time lag, producing a 'then and now' of an area (Webb, Boyer & Turner 2010).

In contrast to the triumphal images from the 1970s, a contemporary visitor to Welkom cannot help but be struck by what one would be hard-pressed not to refer to as a sense of decline. In contrast to the verdant images of Central Park in *Beauty is Necessary* (1971: 70–71), Welkom's public lawns are now patchy and the parks in general are unkempt, unclean and unsafe. There is litter strewn about; numerous alternative medicine posters advertising penis enlargements, same-day abortions, and hip and bum enlargements paper the walls of Central Park. There are four professional photographers working on the Tulbagh Street side of the park, and a wall of the adjoining shopping centre has been painted white as a backdrop for photography. In addition, the green belts are visibly unkempt and the centres of the thirty-nine large traffic circles (for which Welkom is renowned) are scruffy. Paths are worn into the lawn from pedestrian foot traffic taking alternative routes. The trouble with the notion of decline is that, if critics are to be believed, Welkom's failures are obviously the result of ANC corruption. Implicit in this kind of logic – applied also to Joubert Park, as we will see in Chapter 4 – is a racial essentialism, which is of no help in explaining what seems to be the (post-apartheid) failure to sustain the promises of modernity. Of course, it could also be argued that these 'failures' point to the implicit impossibility of the English garden model in an African context. The failure, then, is not a black one, but rather the original white one. Ferguson's questions are the right ones, I think: 'What does a widespread and prolonged perception of decline mean, when scholarship and popular ideology alike have for so long depended on tropes of development and progress, emergence and advance? How are our intellectual and methodological traditions of interpreting African urbanity within a certain

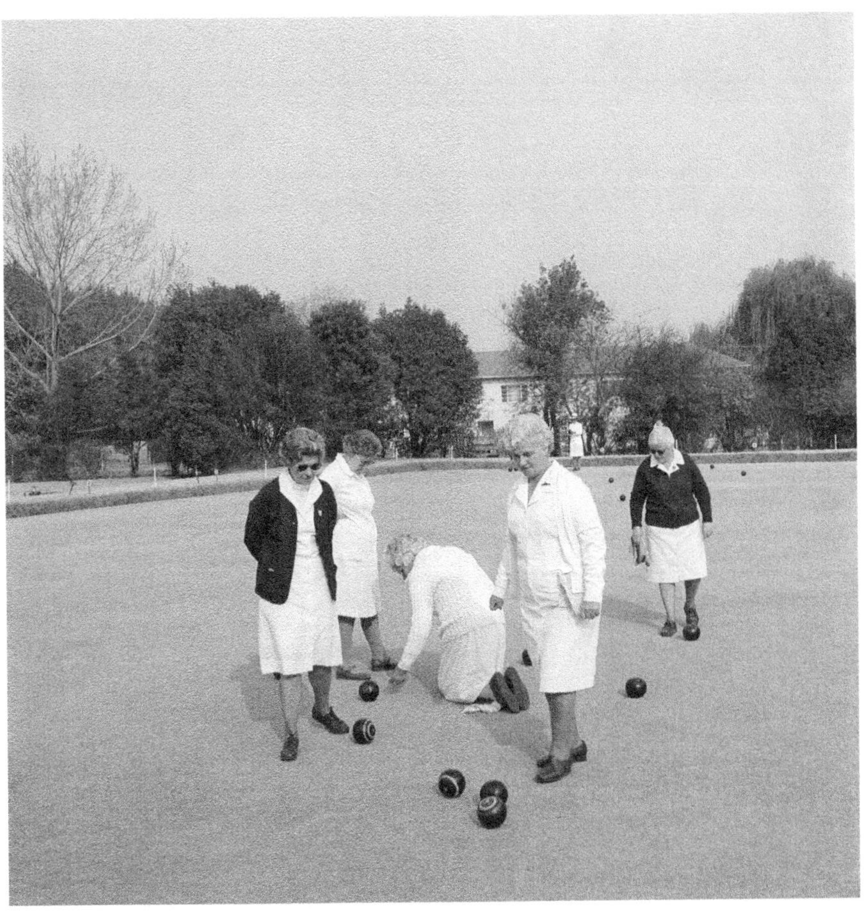

Plate 1: David Goldblatt, *Saturday afternoon: bowls on the East Rand Proprietary Mines green. June 1980*. From the series 'In Boksburg' (1982), Goldblatt's photograph of elderly white ladies on the bowling green exemplifies both the photographer's interests in 'everyday' life under apartheid and the seemingly genteel culture of the lawn. (Photograph by David Goldblatt. © David Goldblatt, courtesy of the Goodman Gallery, Johannesburg.)

HOW CAN ANYONE BE UNHAPPY WHO LIVES IN SUCH A SPLENDID DWELLING?

Plate 2: *Top*, Moses Tladi, *The House in Kensington B*. Tladi's painting of his home, from which he was evicted in 1956 under the forced removals, is a counterpoint to his grander paintings of 'Lokshoek' in Parktown, which depict the garden he worked for Herbert Read. (Image reproduced from *The Artist in the Garden: The Quest for Moses Tladi* by Angela Read Lloyd [Publishing Print Matters, 2009]. Courtesy of Mmapula Tladi-Small and Print Matters.)

Plate 3: *Bottom*, Anton Kannemeyer, *Splendid Dwelling*, 2012. A leitmotif in Kannemeyer's work, the lawn is depicted strikingly as red dashes on a lurid green background. This unsettling visual treatment is suggestive of his scepticism towards the polite conformity of the suburbs. (© Anton Kannemeyer, courtesy of the Stevenson Gallery, Cape Town.)

Plate 4: Brett Murray, *The Renaissance Man Tending His Land*, 2008. In the artist's self-portrait, Murray presents himself in ironic fashion as the landed gentry. Wearing a powdered peruke and in blackface, the shirtless gardener mocks the leisurely presentation of whitely gardening. (Image courtesy of Brett Murray. Photograph: Sean Wilson.)

Plate 5: David Goldblatt, *Saturday Afternoon in Sunward Park. 1979*. The heroic, muscular gardener that Goldblatt captured mowing his lawn in Boksburg is an archetype of the respectable white suburbanite performing his weekend duty. Mowing here is not 'work'; it is a claim of ownership through leisure. (Photograph by David Goldblatt. © David Goldblatt, courtesy of the Goodman Gallery, Johannesburg.)

Plate 6: David Goldblatt, *Miriam Mazibuko waters the garden of her RDP house for which she waited eight years. It consists of one room. Her four children live with her in-laws. Extension 8, Far East Alexandra Township. 12 September 2006*. Water is essential to the lawn, a source of stress for many South African gardeners. (Photograph by David Goldblatt. © David Goldblatt, courtesy of the Goodman Gallery, Johannesburg.)

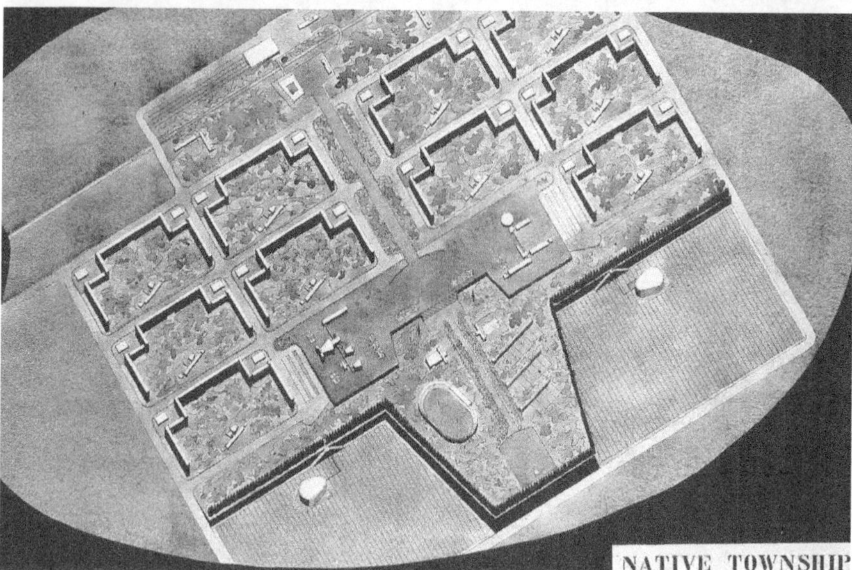

Plate 7: *Top*, W. A. Eden, *Photomontage of Blenheim*, 1935. The montage shows a proposed design for a high-rise apartment block superimposed on top of Blenheim Palace with its iconic eighteenth-century landscape gardens. The modern lawn is the location for revolutionary housing. (Image from *Architectural Review*, March 1935. Courtesy of EMAP.)

Plate 8: *Bottom*, Connell et al., *Native Township General Site Layout*, 1938. The bold plan by a group of Wits students for a high-rise 'Native Township for 20 000 Inhabitants' echoed Le Corbusier and marked the end of a debate in South Africa about the viability of apartment housing for black urbanites. (Courtesy of the Dean of the Faculty of Engineering and the Built Environment, University of the Witwatersrand.)

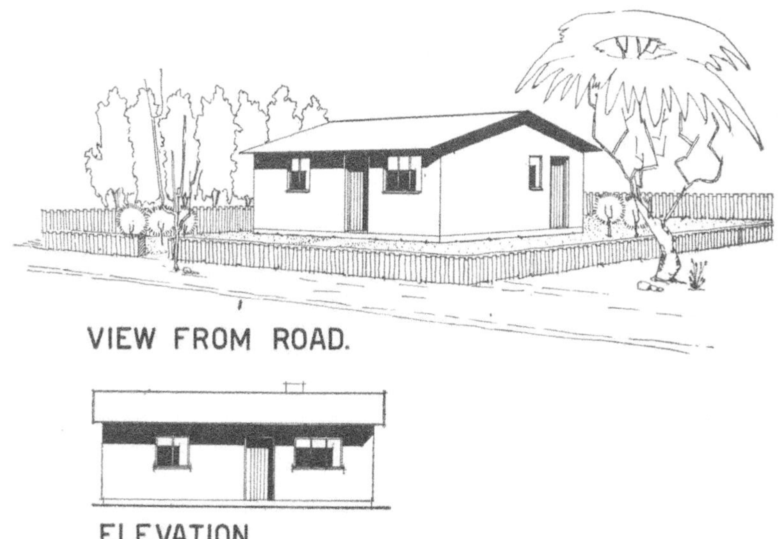

Plate 9: *Top*, D. M. Calderwood, *NE 51/9*, 1953. Often referred to as the 'matchbox' house, the NE 51/9 (Non-European, version 9 of 1951) was devised through studies of existing low-cost houses as well as architectural and scientific experimentation, and became ubiquitous during and after apartheid. (From D. M. Calderwood, 'Native Housing in South Africa', PhD thesis, University of the Witwatersrand, 1953. Courtesy of Wits University Press.)

Plate 10: *Bottom*, D. M. Calderwood, *Proposed New Residential Centre*, 1953. Garden City principles underpinned the master plan for KwaThema. Green belts, sports fields, private gardens and civic space were intended to create a natural environment and healthy neighbourhood. (From D. M. Calderwood, 'Native Housing in South Africa', PhD thesis, University of the Witwatersrand, 1953. Courtesy of Wits University Press.)

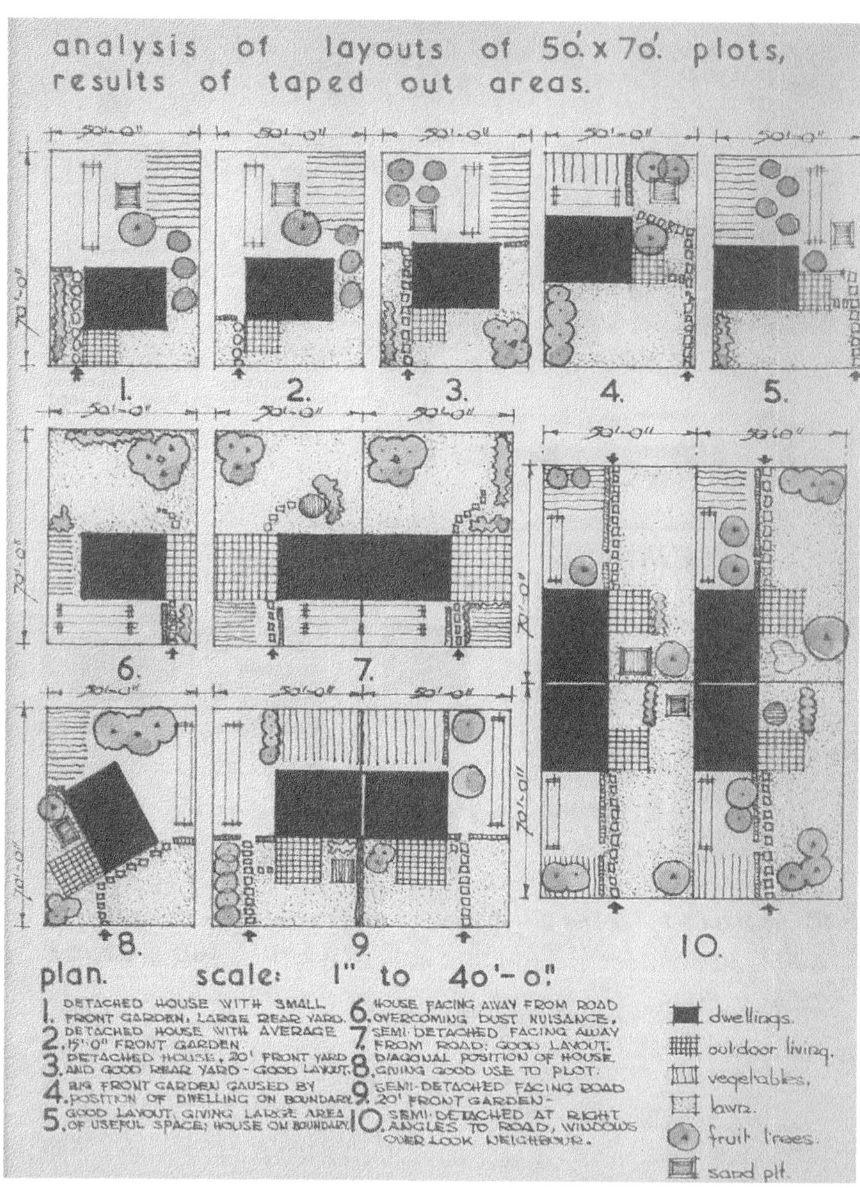

Plate 11: D. M. Calderwood, *Analysis of 50' x 70' plots*, 1953. The modern garden was a technical problem to be solved. Through iterative experimentation, Calderwood argued, useful and efficient residential plots could be planned for black urbanites. (From D. M. Calderwood, 'Native Housing in South Africa', PhD thesis, University of the Witwatersrand, 1953. Courtesy of Wits University Press.)

Plate 12: *Top*, Joane Pim, site of the garden of the Western Deep Levels hospital for mine workers in 1964. **Plate 13:** *Bottom*, The hospital garden three years later. In an homage to Humphry Repton's Red Books, *Beauty is Necessary* presents a before-and-after view of a garden for the mine workers' hospital. Pim deployed eighteenth-century landscape gardening principles to make a garden in the veld. (Images from Joane Pim, *Beauty is Necessary* [Cape Town: Purnell & Sons, 1971].)

Plate 14: *Top*, Roelof Uytenbogaardt, *Nederduitse Gereformeerde Kerk (NGK) Welkom Wes*. A monolith planted in the veld, Uytenbogaardt's church (1966) is at one with – indeed, of – its rough, authentic environment, a fundamentally different view of modernity from that of Pim and other Garden City ideologues. (Original in possession of University of Cape Town Libraries. Courtesy UCT, Special Collections.)

Plate 15: *Bottom*, Jane Alexander, *Security/ Segurança*, 2006. A wheatgrass lawn and the sculpture *Bird* (2006) are 'protected' by razor-wire double diamond-mesh fences; a perimeter of 1 000 sickles, 1 000 machetes and 1 000 used South African workers' gloves; and Brazilian guards, Fabio Silva, André Luiz Marianno, Flávio de Jesus Bastos, Joeferson Goss Oliveira and Alessandro Messias da Rocha. (© 2018 Jane Alexander/DALRO. Photograph: Juan Guerra.)

Plate 16: *Top*, Lungiswa Gqunta, *Lawn 1*, 2016. Gqunta's installation is a disconcerting lawn landscape made from a 242 × 122 mm wooden board studded with upturned broken bottles unevenly filled with surprisingly green petrol. (Image courtesy of Lungiswa Gqunta and Whatiftheworld Gallery.)

Plate 17: *Bottom*, Kemang Wa Lehulere, *Do not go far they say*, 2015. An old-school brown suitcase filled with soil and growing lawn is watched over by porcelain German shepherds. Wa Lehulere's installation challenges the notion that the lawn is permanent and immobile. (© Kemang Wa Lehulere. Courtesy of Stevenson, Cape Town and Johannesburg.)

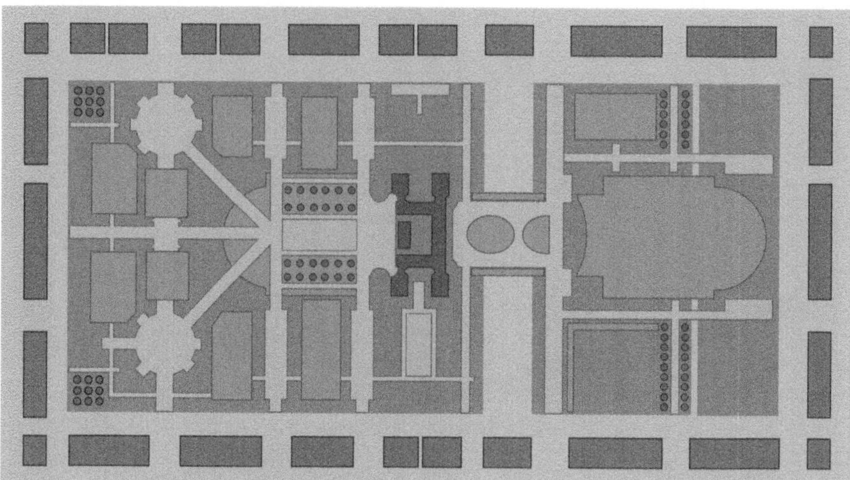

Plate 18: *Left top*, Edwin Lutyens, *Site plan of proposed layout and extent of Joubert Park*. Redrawn by author. Lutyens, architect of the Johannesburg Art Gallery (1915), proposed doubling Joubert Park by spanning the railway tracks and including Union Ground (now the location of Park Central Taxi Rank). The changes would have placed the gallery in the centre of a generous twenty-acre park.

Plate 19: *Left bottom*, Terry Kurgan, *Park Pictures: Aerial map showing the fixed positions of forty photographers working out of Joubert Park in 2004*. As part of her *Park Pictures* project (2005), Kurgan documented the professional photographers who made a living taking portraits in the park outside the Johannesburg Art Gallery. (Image courtesy of Terry Kurgan.)

Plate 20: *This page, top*, Terry Kurgan, *Park Pictures: Photographer Godfrey Ndlovu's unclaimed portrait*, 2005. **Plate 21:** *Bottom right*, Terry Kurgan, *Park Pictures: Photographer Varrie Hluzani's unclaimed portrait*, 2005. The lawn appears in a great number of the unclaimed portraits Kurgan collected from the Joubert Park photographers. As a backdrop, the lawn provides an ambiguous location of urbanity and respectability. (Images courtesy of Terry Kurgan.)

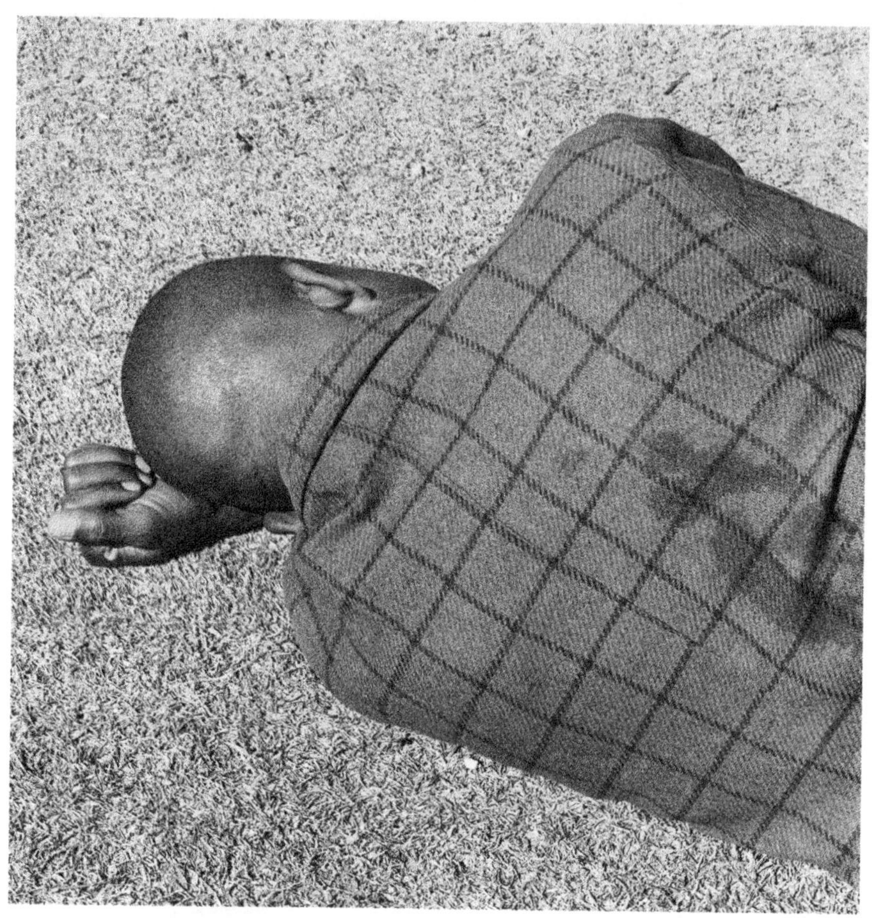

Plate 22: David Goldblatt, *Sleeping man, Joubert Park, Johannesburg. 1975.* Shot during a brief liberal phase after 1974 in which black people were permitted into Joubert Park, Goldblatt's closely observed image of a man sleeping on the lawn ties into long-held racial anxieties about proper comportment, leisure and idleness. (Photograph by David Goldblatt. © David Goldblatt, courtesy of the Goodman Gallery, Johannesburg.)

Plate 23: Sabelo Mlangeni, *A space of waiting*, 2012. Mlangeni's painterly photograph of Joubert Park captures a gentle, even pretty aspect of Johannesburg's inner city. How, we might ask, can the pictorial language of the picturesque be seen as appropriate for representing the post-apartheid landscape? (Image courtesy of Sabelo Mlangeni.)

Plate 24: *Top*, Pieter Hugo, *Aerial View Dainfern Gated Community*, 2013. **Plate 25:** *Bottom*, Pieter Hugo, *Aerial View Diepsloot*, 2013. Hugo's diptych of post-apartheid Johannesburg illustrates the stark contrast between the lush gated compound of Dainfern and the nearby settlement of Diepsloot. While the disparity in these aerial views is indisputable, what ecological subtleties are lost in this kind of visual polemic? (© Pieter Hugo. Courtesy of Stevenson, Cape Town and Johannesburg/Yossi Milo, New York/Priska Pasquer, Cologne.)

teleological metanarrative of modernization to be revised in the face of the non- and counterlinearities of the present?' (1999: 15–16).

The lawn has never been modern

It is important to point out that modernism, even under apartheid, was not monolithic in its conception and reception. As such, its failures were and are not uniform.

As a way of advancing this argument, I propose concluding this chapter by approaching Welkom from the point of view of another kind of modernism, one that was uncharacteristically and uncommonly *against* the lawn, or at least ambivalent to it. As a counterpoint to Pim's British industrialised pastoral modernism, I want to suggest the apartheid modernity of Roelof Uytenbogaardt's Nederduitse Gereformeerde Kerk (Plate 14).

A monolith planted in the veld, Uytenbogaardt's brutalist church drew criticism from its conception in 1965. Elders, church members and the popular press resisted the emphatic modernity of the building (Peters & Kotze 2013). An uncompromising concrete and brick 'abstract sculptural object' (Murray 2010: 90), Uytenbogaardt's church was originally conceived of as 'starkly juxtaposed against the flatness of the area and surrounded by bleached grass and wide open space'. The austerity of the plan is echoed in every specification: bare concrete interiors, custom-designed wooden pews, carpetless concrete floors and certainly no sweeping lawns.

Murray argues that, for Uytenbogaardt, the emergent landscape of 'green' suburbia was 'less important than his vision of the church in the "veld" (open grasslands) upon which he based his conception of the design' (2010: 90). Uytenbogaardt's plans from the archive show no garden or landscape specifications. Early photographs show lawn trimming on some sides of the church building; however, overwhelmingly the image of the church was expressed through dramatic landscape photographs, which placed the building in its striking landscape context.[12] Published in the magazine *Huisgenoot* in 1967 and *Credo* in 1969, the photographs present the church in a manner that accentuates its plantedness.[13] The images suggest a building at one with, indeed *of*, its rough, authentic environment, a fundamentally different view of modernity from that of Pim and other Garden

City ideologues, and a valorisation of the very landscape that Pim had worked so hard to carpet over.

During the last half-century a number of the church's rough edges have been softened – concrete-coloured carpets installed, wood-toned cushions fabricated for the pews, awkward pot plants find themselves dotted around the church, a homely tablecloth on the once bare Eucharist table – and, most incongruously, a neat lawn has been established over the entire property, which is now enclosed by metal palisade fencing. One wants to ask: were there church meetings about the veld surrounding the church and its need to be grassed over, as there must have been debates and meetings about carpets, cushions and tablecloths? The rationale for the cushions seems obvious, and for the carpets it was undoubtedly the cold in winter, but what would the practical argument against veld have been? It seems to me that cushions and carpets share a common domesticity with the lawn. Since the lawn often functions rhetorically as an outdoor carpet, tearing up the veld and replacing it with turf is a perfectly understandable softening, possibly even feminising, domestication of the unyielding church architecture. (It is difficult not to take up a position of Corbusian contempt for the parochial garden with its quaint pot plants and neat lawn.)

That the lawn is theoretically always set in opposition to some kind of wilderness is an orthodox proposition. Whereas the lawn is improved and domesticated, nature interpreted, the wilderness is nature that is unimproved or not yet improved. John Buchan presented this tension in his description of the contrast between the 'common veld' and the garden, between the 'temperate home and the rude wilds' beyond the park walls (Buchan 1903: 127).

The lawn/veld dialectic underpins a number of other texts. For example, in David Goldblatt's photograph *Saturday Afternoon in Sunward Park. 1979*, the rationally mowed lawn in the foreground is set in contrast to the veld across the street. The modernity of the garden, the electric lawnmower and the white suburbanite are framed in relation to the timeless, unchanging veld, but also in relation to a veld that was likely to become future lawn in a growing suburb. In Doris Lessing's *The Grass is Singing*, Mary Turner nurses the foreboding that once she is dead her little home will be 'killed by the bush, which had always hated it, had always stood silently waiting for the time when it could advance and cover it, forever, so that nothing remained' (Lessing 1994: 195). Mary experiences the veld as a threat to her domesticity and indeed to her life. Elsewhere in the novel, Dick Turner describes the contrast he observes between the 'veld he knew so well' and 'ugly scattered suburbs ... stuck anyhow over the veld, that had no relationship with the hard brown soil and the arching blue sky ... He felt he could kill ... all the people who built prim little houses with hedged gardens full of English flowers' (45). The lawn and wilderness are set in a more or less antagonistic relationship.

The image of the veld is not historically stable and without ambiguity. Jennifer Beningfield (2006a) and Jeremy Foster (2008, 2009, 2012) have both provided intelligent analyses of the veld discourse, which demonstrate the ways in which the trope functioned for different racial and language groups at different times. For instance, Foster shows how as part of early twentieth-century Reconstruction discourse the 'cult of the veld' emerged as a way for white English speakers to locate themselves in the 'vastness, emptiness, and desolation' of the Transvaal (2008: 66). The unspoilt veld was perceived by cosmopolitan English elites as a foil to the 'materialism and philistinism' of industrialising Johannesburg (Foster 2012: 48). In parallel, via analysis of early Afrikaans poetry, Beningfield demonstrates how the veld signified an 'attempt to bring the enigmatic wilderness under' control of the white Afrikaner (2006a: 9). The veld's wildness, she writes, was 'both present and held at bay through the natural knowledge of the volk'. She continues: 'The veld therefore was an interpreted wilderness, a means to argue that the plains of the interior were destined for the occupation of the Afrikaner and to familiarise the volk with the "empty" landscape. In other representations, however, the veld emerges as an unstable image, one whose ownership is contested and whose boundaries are illusive.'

The veld is not monolithic. It is, however, generally characterised as unimproved and undomesticated. Because it is unimproved, it holds the promise of potential improvement and thereby the demonstration of the right to domination by the improver's hand; at other times the veld's unimprovedness is a potent source of raw nature, latent not with possibility but with authenticity (Beningfield 2006a: 9).

It is obvious to say that the veld is undomesticated, wild; nevertheless, this wildness needs to be qualified. Take, for instance, Pim's treatment of the green belts in Welkom, planted with indigenous grass, which was to be roughly trimmed (Pim 1956). In addition, writing about the *Collective Thesis*'s unbuilt township, Foster reads the park-like spaces between the super-blocks as 'large interstitial pieces of veld' intended to accommodate the 'community-consciousness that was deemed to characterize the life of most Africans' (2012: 52). As far as I can tell, Foster is the only commentator who has suggested that these parks were pieces of veld, which is clearly the most realistic assumption but not, it seems to me, what the thesis writers were describing in their plans as the green ground surface (Kantorowich 1939: 119). If Foster is correct, is it not also then practically true that the interstitial spaces would need to have been replanted as veld with indigenous grass after the likely degradation during construction? Indeed, while Uytenbogaardt's church had the appearance of being dropped into the untouched veld from above, what kind of veld gardening took place after building was complete?

Aside from the argument above, it is also essential to note that while the veld resonated as that terrain fundamentally outside of human control, it functioned very often within the domestic domain. Beningfield (2006a: 15) argues that while the farm stood for a particular kind of mastery over nature, the veld was easily accommodated within the boundaries of the farm. Indeed, the real power of the veld in political discourse was its ability to be domesticated by the knowledge of the *volk* (Afrikaner nation) without appearing to be brought under control. It was the veld's ambiguity, its appearance as a 'landscape apparently not mediated and altered though cultivation', that made the veld so resonant (31).

How is it that Uytenbogaardt understood the veld as an ideal landscape context for his strain of Afrikaner modernism?

Murray (2007, 2010) argues that one of the key architectural 'moments' in South African architecture was 'Afrikaner/apartheid' modernism, a moment in which modernism was 'domesticated' as the style of choice for serving Afrikaner nationalism. In '"Ons Bou vir die Bank": Nationalism, Architecture and Volkskas Bank', Melinda Silverman argues that the 'formal elements of European modernist architecture' enabled the Afrikaner nationalists to both break with British imperial styles (1998: 129) and to express 'the notion of progress and a more inclusive, cosmopolitan South African identity' (136).

Murray contends that Silverman's argument about the self-conscious modernity of *volkskapitalisme* (nationalist capitalism) can be equally applied to the modern architecture of the Afrikaans Protestant churches. Goldblatt has made a similar argument in his writing and photographs for *The Structure of Things Then* (Goldblatt 1998). In his study and interpretation of a number of Afrikaner churches (17–20), Goldblatt seeks to place their architecture within the physical and cultural landscape of South Africa. His image *Dutch Reformed Church Edenvale, 1983* (19) displays a remarkable similarly to Uytenbogaardt's photograph of the newly built church. They both function as sculptural objects, brutalist masses of concrete and brick, with a foreground of honest and tough veld grass.[14]

Nevertheless, veld settings are not the norm in Goldblatt's church archive. Even *Dutch Reformed Church Edenvale* appears to be a photographer's conceit, shot from outside the church grounds. We can see a mean little fence and imagine the precise lawn that abuts the monolith. Goldblatt's photograph, like his work in general, is an attempt to make sense, and it seems that the veld, in this instance, made sense.

Deon Liebenberg (2014) has performed a fascinating close reading of a number of canonical texts by theologians writing about the principles and precepts of Afrikaans Protestant church design. His analysis of these design 'guideline texts' is helpful in explaining the place of the landscape in the ecclesiastical scheme.

Through his reading of Adrianus van Selms's *Beginsels van Protestantse kerkbou* (1954) Liebenberg argues that there is evidence of the Calvinist church's attempts to locate an authentic and 'indigenous Afrikaans' style. He points out the unsurprising affinity Protestantism felt for modernism's rejection of the ornament and decoration, which they associated with Counter-Reformation Baroque. Echoing Adolf Loos's famous rejection of ornament, Van Selms argues that '*die skoonheid van 'n gebouw is nie 'n toegevoegde ornament nie, maar die harmonie van lyne, vlakke en kleure*' (the beauty of a building is not an additional ornament, but in the harmony of lines, levels and colours), concluding that, in fact, '*die ornament sinvol moet wees*' (ornament must be meaningful) (Van Selms 1954: 85). Van Selms enunciates, in almost neurotic detail, the orientation of the organ, the shape of the ceilings, the arrangement of pews, the placement and material of the pulpit, the height and arrangement of fenestration, floor finishing and design of the *nagmaaltafel* (Eucharist table). The righteousness of the guidelines' author, however, specifically does not include what Van Selms called '*die res*': '*die plasing van die geheel op die aangewese terrein … die hek werk en die plantsoen … Dit is die boumeester se saak*' (the rest: the placement of the whole on the designated terrain … the fencing and the plantings … This is the building master/architect's business) (1954: 91).

What is apparent from the foundational texts is that theologians considered (1) the relationships between the building and the broader landscape and (2) the relation between the landscaping/garden and church to be technical concerns, not immediately (or at all) affecting the conditions of worship. As a non-architect, Van Selms trusted that lawns or veld should be dealt with by professionals. This devolution of control is remarkable, considering the detail with which so many other elements were treated. Van Selms sets up, what seems to me, a rather spurious opposition between the holy inside and the secular outside. In any case, what his pronouncements confirm is a widely held belief that the landscape is neutral, outside of politics, best left to professionals.

The issue of professionalism has been at the forefront of this chapter. I have drawn a distinction between the gardener-worker on the one hand and the professional landscaper-architect on the other. The professionalisation of the landscape, as it emerged within modernist discourse, resulted in a profound disjunction between the plan(ned) and the lived. It is not as if the vernacular or unplanned lawn has not failed to fully approximate the lawn ideal in terms of its creation, maintenance and use. The difference is perhaps that the disjunction is so much bigger and the failures are more visible, easier to trace because we have concrete plans by which to judge the lawn's allegiance to the ideal. Professional landscape practice is characterised by the muscularity with which actors are able to impose their visions. Both the green belt and the lawn are impositions on the landscape, devised in accordance with theoretical, aesthetic, sometimes nostalgic and political ideas. Within this scheme the lawn often stands out, paradoxically, as the element that is not explicitly articulated or drawn onto the plan. This absence is very telling. The lawn sometimes functions as a particular kind of silence and can insinuate itself into the landscape. The lawn can be very sneaky. Indeed, as I argue in the following chapter, the lawn can be quite insidious.

The binaries – before/after, green/brown, healthy/sick and so on – which frame the landscape chronologically seem insufficient to account for the messiness of lived space both during and 'after' modernism. In the next chapter I continue to challenge the binary construction of landscape through analysis of the history of Joubert Park in Johannesburg. This park plays a central role in the artistic imaginary of the city and presents numerous instances of what would be considered failure, decay or misuse, which nevertheless provide examples of lived modernism, of what people actually do. It is abundantly clear from the literature in this chapter how seldom social scientists, both in South Africa and abroad, actually ask people how they live, what they want from their landscapes, what their lawns do for, to and with them.

Chapter 4
No Fucking up/on the Lawn

i don't want that suburban house
i don't want a second car
a swimming pool a lawn a boring Sunday

— Wopko Jensma, *i must show you my clippings*[1]

We recognise the impossibility of landscape achieving its illusion of permanence, its claim of completion or its totalising claim on its future. This chapter is about decay, ruin, inappropriateness, incorrectness, about doing the wrong things to the lawn, with the lawn and on the lawn. It is also, perhaps, about the lawn's failure to do what it *wants*.

I begin with the issue of movement – not often brought to bear on the landscape itself, though it is acknowledged with regard to active subjects who move on or across the landscape. That some subjects have been and still are forbidden from moving on and across the landscape is important to note here. As a deliberate provocation (like W. J. T. Mitchell's contention that the landscape is a verb) I provide a study of *Pennisetum clandestinum* (kikuyu grass) to explore ways in which the immobility of the lawn is established discursively, only to be undermined.

The following notions challenge the inactivity and passivity of the lawn: (1) the underground life and movement of the grass; (2) the horizontal spreading of the grass (particularly rampant in the case of kikuyu); (3) the illegitimate uses of the lawn in relation to the fixed or ideal uses envisioned by the literature (the middle-class repose, for instance); and (4) the alienness of kikuyu, which connects it to ideas of belonging and indigeneity. The overarching point is that there is something transgressive about the lawn.

The notion of immobility points to two things. Firstly, the systems and structures that *do* limit access and movement, especially of black bodies, on and across the landscape/lawn; secondly, and in contrast, the provocation provided by thinking of movement on the lawn but also movement *of* the lawn. Lawn may be thought of as a trans-plant: moving across the world as part of a botanical exchange, and moving above and below ground as part of its biological growth pattern (the prefix *trans* being derived from the Latin 'across').

Joubert Park in Johannesburg serves as the location to interrogate unsanctioned uses of public space broadly and of the lawn specifically. Public homosexual sex, vagrancy, drugging and informal trading – all activities at odds with the Victorian discourse of 'rational leisure' – are examined in this chapter principally via images taken by photographers at work in the park. How amenable is the lawn to alternative uses, or to being used as a mode of getting by and making do? How possible is it to represent the post-apartheid lawn in ways other than through the trope of degeneration and decay? How do we use and represent the lawn *after*?

The chapter concludes with a study of failure from the novel *Triomf* (1999) by Marlene van Niekerk. The inability of the novel's white protagonists to transform themselves into respectable citizens, to manage their own garden in acceptable and rational ways – in short, to be domesticated and also to domesticate – points to the limits and limitations of the lawn. How powerful is the lawn, really? Van Niekerk's novel presents the lawn, following Bettina Malcomess and Dorothee Kreutzfeldt (2013: 40), as an 'event'. The poor white family ends up using the lawn in ways that are contradictory to the normative manner of use. Where the lawn ought to be peaceful and gentle, they make it violent and anguished; where it ought to be kind, it is cruel; where the lawn ought to have an ending, they make it burst its bounds, flow into the street and invade the neighbourhood. The lawn divides, disrupts, damages. Maybe it is incorrect to describe these events as the failure of the lawn to secure what it wants. Indeed, perhaps what the lawn wants, after all, is for you to fail?

No lawn

The Introduction presented the argument for the relevance of failure as an interpretive tool in the study of landscape. Jack Halberstam argues in favour of failure as a 'worthy alternative' to the 'legacies of violent triumphalism', to the persistence of futurism, to the profit of neoliberalism (2007: 69). Halberstam's approach is profoundly influenced by 'anti-relational' queer theory (Halberstam 2008). The anti-social approach, a strand of queer theory most associated with Leo Bersani and Lee Edelman, is at odds with neoliberal agendas, which have tended to coalesce around, for instance, activism for gay marriage, adoption and gay parenting and other high-minded liberal ideals. The queer subject, Edelman argues, has always been 'bound epistemologically, to negativity, to nonsense, to anti-production, to unintelligibility', and so, instead of fighting these ascriptions and working towards assimilation, he proposes that queers should embrace 'the negativity that we anyway represent' (2007: 83). The anti-social thesis is resonant with a number of what Halberstam calls 'shadow feminisms' (Halberstam 2011: 4), which haunt feminist discourse that is deemed respectable, tolerable and positive. The power of the anti-social thesis is its potential to replace 'the forward looking, reproductive and heteronormative politics of hope' (2008: 141).

Failing presents an opportunity for escape: from the punishing norms of disciplinary society; from capitalism, which is in any case structured by the necessary failure of some other person; from 'toxic positivity', which is the denial of structural injustice in favour of positive thinking; from modernity (Halberstam 2008); from compulsory heterosexuality and reproductivity; from teleology. Róisín O'Gorman and Margaret Werry argue that failure 'is neither a dead end nor a pit stop on the path to success but a generative, unsettling and revelatory force' (2012: 1).

As a modality of resistance, failure constitutes what James Scott (1998) calls a 'weapon of the weak', or what Michel de Certeau (1984) conceptualises as a 'tactic'. Saidiya Hartman (1997) argues that such oppositional tools explain the 'subtle resistances to slavery', evident in practices such as working slowly or feigning incompetence. Halberstam postulates that we should 'recategorize what looks like inaction, passivity, and lack of resistance in terms of the practice of stalling the business of the dominant' (2007: 88).

This raises a question in relation to my analysis of the lawn. How does the (white) history of unproductive and incompetent 'garden boys' change when interpreted through the emancipatory logic of failure? The concept of failure proposes an inefficient, unproductive, non-reproductive way of dealing with the natural world. What does negative, non-reproductive gardening look like? Failure's analytical promise lies in its capacity to unravel the certainties of knowledge, competence, representation, normativity and authority that discursively define the lawn.

Indeed, much of what the embrace of failure potentially offers is an escape from modernity: from the teleological vector of becoming a new person, of transformation, of arriving. Arjun Appadurai suggests that whatever else the project of modernity 'may have created, it aspired to create persons who would, after the fact, have wished to have become modern' (1996: 1).

Lastly, it is essential to note that failure constitutes, as Scott Sandage argues in *Born Losers* (2005), a 'hidden history'. If the archive of failure, in general, is hidden, the record of the landscape failing is especially absent. This chapter requires scouring the archive for silences, shadows and ghosts in order to argue for a negative ecology.

No walking on the lawn!

Humans, in contrast to plants, are known to move on and across the landscape, on and across the lawn in prescribed and non-prescribed ways. The proscriptions include probably the most famous one, 'Don't walk on the grass!' but include other, more subtle ones, such as, 'Don't sleep on the lawn (especially if you are black)' – this injunction is explored fully later in this chapter.[2]

By its very definition the lawn is always bounded. Whether the lawn's boundary is articulated by a ha-ha, a precast concrete wagon-wheel fence or a fence fashioned from bits of junk, a herbaceous border or simply by abutting the veld, the lawn must end somewhere. What has not always been open for debate is whether the lawn is being kept in or the wilderness kept out. 'Aggressive' lawn grasses like kikuyu are surprisingly invasive, occupying the veld and pasture grasses, and presenting a real challenge for containment.

The boundary is conceptualised as that which is between the lawn and the wilderness. Writing about game lodges in *Blank____ Architecture, Apartheid and After*, Njabulo Ndebele observes that in the middle of the bush there will be a clearing 'signifying civilization. This clearing will have neat green lawns, which contrast with the dense, chaotic bush just beyond their trimmed edge. That clean-cut edge is crucial. It indicates the perimeter of civilization' (1998: 119). From this, it follows that if the lawn is not cared for and protected, the wilderness will engulf the garden. The lawn must be defended.

Perhaps the opposite is also true. Take, for example, Jane Alexander's installation *Security/Segurança* (2006), made for the 27th Bienal de São Paulo (see Plate 15). The original installation was built around a central verdant quadrangle bounded by two razor-wire security fences. Inside the perimeter were 1 000 sickles, 1 000 machetes and 1 000 used South African workers' gloves. At its centre – 'watchfully protected, or imprisoned' – was a single sculpture, 'part bird, part human, part something harder to define … a useless creature, its cruel beak leaning out from a torso without either arms or wings, supporting itself on oddly bent legs seemingly unequal to the task' (Powell 2007: 36). The inner 'lawn' was composed of germinating, growing and dying wheatgrass. The securitised lawn points to parallels in paranoia between Brazil and South Africa, problems of migration and the privatisation and militarisation of security. The wheatgrass lawn – either dangerous or precious; or perhaps both dangerous and precious – was contained by the gallery, by the white/grey modern cube, by the concrete floor, which made it impossible for the grass to take hold and grow, to move.

Alexander's installation was endowed with an added layer of ambiguity in 2010, when, at the exhibition 10 Years of South African Sculpture, a similar version, *Custodian with Bird*, was planted within the rolling verdure of the Patrick Watson-designed Nirox Foundation sculpture park. Federico Freschi suggests that the 'self-consciously picturesque landscaping of Nirox Estate cannot also help but evoke the notion of an Arcadian idyll, suggesting, as it does, a lyrical, nostalgic evocation of a golden age of prelapsarian peace and innocence' (2009: 39). In principle, the lawns of Nirox, and many other sculpture parks, can be thought of as the equivalent of the 'neutral' white/grey cube of the modern art gallery/museum.

Critics have long since argued that the 'white wall's apparent neutrality is an illusion ... the perfect surface off which to bounce our paranoias' (O'Doherty 1999: 79). The ideological function of the white cube is to 'actively disassociate the space of art from the outer world, furthering the institution's idealist imperative of rendering itself and its values "objective," "disinterested," and "true"' (Kwon 2002: 13). In the modern sculpture garden, lawn could be said to function in the same way, providing a seemingly non-political and uncontaminated pastoral context. Of course, as I have shown, the pastoralism of the eighteenth-century garden, the logic on which Nirox is based, is far from neutral and interpellates a particular kind of viewer and mode of relating to the landscape.

When *Custodian with Bird* was installed at Nirox, the ground of the sculpture park itself replaced the germinating and dying grass of earlier gallery iterations. Simply installing it in Johannesburg annexes anxieties about crime and post-apartheid racial exclusion in the form of electric fences, razor wire, illegal road closures and gated communities. However, that the artwork was mapped over the already existing lawn meant that *Custodian with Bird* became suddenly porous, its quarantine broken. As a thought exercise, we could imagine Nirox Foundation as the scene of a science fiction disaster, *circa* 2075, where the lawns are contagious and, having swallowed the entire sculpture park, are now at war with the surrounding veld.

The treacherous lawn appears in artist Lungiswa Gqunta's installation *Lawn 1* (2016), a disconcerting landscape made from a 242 × 122 mm wooden board studded with upturned broken bottles unevenly filled with surprisingly green petrol (see Plate 16).

Exchanging the soft, evenly mowed lawn with sharp, rough glass shards is a provocative and uncanny manoeuvre. What should comfort now cuts; what ought to soothe now seethes with urgent political disquiet. Whereas the lawn in general tends to naturalise land ownership, Gqunta's *Lawn 1* deterritorialises property after apartheid. In light of political machinations regarding land redistribution and anxieties about safety, Gqunta unsettles the polite order of suburban life.

The broken bottles invoke the shards of glass atop many boundary walls. These symbols of suburban anxiety, emphatic statements of property ownership, are homemade protections. The bottles and petrol also invoke the Molotov cocktail and the call for radical land redistribution; an accusation against the inherent violence of white settler occupation, black embourgeoisement and a challenge to the claim of ownership based on the improvement of land.

What is most stimulating about Gqunta's artwork, however, is the flattening of the wall into a lawn. The boundary, so essential for the South African lawn, has been widened and then flattened down to form the surface of the garden. The wall has become the floor; that is, the boundary has become the interior; the structure that provides protection, keeps the outside out, has become instead a dangerous inside.

Gqunta offers an alternative take on domesticity, one that is not safe, not a safe return from a chaotic and dangerous world outside. At best, it presents a futile wall, a useless boundary that cannot protect us.

No aliens

An investigation of South Africa's best-known lawn grass, kikuyu or *Pennisetum clandestinum* Hochst. ex Chiov.,[3] will further challenge the notion that the lawn is gentle, stable and kindly.

In *c.*1910 botanist Joseph Burtt-Davy received from his friend David Forbes a root of kikuyu grass (Stapf 1921: 85), 'planted in a small milk-tin', which he had carefully carried from his cabin near Lake Naivasha in the East Africa Protectorate to Pretoria (Burtt-Davy 1915: 147). The root was planted in one of the plots of the Botanical Station at Groenkloof, Pretoria (Stapf 1921: 85). It was primarily for its grazing potential that Burtt-Davy and Stapf were interested in kikuyu, as Stapf makes clear: 'I can say with every assurance that Kikuyu is one of the most palatable grasses. All stock eat it greedily and will leave most grasses to get to it. If stock are allowed on a patch of Kikuyu it will be seen that they will graze contentedly, and when they have had their fill they like to lie down on it, for the Kikuyu forming such a dense turf provides a very comfortable rest' (86).

The turf produced by stock grazing provides a comfortable spot for an after-dinner nap! The potential of kikuyu for lawns was not lost on these early fans of the grass. As early as 1913, Illtyd Buller Pole-Evans used kikuyu for the lawns of the newly built Union Buildings in Pretoria (Fairbridge 1924: 36; Stapf 1921: 88). When in 1915 the first 'very meagre specimens of the grass' reached Kew

Royal Botanic Gardens from Pretoria, they were recognised as identical to 'some fragments of *Pennisetum*, which in 1906 had been received from A. Linton among pieces of *Cynodon dactylon*', and, indeed, as identical to an even earlier specimen from 1903, which led Emilio Chiovenda to accord the grass the status of a species (Stapf 1921: 89).

The centrality of Kew Royal Botanic Gardens in the circuit of colonial capitalism is well known. Lucile Brockway argues that institutions like Kew 'played a critical role in generating and disseminating useful scientific knowledge, which facilitated transfers of energy, manpower, and capital on a worldwide basis and an unprecedented scale ... Kew became a clearinghouse for the exchange of plant information and a depot for the interchange of plants throughout the empire; it sent plants wherever it saw commercial possibilities' (1979: 450–453).

Kikuyu was one of the less remarkable botanical transfers that made its way through Kew and has attracted no scholarly attention. More important commercial and medicinal plants like cinchona, rubber and sisal and their places within circuits of colonial capitalism have been well studied (see, for example, Beinart & Middleton 2004; Brockway 1979; Crosby 1986; Drayton 2000; Grove 1995; Pollan 2003). The banality of *P. clandestinum*, one of a multitude of botanicals that were registered, collected, propagated and transmitted to other areas of the world, makes its story profoundly central to the narrative of the exchange because of its everydayness. Because it is 'accommodating and versatile' (Sheat & Schofield 1995: 19), 'tough' (Quattrocchi 2006: 1637), 'hardy and vigorous' (Stapf 1921: 86), kikuyu has managed to thrive in the diverse geographic and ecological zones to which it has migrated and is now naturalised in northern and southern Africa, tropical Asia, Australia, New Zealand, south-west mainland United States, Mexico, Central America, South America, Melanesia and Polynesia (Mears 1970: 140).

In addressing the morphology of *P. clandestinum*, we can discern the theme of movement in two ways. Firstly, the common name 'kikuyu' – from the Agikuyu tribe of Kenya, meaning 'a huge sycamore tree' – has everything to do with location: it indicates the *place* where the grass was picked from, a colony of Britain, a kind of starting point where the grass was native; a native grass named after a 'native' tribe. The name is also arboreal, further suggesting a plantedness, fixedness in a location. Inherent in this name is a fascinating tension between human/plant, indigenous/alien, collective (lawn and tribe)/singular (sycamore) and micro and macro scales. There is also a botanical circularity (incestuousness) between the tree and the grass.

In most plants, the area of growth, called the meristem, is located at the plant's tip (an apical meristem), but in lawn grasses the meristem is 'subapical', well below the tip. Because the growth area is uniquely low down on the stem, the reproduction centre of grasses, and thus their ability to continue producing shoots and leaves, is protected from mowing or grazing. Edward Johnson and Kiyoko Miyanishi (2007: 400) explain that the precise location of the meristematic activity allows the grass to 'tolerate disturbance'; indeed, to thrive despite disturbances such as mowing. When the grass stem is first developing a leaf or primordia, the leaf is 'initially entirely meristematic', possessing the ability for cell division; however, soon afterwards, the meristematic activity becomes isolated lower down in the area called the 'intercalary region', the base of the leaf blade, sheath and stem internodes (Gibson 2009: 43). Thus, if a disturbance like the mower's blade removes the leaf, the portion cut away is quickly replaced by the intercalary meristem through the 'elongation of the leaf', encouraging extra stem growth (tillering) and making it possible to 'maintain dense artificial grasslands (lawns) by artificial grazing (mowing)' (Johnson & Miyanishi 2007: 400).

Kikuyu's reproduction is both rhizomatous and stoloniferous, which makes it particularly 'aggressive' in its movement (Quattrocchi 2006: 1637). Its slender, branched rhizomes grow laterally underground, while above the ground long multi-branched stolons move horizontally and prone.

The notion of the rhizome is taken up by Gilles Deleuze and Félix Guattari in *A Thousand Plateaus: Capitalism and Schizophrenia* (1987) in order to describe a way of thinking not structured by binaries or by the logic of cause and effect, but nevertheless not conceived in opposition to Western logic. The image of the tree claiming singularity and truth is replaced by the networked, horizontal image of the rhizome (Sutton & Martin-Jones 2011: 4–5). The rhizome, according to Deleuze and Guattari, 'is comprised not of units but of dimensions, or rather directions in motion. It has neither beginning nor end, but always a middle (*milieu*) from which it grows and which it overspills. It constitutes linear multiplicities with dimensions having neither subject nor object, which can be laid out on a plane of consistency … the rhizome is made only of lines; lines of segmentarity and stratification as its dimensions, and the line of flight or deterritorialization' (1987: 21). Approaching the lawn under the theme of the rhizomatic invests it with dynamism and momentum that is denied it when it is treated as an inert surface.

Kikuyu grass also has very short flowering culms (aerial stems), which are hidden among the leaves, and the inflorescence of the grass is therefore described as clandestine (hence *clandestinum*). To be clandestine is to be secret, private, concealed, usually in a negative sense, implying craftiness or deception; underhand, surreptitious (*Oxford English Dictionary*). Indeed, there is something devious about the grass and its habits. Take, for example, Otto Stapf's description of kikuyu in the *Kew Bulletin* (1921: 87–88): 'Kikuyu is so aggressive that … when planted on the veld it will establish itself against any of our veld grasses.' The *CRC World Dictionary of Grasses* describes kikuyu as 'troublesome, a noxious weed', a 'vigorous and aggressive' invader, an 'excellent colonizer' (Quattrocchi 2006: 1637). Elsewhere the grass is described as 'very greedy' (Sheat & Schofield 1995: 19) and 'aggressive and strong' (Omole 2011). Kikuyu, the building block of the civilised lawn, is, in short, a weed.

The 'discovery of the indigenous', the appreciation – respect for, enjoyment of, affective response to, collection, promotion, protection and propagation – of native plants should be understood as connected to racial, political and class discourses (Ballard & Jones 2011; Comaroff & Comaroff 2001, 2012; Mabey 2010; Van Sittert 2003). The corollary is also true: the appreciation of exotic – alien, non-native, non-indigenous – plants is discursively constructed. Just as the vogue for exotic botanicals in South Africa – the jacaranda tree, kikuyu, chrysanthemums (and all the trees and bushes specified for KwaThema by Douglas McGavin Calderwood) – was historically specific, the contemporary revulsion towards them is temporal. Lance van Sittert (2003) has shown in his research of the Cape floral kingdom how the taste for fynbos was closely linked to race/class positions and political ideology. The 'discovery' of indigenous botanicals also meant the discovery of threats: extralegal flower harvesting and street selling by so-called locusts (Van Sittert 2003: 119), veld burning and, lastly, invasive alien species. In their iconic studies of the fynbos fires at the Cape, Jean Comaroff and John Comaroff (2001, 2012) show that not only does the taste for the indigenous develop along with a distaste for the alien, but also that flora come to 'signify what politics struggles to name' (2001: 639) – who is and is not a citizen of the postcolonial state. Xenophobia, racism and national chauvinism can bubble to the surface in discourse about 'nature'. Kenneth Olwig argues that 'discourses concerning the threat of alien species to national landscapes have a curious tendency to bleed into discourses concerning the threat of alien races and cultures to the native people and culture of these same nations' (2003: 61).

I wish to disrupt the impression that the lawn's rootedness is evidence of its lack of desire to travel. The lawn-as-traveller is nowhere more elegantly evoked than in Kemang Wa Lehulere's installation *Do not go far they say* (2015) (a portion of which is shown in Plate 17). Consisting of old-school brown suitcases filled with soil and growing lawn, and watched over by tacky porcelain German shepherds, the installation invokes homelessness, statelessness, dislocation and death. The earth and grass recall the lawn from the Ferncliff Cemetery outside New York, some of which, while visiting the grave of exiled writer Nat Nakasa in 2013, Wa Lehulere dug up and transplanted back to his studio in Europe. Nakasa, who had left South Africa on an exit visa with no possibility of return in 1964, committed suicide a year later. The suitcases packed with portable lawns suggest a radical rethinking of the lawn as permanent.

No gays, no blacks, no dogs

I now turn my attention to Joubert Park in the densely populated centre of Johannesburg. Attached to the distinguished Johannesburg Art Gallery (JAG), it was once the premier promenading ground of the Edwardians, and later a thriving core of bohemian, semi-multiracial, high-density urbanism. It has, since the so-called white flight into the suburbs during the 1990s, become a complex neighbourhood of migrants and foreigners making new uses and making do. It is singular in its ability to evoke a peculiar form of urban nostalgia and the associated melancholy of failed urbanity. As Aubrey Tearle, the grumpy narrator of Ivan Vladislavić's novel *The Restless Supermarket*, says about Hillbrow's decline: 'Where once there had been benches for whites only, now there were no benches at all to discourage loitering. The loiterers were happy to lie on the grass, but, needless to say, I was not' (Vladislavić 2001: 15). The idea of reuse, of getting by with remnants, is at odds with the established concept of the lawn, which does not suggest a proliferation of alternatives and multiple uses. There is a singularity about the lawn's intention. Inherent and often explicit in the lawn trope are a number of exclusions, prohibitions, injunctions and exhortations. The commandments of the public lawn are directed towards the formation of well-behaved and respectable subjects. By examining some of the least respectable practices and those subjects who have used and been forbidden to use the park historically, it is possible to offer a queer analysis of this landscape's dark side.

Joubert Park was established in 1887 at the request of the Diggers' Committee, Johannesburg's earliest local government, as a 'public park or garden to be planted with trees' (Bruwer 2006: 107). Marked Joubert's Plein on an 1889 stand map, the park was named after General Piet J. Joubert, commander-in-chief of the Transvaal military forces (105). The land was ploughed in 1891 and planted with seeds and seedlings, some of which were donated by Kew Royal Botanic Gardens (Van Rensburg et al. 1986: 177), and by April 1892 *The Standard and Diggers' News* reported that the park 'speaks volumes for the richness of Rand soil. Already the grounds are perfectly lovely with shrubs and flowers' and the benches 'are always occupied by engrossed couples' (quoted in Bruwer 2006: 105).

In 1895 some indigenous trees were added to the botanical transplants, followed by a central ornamental fountain with a rockery and water flowers (Bruwer 2006: 105), and in 1898 a conservatory, bought from the Wanderers Club, was added. In 1906, Joubert Park was donated by the government to the Johannesburg Municipality 'for the purposes of or incidental to the recreation and amusement of the inhabitants' (Crown Grant No. 268/1906, 22 May 1906, Rand Townships Registrar, Johannesburg).

JAG was conceptualised by Florence Phillips and Hugh Lane, and opened in November 1910 in temporary premises before moving to its final home in 1915. As part of Edwin Lutyens's design, he proposed doubling the size of Joubert Park by constructing a wide causeway to span the railway tracks and include Union Ground (later known as Jack Mincer Park and now the location of Park

Central Taxi Rank). The changes would have placed JAG in the centre of a generous twenty-acre park. As can be seen in Plate 18, Lutyens's plans envisaged Joubert Park as the rear garden, with the front park being treated as a *cour d'honneur* (three-sided courtyard) with formal lawns. The proposed park drew on a 'mixture of grand scale and intimate elements, related to major, minor and converging axes' (Bruwer 2006: 108).

Joubert Park had neither a singular designer nor a singular design, but the cumulative intentions – sometimes ad hoc, sometimes formalised, as was the case with Lutyens's plans – were in accord that the park should be a place for the conspicuous display of wholesome leisure. The goal was 'to design a park which required becoming behaviour; behaviour which would fit the visitor not just for an afternoon's polite stroll, but also encourage him to fulfil a role deemed appropriate and useful within the community' (Taylor 1995: 214). The formal architecture of the eventual park design, set on an axis with a symmetrical arrangement, created not only a sense of order and clarity in the dusty mining town but also spaces for public sitting and promenading. The Victorian idea of conspicuous performance is evident in a number of turn-of-the-century postcards (Norwich 1986: 76), which show scenes of white women in 'pouter pigeon' blouses and trumpet skirts with oversized hats strolling with men in three-piece suits and smart hats. In these postcards, the lawns have been tinted in an optimistic green and the bedding schemes painted with sharp and bold colours.

In 'The Virtuous and the Verminous: Turn-of-the-Century Moral Panics in London's Public Parks', Nan Dreher (1997: 252) argues that the discourses of 'rational recreation' and 'social purity' were the two most important concepts at work in late nineteenth-century metropolitan crises over public indecency. On the one hand, proponents of so-called rational recreation (sports, family picnics and the enjoyment of nature) pictured idealised middle-class citizens as models of sober, abstemious public comportment; the performance of respectability was hoped to have what was then called a 'healthful influence' (253). On the other hand, social purity advocates mapped fears about hygiene and health onto public sexual activities (courtship and prostitution) and the public visibility of homeless or 'verminous' persons (258). That these concerns could be located on the lawn is clear from the archival material Dreher collected. For instance, in 1918 the London Council for the Promotion of Public Morality complained: 'Twenty or thirty years ago the limit of alfresco courtship recognised by ordinary folks extended as far as placing an arm round a lady's waist, whilst sitting on a seat. Now the seats ... are discarded in favour of lying full length upon the grass' (quoted in Dreher 1997: 257).

No sex

In *Queer Ecologies* (2010) Catriona Mortimer-Sandilands and Bruce Erickson point out that the emergence of European public parks in the mid-to-late nineteenth century coincided with a growing social panic about the proliferation of non-normative sexual types and expressions. They argue that the 'naturalisation of (apparently fragile) heterosexuality' found expression in the conspicuous display of middle-class respectability and the promotion of the park as site of moral upliftment, especially of the working-class (2010: 13). Conversely, Mortimer-Sandilands and Erickson suggest that in this context what is significant about sex in parks is that it is public,

> meaning that it overtly challenges heteronormative understandings of what is appropriate behavior for public, natural spaces. Here, we must remember that public parks are *disciplinary* spaces, in which a very narrow band of activities is sanctioned, practiced, and experienced; only certain kinds of nature experience are officially allowed. In this context, one can consider public gay sex as a sort of *democratization* of natural space, in which different communities can experience the park in their own ways, and in which a wider range of natural experiences thus comes to be possible. (2010: 26)

Matthew Gandy offers the notion of 'unruly space' for describing arenas that 'do not play a clearly defined role, or which are characterized by ill-defined use or ownership, or that have been appropriated for uses other than those for which they were originally intended' (2012: 734). He argues that activities like public sex and cruising are 'forms of site-specific spatial insurgency'.

Mark Gevisser's research provides a singular resource for the exploration of Joubert Park's public sexual exuberance.[4] As co-editor, with Edwin Cameron, of the groundbreaking queer volume *Defiant*

Desire (published in 1995), in his role in co-curating the exhibition Joburg Tracks in 2010, his involvement in the documentary film *The Man Who Drove with Mandela* (Schiller 1999) and in his book *Lost and Found in Johannesburg* (2014), Gevisser has gathered together one of the very few collections of fragments about this central space. Two recurrent characters – Phil and Edgar – provide the narratives for much of Gevisser's memory making. Both men were 'after nines'; that is to say, black gay men who lived ostensibly heterosexual lives before nine o'clock at night, when, with their family asleep in the township, they would pursue queer encounters, often in the 'white' city. Gevisser writes about Phil and Edgar's youth, around the time of the Second World War, when Joubert Park began to take on an important role for male gay life:

> Having delivered the goods for his mother, Edgar told me, he would go 'fishing' – as he liked to put it – in Joubert Park or at Park Station on his way back to [Pimville]: 'I was sixteen, a Zulu boy. Hefty! Plumpy! I wore shorts, very tight shorts! I was a fit young boy; men of all races would be attracted to me.'
>
> Delivering washing for his mother provided Phil, too, with access to the city: he was seduced by one of her clients, and realised the possibilities of the world beyond Soweto. He dropped out of school, much to the fury of his parents. 'I was too streetwise,' Phil explained to me. 'I liked the money. It was my chance of meeting men.' One of Phil's favourite haunts was Union Grounds, in Joubert Park, where white soldiers were barracked after the war. 'He is on one side of the fence and you are on the other, he pulls down his pants, and puts his whatsisname through the fence, and you put your hands through the fence to get hold of him, and you do your thing. There and then. And he gives you two and sixpence.'
>
> When I asked if he was worried about being seen, he deadpanned back: 'The lights in those days were not as bright as the lights today.' (Gevisser 2014: 194)

The tightly circumscribed domestic arrangements of family life, embodied and structured by the tiny black family homes of the townships where Phil and Edgar lived, influenced the spatial order of their sex lives. In the patriarchal order, under the apartheid vision of black family life and gender roles, places like Hillbrow and Joubert

Park potentially provided blurred spaces for the articulation of difference and subversive connections. On a practical level, Joubert Park was one of the very few places where black and white men could encounter each other. Phil and Edgar describe the 'possibilities of the world beyond Soweto' as a certain kind of worldliness, a world of interracial relationships (characterised, of course, by profound asymmetry), money, sexual liberation and physical freedom to wander. The following is from the film *The Man Who Drove with Mandela*:

> Gay life in Johannesburg was very tough. To be gay back then as a black man, one had to be rich, because, point number one: you had to have your own privacy. Blacks by then, if you are not married, you were not allowed to have a house. Number two: you wouldn't come into town to enjoy your gay life, to stay in a hotel. There were no hotels for blacks. We had to stand outside the gates of Joubert Park or go to the Union Grounds' soldier barracks; there were a lot of soldiers there. They were white. Nobody who was not gay would come near the fence. (Schiller 1999)

The film also includes the following monologue attributed to Cecil Williams, reminiscing about early life in Johannesburg:

> On my way from the university I used to linger in Joubert Park. I was quite taken aback when an older man struck up a conversation with me and invited me to his flat. Really, I'm amused when I think about it now. The mere mention of the word flat – a flat, oh. The connotations were fabulous. One knew that all sorts of abominable things went on there. My seducer offered me a drink: a gin and lime. For years after just the smell of gin and lime signalled a sexual experience. (Schiller 1999)

By the time the soldiers eventually left, a gay subculture had stubbornly planted itself in Joubert Park and in Hillbrow more generally. Park Station, adjacent to Joubert Park, became a famous site for cruising (Gevisser 1995: 18–19) and picking up rent boys (Galli & Rafael 1995: 136). There were also bars, clubs, bathhouses and gay-friendly bookstores. Through the 1950s and 1960s, there were periodic crackdowns on homosexual activity, particularly at those edges of the park where black men and white men met, such as the post office steps on Wolmarans Street (Gevisser 2014: 197–198), leading to numerous embarrassing arrests. After the decriminalisation of homosexuality, Hillbrow accommodated some racial mixing in gay bars and the first pride march in 1990 (172).

No rest

In London at the end of the nineteenth century, members of the public expressed outrage about the 'thousands of verminous and infected people lying on the grass' in public parks (quoted in Dreher 1997: 265). Their anxiety about indolent men, and especially the potential of their spreading communicable diseases, caused the London Office of Works, in 1913, to consider the issue of disinfecting lawns: 'The question of disinfecting the grass has been considered but the use of a solution of paraffin or similar liquid would be very objectionable and disinfectants would tend to destroy the grass' (quoted in Dreher 1997: 264). Dreher presents a 1902 photograph of St James's Park depicting sleeping men 'strewn thickly over the grass' (262).

Contemporary South African writers and artists have not missed the opportunity to observe (black) men sleeping inappropriately on the lawn. For instance, in *Johannesburg Circa Now* (2005) Melinda Silverman and Msizi Myeza compare a vintage postcard showing promenading white Edwardians in Joubert Park *circa* 1904 with the parallel image of black men sleeping on the park's lawns '*circa* now'. On the one hand, the observation is surely true enough: as they point out, a century later there are fewer white people, more black people, fewer women and more people sleeping. It is the same observation one could make of Welkom Central Park comparing 1955 and 2005. On the other hand, one has to ask: what is at stake in pointing out *this* particular use as opposed to, for instance, excavating the unsavoury sexual patterns of the park?

In his blog *The Death of Johannesburg* the 'Real Realist' explains that Joubert Park 'used to be a place where the city council put up Christmas lights, where choirs would sing Christmas carols … nowadays it's just a slum with squatters living there'.[5] The blog features a few grainy shots of the park from a car window, which the author – and the many readers who have commented in the threads attached to his blog – seem to believe makes a compelling case for an apparent racial cause for current failures. There is, as elsewhere in the discourse around Hillbrow, a vivid nostalgia for 'the good old days', emblematic of a broader concern with the city in decay and the loss of a way of life. In a similar fashion, Vladislavić's Aubrey Tearle catalogues the 'decline' of Hillbrow, describing, in explicitly hygienic terms, the 'new varieties of dirt on the pavements':

> Sticky black scabs on the cement flags, blotches, bumps, nodules that cleaved to the soles of my brogues. More of them all the time, like some skin disease. What is this stuff? Where on earth is it coming from? You never saw it falling from the sky or spilt by a human hand. It seemed to be *striking through* from beneath, like some subcutaneous festering. A less fastidious man than myself, a man more accustomed to taking specimens, an indigent geologist, say, a botanist, a pathologist, might have made a study of it to determine its origins. Animal or vegetable? (Vladislavić 2001: 51–52)

Tearle's affective inventory of decline is written as a diagnosis, observed with the eye of a pathologist.

Terry Kurgan, as part of her *Park Pictures* project, mapped onto a large aerial photograph the location of the forty portrait photographers who worked in Joubert Park at the time (see Plate 19). This cartographic work indicates the concentration of photographers on the east–west axis, the major vector of movement through the park. The photographers and many of their clients have roots elsewhere: 'They have migrated to Johannesburg from other parts of the country and the continent to find work and better lives. The position each photographer occupies is sacred, and the right to occupy a particular wrought iron bench, a large rock on the grass or a low wall perch along a cobbled pathway, is often purchased or negotiated as far away from the inner city of Johannesburg as a rural village in Mozambique or Zimbabwe' (Kurgan 2003: 468–469).

Tamar Garb points out in *Figures and Fictions* that the park's lawns, fountains and gallery produce 'ready-made picturesque settings' (2011: 68). Through the clients' photographic interactions, the park becomes a situation, one in which the scenic potential of colonial/modern aesthetics becomes the set for staging a claim on a kind of urbanity and black modernity, a form of 'cityness'. David Bunn argues that the park is 'part of the mise en scène of a larger plot involving Johannesburg and the continental imaginary: the desire of migrants and work seekers, from Kinshasa to Beira, to find jobs and enrichment in Johannesburg, and to move through the city fluently, like a native. For African working-class subjects, this drift into the city has always, since the origins of migrant modernism, been anchored with representational acts' (2008: 157).

The lawn appears in a great number of the images Kurgan collected from the park photographers. By buying up numerous uncollected images – those prints the photographers had kept for clients who did not return – Kurgan built up a fascinating archive (see, for example, Plates 20 and 21). These images were curated inside JAG, spliced with portraits from the gallery's permanent collection and with formal portraits of the park photographers taken by Kurgan. In addition to the curatorial component of her project, Kurgan collaborated with the photographers to fund and construct a mini studio, which featured printed backdrops. The choices made by both photographers and clients regarding the backdrop imagery and their poses and gestures highlight modes of meaning making and self-articulation. The two-dimensional backdrops partly screen off the 'real' life of the park while the lawn persists as a remainder and reminder of the park.

South African photographers David Goldblatt and Pieter Hugo have both trained their lenses on black men sleeping on the lawn. Hugo's *Green Point Common, Cape Town, 2013* is shot on the contested Cape Town promenade late after apartheid.[6] In this colour photograph, the grass is dense, spongy and comfortable. The man lies flat on his stomach, fast asleep. Goldblatt's black-and-white photographs were made much earlier, during a brief liberal phase after 1974, when the Johannesburg City Council relaxed the application of the 1953 Reservation of Separate Amenities Act and allowed black people to access Joubert Park and JAG (Silverman & Myeza 2005: 44). *Man sleeping, Joubert Park, Johannesburg. 1975* and *Sleeping man, Joubert Park, Johannesburg. 1975* (see Plate 22) were part of a series called 'Particulars', which is an unusual collection for the close attention it pays to small gestures and close-ups of body parts, and because of its strange sensuality. Men and women – sleeping, waiting, sprawled, at play, smoking, dressed for an occasion – are observed with unnerving clarity.

Goldblatt appears to have shot the sleeping men at midday: the grass is overexposed and rough-looking and does not suggest a comfortable resting place. Sean O'Toole writes that 'clasping his hands over his head … rest is something to be defended as much as stolen' for Goldblatt's sleepers (2014: 8). Rest assumes a comfortable resting place and can be construed in a binary opposition with gainful employment. These photographs depict neither rest nor leisure, but rather exhaustion. The photographs only become readable against the background of the history and ideology associated with the lawn. From that perspective, sleeping on the lawn in the way the two black men do is undoubtedly a desecration: an appropriation of the lawn for purposes that are foreign to its intent. Hannah le Roux has suggested two alternative ways of conceptualising modernity *after* the end of colonialism, apartheid, modernity itself, the belief in modernity's promises:

> Vision 1: The project of modern architecture is a failure in Africa. The buildings are shells, void of any aesthetic qualities that are respected by their tenants, and impossible to maintain. Vision 2: The buildings are, on the other hand, highly lively and animated settings, replete with sounds, social relations and multiple functions. In this vision they are preferable to the sterile modernisms of Western institutions that are the backdrop to everyday lives characterised by monotony, order and cleanliness. (2005: 52)

The first mode is exemplified by the 'Real Realist' and his neurotic photographs of the outside of the park, shot from a moving car. The second is less common. Take, for instance, a little-known landscape photograph, *A space of waiting* (2012) by Sabelo Mlangeni (see Plate 23). In a strangely compelling, romantic treatment, the image is shot from a shady location facing south from the north side of Joubert Park. A dark coulisse on the left side frames the scene according to a Claudian scheme. The trees, captured with a painterly quality suggesting swirling clouds, cast shadows in the foreground. The neo-classical treatment makes it easy to imagine a leisurely picnic happening under the shade. One has the distinct impression that Mlangeni was sitting (lounging?) when he took the photograph. While the 'Real Realist' shoots from his car at speed and Goldblatt is the *flâneur*, Mlangeni waits. In *Apartheid & After* O'Toole suggests that Mlangeni's power is as 'an observer of people. His own presence goes unnoticed … His playful observations are nevertheless rendered with great eloquence and precision' (2014: 10). The photograph captures a profoundly un-anxious, gentle and even pretty aspect of the park. How, we might ask, can the pictorial language of the picturesque be seen as appropriate for representing a place like Joubert Park after apartheid? What is at stake in the deployment of a postcolonial picturesque idiom? Waiting assumes a different kind of space to a space in which one spends only limited time. The photograph clearly is a polemic against the idea of a decaying park and it makes references to European landscape painting. This is a new kind of appropriation of the park, by a black (queer) person, and it could be read as an expression of both despondency and hope.

No shame

I investigate three issues in a reading of Marlene van Niekerk's novel *Triomf*. First, I address the question of depth, which is to say, the failure of the lawn to cover what is beneath, the failure of erasure; at the same time, it is also the failure of the lawn to facilitate a kind of integration of the past, to make any kind of ecological reconciliation possible. Essentially, I aim to emphasise the depth of the lawn, and to tie together a number of examples discussed up to this point that illustrate the verticality of the lawn. Second, I aim to queer the ecology of *Triomf* through a contrapuntal reading of the lesbian neighbours who are replaced by black residents once they move away. Both the lesbian couple and the black suburbanites are counterintuitive models of queer reproduction. I nevertheless attempt to locate the lawn in relation to queer modes of gardening with reference to these characters. Third, I examine violence and the failure of respectable whiteness, looking at the limits of domestic cordiality and the threat of the lawn as a weapon.

No money for fertiliser

Between 1955 and 1960 around 60 000 people of colour were removed from Sophiatown and mostly resettled in the new dormitory township of Meadowlands (Beningfield 2006a: 232). The destruction of Sophiatown has passed into legend, coming to stand, along with District Six, as metonymic for the forced removals of the period. Once bulldozed, the town was rebuilt, as Maureen Isaacson puts it, as a 'cheap white suburb', with 'pretty white' houses and 'tidy green gardens guarded by bright Plaster of Paris gnomes' (1990: 16, 18, 12). The new houses built for 'poor whites' by the Department of Housing were single-storey bungalows with plastered brickwork walls, face-brick plinths, pitched corrugated iron roofs, standard steel windows, asphalt tiles and curtain rails in all rooms (Beningfield 2006a: 245–247). The houses, built from five standardised plan types, were laid out with open ground separating each house and creating front and back gardens. The suburb was 'tactlessly and cruelly' named Triomf (Beall, Crankshaw & Parnell 2002: 3).

That Triomf was not in fact a triumph – of National Party ideology, mid-century modernist planning, poor white upliftment or Afrikaner urbanisation – is the premise of the novel *Triomf.* The failure of Triomf to flourish, its sterility and barrenness stand in contrast to the mythological vitality of Sophiatown prior to its destruction. Don Mattera describes Sophiatown as 'picturesque and intimate like most ghettos. Double-storey mansions and quaint cottages, with attractive, well-tended gardens, stood side by side with rusty wood-and-iron shacks, locked in a fraternal embrace of filth and felony' (1971: 31). Sophiatown incorporated 'enormous complexity and vivid contrasts. The place had squalor and charm, violence and companionship, bleakness and vitality, light and darkness, hope and despair' (Hart & Pirie 1984: 43).

Jennifer Beningfield argues in *The Frightened Land* that Triomf's infertility can be attributed to the 'debris of the past that still thwarts attempts to coax the land' into growth (2006a: 223). Indeed, she argues, landscape in this instance could be seen as a 'veneer, a thin edge', which conceals the destruction of past lives, buildings and inhabitations.

Within the neighbourhood ecology of *Triomf*, it is 127 Martha Street that embodies the kind of infertility Beningfield is pointing to. The garden of the Benades consists of nothing but a 'bare yard', a 'yellow lawn' and a solitary fig tree (Van Niekerk 1999: 1–9). Their failed garden is attributed to, among other things, the detritus that constantly emerges from the soil and that prevents plants from rooting deep into the soil. Pop, the oldest Benade, explains that the 'roots struggle to get a grip'. The narrator says: 'They first have to grow all the way through Sophiatown's rubble. Pop says you have to dig six feet under Triomf's tar before you find the old topsoil. In between there's just rubbish. It takes a tree three years to find the soil ... That's why they never planted anything on their own plot' (260). A number of remnants of 'kaffir-rubbish' resurface throughout the novel, particularly objects dug up by Lambert – the family's epileptic and violent inbred son – which he collects in his room in a heap: the 'bricks, bottles, window-frames, drainpipes' (36).[7]

The significance of the rubble that lurks beneath the lawn is twofold. First, it serves as 'a constant reminder that the inhabitants of Triomf do not possess the land on which they live – they have no historical claim to it' (Buxbaum 2011: 34). Indeed, the rubble reinscribes the history of black suffering back into the supposedly flat, hygienic, racially pure suburb. Second, as anthropologist Gastón Gordillo argues in *Rubble: The Afterlife of Destruction* (2014), rubble is never 'simply a figure of negativity. Rubble exerts positive pressure on human practice and is constitutive of the spatiality of living places' (2014: 11). As much as the 'material, cultural and linguistic rubbish' that surrounds the Benades disrupts their attempts at successful white family life, Nicole Devarenne argues that, in fact, it is upon the 'suppressed (black) history [that] their collective identity is built' (2006: 113). Thus the 'kaffir-rubbish' is not only a disruption of the status quo but actually the foundation on which their very lives are built. Miriam Tlali points out the contradictions upon which Triomf is constructed: 'What triumph? All those black cockroaches, bed-bugs and lice they have built their beautiful houses on ... where is all that pride of theirs? All those nice gardens of theirs where they have planted lawns and flowers are fertilized by the urine and stools of the black children who used to run all over naked, neglected and starving, while their mothers cared for their white kids' (1975: 143).

Tlali's mordant critique foregrounds a number of important issues. First, in light of the hygienic discourses that partly animated the expulsion of the 'slum' dwellers, it is ironic to reinvest the soil – to fertilise it – with vermin. Second, Tlali makes transparent the relationship between white domesticity and black domestic work that makes Triomf's 'nice' lawns possible. Third, by writing body fluids into the soil, into the garden and into the landscape, she inverts the dominant conception that the remnants of Sophiatown poison the soil. Indeed, elsewhere in the same text Tlali points to 'the place where the tears of the African women and children fell and soaked into the soil. I do not think they will ever dry. They, the whites, have built their Triomf on top of them' (1975: 142). The tears, faeces and urine of black mothers and children are the abject materials that disrupt the symbolic order.[8]

The goal of the current analysis is to work towards thickening the lawn surface as part of the broader attempt to argue against the lawn's presumed thinness. The lawn's horizontality and the common-sense understanding of it as only a surface elide questions about its rootedness, connectedness, depth and its relationship to what is beneath it. For instance, instead of conceiving of the lawn as an outdoor carpet, it might be more useful to consider it as only one layer of sedimented biological matter in the landscape. What if the lawn is not theorised as on-top-of, but rather in a troubled and troubling relation to an articulated and sedimented array of human and non-human agents? In her introduction to the volume *Imperial Debris: On Ruins and Ruination* (2013) Anne Stoler argues for the concept of 'ruination' as a verb that refocuses our attention on the '*connective tissue* that continues to bind human potentials to degraded environments, and degraded personhoods to the material refuse of imperial projects – to the spaces redefined, to the soils turned toxic, to the relations severed between people and people, and between people and things' (2013: 7–8).

It is not only rubble that troubles the suburban order; other non-human actors interfere with the present, too. For example, in *Triomf* Treppie likens the other holes in their domestic life to moles, which push up molehills on the lawn: 'Walls full of plaster cracks, and our roof that leaks onto our heads, and our floor full of holes, and the moles who make molehills on the lawn' (Van Niekerk 1999: 343). Lambert depicts the 'little hills on the lawn' in the mural on his bedroom wall (164–165). In addition, dogs – both alive and dead in the form of bones and as ghosts – haunt the Benade property. Treppie and Lambert, along with their dogs Toby and Gerty, stand on the lawn and howl, disrupting the neighbourhood. Van Niekerk writes that it is 'as if they are sucking the sound up through their bodies, from deep under the ground, from the hollows of Triomf' (19). The 'hollows' beneath the town are particularly unnerving for Mol: 'It's hollow on the inside. Not just one big hollow like a shell, but lots of dead mines with empty passageways and old tunnels' (194). Her suspicions are, of course, correct.[9]

In *Johannesburg: The Elusive Metropolis* (2008) Sarah Nuttall and Achille Mbembe argue that the 'underneath' of the city is fundamental to unlocking the secrets of its modernity (2008: 23). The city of Johannesburg, and indeed the whole of the Rand, is founded on an 'originary tension', built into its morphology and geological structure, between life below the surface and what is above (18). Nuttall and Mbembe argue that 'beneath the visible landscape and the surface of the metropolis, its objects and social relations, are concealed or embedded other orders of visibility, other scripts that are not reducible to the built form, the house facade, or simply the street experience of the metaphorical figure of the flâneur' (22).

In the same volume, Bunn takes up the question of surface/depth in relation to art practices in Johannesburg. He argues that the 'rhetoric of the surface has been implicated in an act of historical repression': 'the inability to come to terms with the real origins of surplus value, in the apartheid labor practices, and especially in the buried life of the black body, instrumentalized and bent in contact with the coal face, or ore seam, in the stopes below (2008: 137). Bunn argues that in one of the key artistic traditions of the city the surface is portrayed as an 'integument' beneath which an 'irreducible body of truth lies hidden' (139). He suggests that Gordimer's novel *The Conservationist* (published in 1974) treats the surface as a 'meniscus', 'a tense field of pressure against which buried bodies strain' (141). The lawn surface in *Triomf*, particularly in the garden at 127 Martha Street, falls within this discursive tradition.

Thus far this book has noted two other examples where the lawn is constructed in direct relation with mining. The first is the narrative by Dorothea Fairbridge (1924) in Chapter 1, where the pure and loved domestic lawn is 'raped' by the mineshaft. In this instance, domestic labour, explicitly feminine and non-capitalist, is set at odds with masculine industrialisation. The lawn is romanticised and imagined as an antidote to the brutality of mining, but in the end is not able to sustain its oppositional role. In Chapter 3, the horizontality of the lawn is conceptualised by Joane Pim (1956) as an antidote to the brutality of mining, but she sees the lawn as complementary to industry. Her lawn is dialectically produced in relation to mining. Indeed, it draws on two discursive themes: flatness, which denies the obviously existing depth below, and the notion that the lawn refreshes, that it has a therapeutic effect. Read in conjunction with the spectre of mining in *Triomf*, the problem of depth is a compelling challenge to the lawn's thinness.

In order to reckon with Triomf's landscape, Beningfield argues that one should understand the landscape as a 'hybrid representation, the meaning of which is inseparable from ambiguity and uncertainty' (2006a: 273). Thus landscape functions not as a 'stable "way of seeing" but rather as unstable ground which is dug deep into the earth, full of memories and debris'. The unsettled landscape is a reminder that attempts to be 'at home' are complicated by the claims of other histories and an incitement to reconciliation.

No meat

The Benades maintain equally contentious relationships with their above-ground community of neighbours.

Across the street lives a lesbian couple, who are, as Mol points out, not their 'class of people'. They look like the type with 'money for fertiliser' (Van Niekerk 1999: 189). The same-sex couple is a peculiarity that the Benades struggle to make sense of, variously claiming they must be 'vegetarians' (188) or 'communists' (189). They wonder 'what they think they're doing here in Triomf, and why they've got so much time for gardening' (189). These 'dykes' are a fecund presence on the street. Indeed, counterintuitively, they are the reproducers: their multitude of plants grows well in their 'secret garden' (193). Indeed, Treppie says their sweet peas are the healthiest he has ever seen in Triomf. Even their sex (apparently seen by Lambert, the peeping Tom) is described in vegetal and botanical terms. Lambert explains that they stuff 'fruit salad wherever they can find a hole. Nose, mouth, ears, backside, frontside ... there's so much juice they both look like tropical forests' (191).

Although minor characters in the novel, the lesbians offer a contrapuntal reading of the Benades and their garden. As Jessica Murray points out, although the lesbianism of the characters in *Triomf* is largely peripheral to the main plot, 'a close reading of the characters' roles in the texts can offer valuable insights into the extent to which heteronormative pressures continue to structure understandings of lesbian desire' (2012: 88). Building on this queer reading, I suggest that the black residents who move into the property once the couple moves away to 'greener pastures' might equally be read as queer in this context.

To develop the queer reading of *Triomf*, I suggest examining Van Niekerk's underappreciated short story 'Labour' (2007). A putatively autobiographical narrative, the story recounts the author's attempts to negotiate the pitfalls of labour in her new suburban house and garden in Stellenbosch. 'Marlene', the protagonist, is angst-ridden about being interpellated as a 'madam' and she struggles against an unequal system of domestic labour, only to find herself co-opted discursively and materially into the racist and heteronormative system she tries to oppose. Unlike the Benades, who cannot afford to do so, both Marlene in 'Labour' and the lesbian couple in *Triomf* employ black labour. The class position and the political liberalism of the lesbian characters become manifest in their queer approach to their gardeners.

For instance, while the Benades subsist on polony and white bread, they are amazed that the lesbians 'give their garden-kaffir a knife and fork to eat his bread and wors with' (Van Niekerk 1999: 189).[10] Not only do they feed their gardener better food than the Benades can afford for themselves, but also 'they all sit together on chairs around a plastic table in the back garden'. This convivial attempt at social levelling strikes Treppie as symptomatic of not being 'properly connected with the world'. It is unrealistic, he argues, to think they can just 'make their own connections'. Lambert suggests that the awkward gardener 'doesn't know where to look … what to stick his fork into, or what to cut with his knife'.

As if reflecting on this (uncomfortable) white liberal attempt to subvert dominant relations in the garden, Van Niekerk writes in 'Labour' about a salad Marlene prepared for her new gardener, Piet. She is quick to point out at the beginning of the story that Marlene 'used to do all her own gardening. But now she is forty-six [and] is dependent on labour. But she's not scared. She'll be cautious and correct. Firm and friendly, with distance' (2007: 853). When she asks Piet what he wants for lunch on his first day of work at her home, he replies that against expectations he's 'actually a salad man' (854). So, as requested, the 'madam' prepares a 'delicate and well-dressed salad', which she sets out on the garden table, with balsamic vinegar and olive oil and a big jug of fruit juice with ice. Piet is a 'genuine gardener' and they enjoy each other, 'the woman and the labourer' (855). However, by breaking the implicit rules that govern these kinds of interactions, she disrupts the social balance, as she finds out when Piet's other employer telephones her to complain that (1) not only is she paying him too much, but (2) suddenly now Piet likes lettuce and is asking for cheese, olives and dark brown vinegar, as well. 'You're setting a dangerous precedent,' she is warned. 'You don't know what it can unleash.'

Van Niekerk's queer 'communism' partly disrupts the normal functioning of labour in the South African garden. In a similarly subversive fashion, Marlene instructs Piet and another gardener to tear up her 'devil's grass' (*Cynodon dactylon*/Bermuda grass) lawn to make a water-wise gravel garden (Van Niekerk 2007: 864). She watches them wage war with her lawn from inside the safety of her home. Through the window, she admires their 'five-days-a-week bodies'. Van Niekerk draws on, and experiments with, the literary conventions I have already pointed out regarding heterosexual lust for the black body, the fear of the black rapist and the structural power relations between madams and boys. These attempts at subversion are, however, limited. (As Treppie notes of the *Triomf* lesbian couple: one cannot just make one's own connections.) In the end, after a number of mostly failed attempts at ethical gardening, Marlene loses her temper with one of the workers: 'I'm not your madam,' she says. 'My name is Marlene and if you want to be a boy that's your business' (867).

It is interesting to compare this with two provocative postcolonial short stories that queer the master/boy relationship: 'Shoga' (2011) by Diriye Osman and 'Apollo' (2015) by Chimamanda Ngozi Adichie. In 'Shoga', the black teenage 'master' of the household has sex with his grandmother's 'boy', a refugee from Burundi. The teenager's observations of the 'boy' follow and also subvert the tropes of the black working body: 'I saw prime beefcake. Papi was beautiful and he looked like he was packing. I licked my lips and locked and loaded. Every day I'd go to my window and watch him wash clothes outside. When it became humid, he'd remove his shirt, fold it and place it on the ground. His pectorals would be slick with sweat. Whenever he saw me, he'd smile and wink. I'd stick my tongue out' (Osman 2011).

Similarly, in 'Apollo' the twelve-year-old black 'master' develops a crush on Raphael, the new houseboy, an 'ordinary-looking teen from a nearby village'. They develop a close (but not sexual) relationship, often play-fighting in the garden on the soft lawn. 'My parents did not notice how close Raphael and I had become. All they saw was that I now happened to play outside, and Raphael was, of course, part of the landscape of outside: weeding the garden, washing pots at the water tank' (Adichie 2015). Raphael's body, as observed by the young narrator, is strong enough to 'disembowel a turkey and lift a full bag of rice'; he is admired for the 'smallness of his shorts … and how the muscles ran wiry like ropes down his legs'.

Neelika Jayawardane and Ainehi Edoro argue that the 'allure of the "boy"' as the 'bearer of sexual difference in the household resides in the contradictions inherent in the figure' (2015). While he is a man who performs feminine roles, he is also 'an avuncular figure who is portrayed as virile, muscled, and stereotypically masculine'. As an 'intimate stranger', the 'boy' 'comes from outside to inhabit and share the intimate life of the household. And in so doing, he clears out a space where the male child can discover and experiment with desire.'

The queer approach to gardening continues in *Triomf* when the lesbians eventually move house, taking with them 'plants, plants, and more plants', their moving truck looking like the 'Hanging Gardens of Babylon on wheels' (Van Niekerk 1999: 466). The Benades' new neighbours are black. Their arrival on election day, right at the end of the novel, is treated very briefly by Van Niekerk. We are left with only one observation from Treppie: 'They're okay on the whole, except they grow mealies on the pavement' (472).

Lindsay Bremner writes that in the post-apartheid city, former categories – black/white, clean/dirty, good/bad, suburb/township, order/disorder, human/inhuman, safe/dangerous – have been overturned (2004: 459). Under the new spatial dispensation, 'the stranger, the mob, the beast, that against which the entire edifice of apartheid had been erected, is within'. The city after apartheid, she argues, is 'rendered permeable, open to infiltration, intervention and contamination. All that apartheid so vigilantly preserved and kept at bay – wildness, brutality, laziness, madness has entered the city.'

The mealies growing on the pavement suggest three salient issues to pursue further. First, we need to problematise the stable Manichean order that undergirded apartheid and its post-apartheid disintegration, because the notion of stable mutual exclusion partly obscures some of the complexities of actually lived space, even before the end of apartheid. Second, there needs to be an examination of the cluster of white anxieties (especially after apartheid) regarding the appropriate use and correct maintenance of suburban gardens by black people, signalled by Treppie's supplemental exclamation – 'except'. And third, there is a need to engage with the typology of the pavement as a marginal, interstitial and possibly queer space.

The irreconcilably polarised nature of the colonial city is famously captured in an iconic passage from Frantz Fanon's *The Wretched of the Earth.* He proposes a 'world cut in two'; the zone of the natives as fundamentally opposed to and non-reciprocal with the zone of the settlers:

> The settler's town is a strongly built town, all made of stone and steel. It is a brightly lit town; the streets are covered with asphalt, and the garbage cans swallow all the leavings, unseen, unknown and hardly thought about … The town belonging to the colonized people … is a place of ill fame, peopled by men of evil repute. They are born there, it matters little where or how; they die there, it matters not where, nor how. It is a world without spaciousness; men live there on top of each other, and their huts are built one on top of the other … The look that the native turns on the settler's town is a look of lust, a look of envy; it expresses his dreams of possession – all manner of possession: to sit at the settler's table, to sleep in the settler's bed, with his wife if possible. The colonized man is an envious man. And this the settler knows very well; when their glances meet he ascertains bitterly, always on the defensive, 'They want to take our place.' It is true, for there is no native who does not dream at least once a day of setting himself up in the settler's place. (Fanon 1963: 38–39)

Fanon's formulation of colonial urbanity echoes discursively on numerous occasions. For instance, in *Moonsongs* Nigerian poet Niyi Osundare (1988: 42) opposes the lush suburb of Ikoyi and the slum Ajegunle:

> Ikoyi
> The moon here is a laundered lawn
> Its grass the softness of infant fluff,
> silence gazes like a joyous lamb,
> doors romp on lazy hinges the ceiling is a sky
> weighted down by chandeliers of pampered stars.

> Ajegunle
> here the moon is a jungle,
> sad like a forgotten beard with tensioned
> climbers and undergrowths of cancerous fury:
> cobras of anger spit in every brook and nights
> are one long prowl of swindled leopards.[11]

Similarly, Lisa Findley writes that from the 'window of an airplane it's all too plain that apartheid has been deeply written into the South African landscape'. She adds: 'Even the smallest town appears as two distinct towns. One features a spacious grid of tree-lined streets and comfortable houses surrounded by lawns. The other, its shriveled twin, some distance away but connected by a well-travelled road, consists of a much tighter grid of dirt roads lined with shacks. Trees are a rarity, lawns non-existent' (2011).

The evocative contrasts outlined above – soft/rough, green/brown, joy/sadness, lawn/dirt, healthy/deformed – are didactically evoked in Pieter Hugo's diptych of post-apartheid Johannesburg, *Aerial View Dainfern Gated Community* and *Aerial View Diepsloot* (2013) (see Plates 24 and 25).

It is not my intention to dispute the grounds for this stark polarisation; it is, however, worth asking what this kind of formulation obscures, what complexities, subtleties and ambiguities it hides. The argument that apartheid was never able to fully totalise lived experience or to fix the landscape is becoming more forcefully made. The lack of attention that has been paid to the botanical exuberance of the townships and informal settlements means that scholars have very little data with which to flesh out a picture of plant life in these environments. Jacob Dlamini makes this point in *Native Nostalgia*, arguing that it 'behoves any history worthy of the name' to take seriously the differences and distinctions between black dwellings, which could be 'as small as the type of lawn one had in one's yard, the type of furniture in each bedroom, or the kind of fencing one had around the yard – whether it was concrete slabs called "stop nonsense" or … wire mesh fence' (2010: 19–20). Dlamini offers a suggestive anecdote about Mr Chirwa, a resident of Katlehong, who was famous for his 'immaculate garden', which boasted the kind of grass planted at Wimbledon, not just 'common' kikuyu (53). This fine-grain sensitivity to grass types, fencing typologies, garden maintenance and aspirational cues focuses the researcher on subtle distinctions of cultural capital.

In the book *Soweto* Niq Mhlongo highlights the 'serious competition' in the township to have a house with 'a beautiful lawn and a well-polished stoep' (2010: 12). This kind of competition was (as in the discussion of Sasolburg in Chapter 2) often stoked by formal competitions, which attempted to socially engineer black people's relationships to gardening. For instance, in Durban in the 1950s, 'the regressive habit of keeping goats or growing maize in the yards was curbed by an annual municipal competition for the best-kept flower garden, preferably around a well-trimmed lawn' (Russell 2003: 154).

In her classic studies on township class and distinction, *Reeftown Elite* (1971) and *Coming Through* (1978), Mia Brandel-Syrier offers limited information on garden design or gardening practices (apart from a discussion of a brief 'craze for rockeries').[12] Through a comprehensive discussion of architecture (wall treatments, garage number and size and so on) and interiors (furniture, kitchens, floor treatments, built-in storage, bathroom colours), she does, however, show the rhythms of adoption and rejection of styles associated with living a 'decent' and 'respectable' life. 'Proper living,' she argues, had at the time of her study, 'condensed, almost as an obsession, into the picture of a house' (1978: 88). Whether that obsession extended also into the garden is unclear, but Brandel-Syrier's detailed treatment of the stoep and fence typologies suggests that there may have been a strong affiliation.

Recently, some research has begun to further clarify the contours of 'vernacular' or 'ethnic' gardening.[13] Extended research could deepen our understanding of certain 'cues to care' (Nassauer 1995), for instance: (1) the stoep and its shininess; (2) '*lebala*', the belief of some groups that the area around their houses should be open, devoid of vegetation and swept, indicating the tidiness of the household (Cilliers, Bouwman & Drewes 2009: 104; McHale et al. 2013: 561); (3) the planting of lawns in water-scarce rural areas (McHale et al. 2013: 562); and (4) fence design and construction.

Nevertheless, since the end of apartheid, black newcomers to previously white suburbs have been confronted with a carefully nurtured and sometimes opaque set of 'cues to care' that frame neighbourhood belonging in relation to 'culture' and not to 'race'

(Ballard 2005: 79). Vladislavić describes such an arrival scene in *Portrait with Keys*:

> For a while the new tenants stayed indoors. Then, as they grew more comfortable in the area, they became more visible. Soon there were children pushing toy cars on the path or playing soccer in the street. Tricycles and dolls lay on the lawn ... 'Why don't they stay inside like normal people? Why are they always lazing about in the yard? Have they got nothing better to do with their time than sit around in the sun?' ... 'What's with the paint tins?' he said grumpily. 'Can't they get proper garden furniture?' (2009: 21)

The mess on the lawn, the idleness and inappropriate outdoor paraphernalia embody a set of white fears about invasion. No suburban practice has caused more anxiety, however, than animal sacrifice. The image (and sound) of an animal being slaughtered on a (quiet and peaceful) lawn transgresses all of the 'acceptably white middle-class ways' (Ballard 2005; Southall 2016: 188) that newcomers are expected to mimic. In 'Slaughter in the Suburbs' Richard Ballard argues that after 1991, when the Groups Areas Act was abolished, 'the task of securing Western, modern, civilized values in suburbs remained as important as ever even though this was no longer expressed in racial terms' (2010: 1073). Animal sacrifices in suburbia have led to the calls for total rejection of the practice in cities, and the advancement of the claim that the rural homestead, farm or kraal is the 'proper location for obviously "African" behaviours, activities and landscapes' (1079). By this logic, Zulu kraals and farms are figured as traditional spaces while suburbs are considered as modern spaces. As Ballard argues: 'This maps onto apartheid's spatial logic, which coded black bodies as inherently out of place in suburban South Africa beyond the need for cheap labour.'

Journalist Vuyo Mvoko, writing in *Business Day*, expounds on the controversy surrounding the *ukukhapha* (send-off) ceremony for his grandfather. The white neighbours who objected to the ceremony argued that the suburban garden was neither a practical nor appropriate place for 'barbaric' and 'uncivilised' animal slaughter. They suggested 'the family should have gone to some open field', but Mvoko explains that an open field was not an appropriate option because the ceremony in question must be done *enkundleni* – in an identified and sacred spot within the family's dwelling (Mvoko 2006).

Such tensions around disreputable and inappropriate garden activities are highlighted in *Triomf* by Van Niekerk's inclusion of the mealie-growing black neighbours, who are okay, 'except'. The anxiety about black people taking over the suburbs and taking back the land also animates the 'Saturday night fuck-around', to which I turn momentarily. Before that, I want to point out that while critical of the mealies on the pavement, Treppie also says he wishes the 'two dilly dykes would come and see their old house so they could take a lesson or two from its new inhabitants. In times like these no one can afford to buy fertiliser for sweetpeas' (Van Niekerk 1999: 472). What would the lesbian couple have thought about the post-apartheid pavement vegetable garden? Even so-called 'guerrilla gardeners' who 'garden without boundaries' (Reynolds 2012) tend to prefer aesthetically pleasing pastoral crops over hardy African crops like mealies, and I would hazard a guess that the *ferme ornée* (ornamented farm) aesthetic of sweet peas and strawberries would have appealed more to the lesbians' class sensibilities.

That said, the pavement is a special spatial phenomenon that functions in post-apartheid securitised suburbia as part of a tense boundary between the safety of the inner garden and the dangers of the multiracial public realm. The pavement is not, however, without its own history. It was the pavement that belonged to the domestic worker on her day off, or the gardener at rest (see Jansen 2015). The 'maid in uniform' listening to a radio on the pavement lawn in Ernest Cole's famous photograph is quoted as saying: 'You have to be punctual on duty, but there's no punctuality when you knock off – you knock off when it suits your madam' (Cole et al. 2010: 115).[14] The ambiguous space of the suburban pavement embodies numerous political tensions, and as a space that is physically outside of the domestic boundary (which may or may not be composed of lawn), it suggests the potential for critique from the margins, from a certain outside. It also extends our scepticism towards the notion of the impermeable boundary wall. In the analysis that follows, the walls between neighbours are transgressed and boundaries fail.

No class

Adjacent to the Benades' property is Fort Knox, the highly securitised home of the other neighbours who feature in the novel. The occupants of Fort Knox are Afrikaners with more financial and social capital than the Benades. They share, however, a profound anxiety about the security of their place in the coming post-apartheid dispensation. This nascent unease is the spark that ignites the 'Saturday night fuck-around' (Van Niekerk 1999: 91–113), a violent event of geopolitical gardening terrorism. Political issues of racial belonging and land ownership are articulated on a local scale through the practice of mowing, the object of the lawnmower, the violation of boundary walls and damage to domestic property.

The fuck-around happens on a Saturday night. Lambert, 'walking around with a hard-on from looking at the *Scope* centrefold' (Van Niekerk 1999: 92), is feeling 'pushed' from 'fucken underneath' (93). The smell of *braaivleis* is in the air, 'thick with smoke' (91).

> He wants to see what those fuckheads next door are doing. He stands in the long grass and peeps over the prefab-wall, into next door's backyard ... They're fucken braaiing again. Them and their fucken meat ... The wors sizzles and drips fat over the coals ... Two women are wearing bikinis, a pink one and a blue one. They're not so bad, even though they don't look as smooth and tanned as the Tuxedo Tyre girls. These ones have dimples on the backs of their thighs. Pink Bikini stands with her arm around a man in blue jeans. The jeans are tight and there's a bulge in front. Blue Bikini stands with her arm around Speedo. It's a black Speedo with an even bigger bulge. His bulge stands at an angle, pointing to one side. (Van Niekerk 1999: 95)

'There's a proper piece of meat,' Speedo says, bunching Blue Bikini's bum in his hand and squeezing it (Van Niekerk 1999: 98). They sit down to eat: plates brimming with banana-and-yellow-sauce salad, pap and sauce, T-bone and wors, so much it 'wants to fall off'. They wonder aloud (half joking) if the 'kaffirs are going to come and take their houses back' after the 1994 elections.

The surfaces of the neighbours' lives suggest the contours of a viable (even successful) apartheid masculinity, in direct contrast to Lambert's impotence. The excess of food and bodies serves to underscore the poverty of the Benades. The flatness of the pin-up women is contrasted with the Benades, who themselves bulge and overflow their bounds in grotesque and abject ways. In the film adaptation of *Triomf* (Raeburn 2008), the production designer chose Astroturf for the Fort Knox garden. This lawn is literally the idea of a perfect lawn, which taunts the Benades' wretched garden. The fertility of the queers and the prurient excess of the heterosexuals foreground the fruitlessness of the Benades.

Lambert's reaction to the braai scene is incredibly provocative: he decides that it is time to mow the lawn and he insists that his old mother is the one to do it (Van Niekerk 1999: 98). The 'garden maintenance' that follows inverts most standards and statutes of the lawn discourse.

To begin with, instead of the home extending outwards into the garden (where the lawn is figured as an outdoor carpet), the garden flows dangerously into the house, erasing the border between interior and exterior. Lambert starts the mower inside the house, sending smoke out the doors, creating pandemonium; with threats and insults, he forces the family into the garden. Second, he 'pimps up' the mower to make it as obnoxious and disruptive as possible: he purposefully sets the mower's blades to rev 'nice and high' and puts in too much oil to create more smoke (Van Niekerk 1999: 98). In addition to the increased noise and smell, the timing of his gardening is very inappropriate. Mowing is never acceptable outside of normal working hours and only on weekends in the most considerate, neighbourly fashion. To mow at night is a hostile gesture.[15] Third, in an inversion of the proper gardening gender and age roles, Lambert coerces his seventy-something-year-old mother to mow while the men of the family drink, watch, cheer, criticise and interfere. Last, the pleasure derived from the mowing exceeds its proper limits. As we have seen so far, the lawn provides pleasure for those who mow and to those who have the privilege of witnessing the beauty of that lawn. Legitimate lawn pleasure derives from real or imagined success at lawn care and proper demonstration of ownership. To be sure, there are aspects of competitiveness, jealousy, insecurity and selfishness in 'normal' mowing practice and those malevolent feelings contribute to a kind of pious superiority to be enjoyed discreetly. It is, however, atypical to read a passage in which lawn pleasure is derived from neither success nor superiority. As part of the grotesque buffoonery, Treppie becomes so drunk that he starts shoving 'handfuls of grass into his mouth, mooing like a cow on the front lawn' (106). It is difficult to picture a more abject scene on the lawn.

Needless to say, Blue Bikini, Speedo and the gang are pissed off: 'Shuddup with that noise! Shuddup! It's fuckenwell eleven o'clock at night! What the hell do you people think you're doing!' (Van Niekerk 1999: 103). However, after the mowing concludes, the neighbourhood seems to settle down again. Emboldened by his incendiary gardening stunt, Lambert continues to spy on Blue Bikini and Speedo while they copulate – 'Soft guava and cucumber power', as he puts it (106). While balancing for a better view, he slips and falls over the wall into Fort Knox, again violating the suburban boundaries. In retaliation, Speedo invades the Benades' property, climbs onto their roof, breaks off their TV aerial, flattens the overflows and rips out the gutters. This is what happens 'to fuckers who peep at other people when they're braaiing,' he shouts. 'Take that, you filthy rubbish!' (108).

The police arrive, 'cool as cucumbers'. They know 127 Martha Street well; no one ever presses charges, they are just here to calm things down. All the way down the street people are coming out their houses, dogs are barking for blocks around because of 'the fucken Benades' fucken late night show' (Van Niekerk 1999: 111). The police look the house up and down. 'Ag, jirre, shame,' they say. 'At least the lawn is nice and neat' (112). Instead of the lawn care functioning as a public statement about proper private behaviour, moral character and social reliability (Robbins, Polderman & Birkenholtz 2001), the Benades' labour attracts a crowd to witness their shame. Shame and mockery are consistently associated with an imperfect lawn. Perhaps the most disturbing thing about this event, however, is not that the lawn is weaponised against the community – is that not always a latent possibility? Rather, it is amazing that after the battle is over, as the police observe, the lawn has actually been well mowed. How did the lawn emerge unscathed, 'nice and neat'?

The Benades' lawnscape requires obscene effort, which seems so unnatural, so difficult, so inelegant. Mol, mowing in her housecoat, is the ideal counterpoint to Goldblatt's image of idealised white male effort: his effortless masculinity, the straight lines he is cutting into his lawn and his safe vantage over the yet-to-be-developed veld embody his control over and hope for a flourishing white future. Possibly, instead of reading *Triomf* as a counterpoint to *In Boksburg*, it is more apt, I think, to read *Triomf* as already implicit in Goldblatt's image. The heroic, shirtless mower is already profoundly anxious, his control over his property tenuous, his confidence in his manhood unconvincing, his future insecure.

Van Niekerk's lawn is therefore not an obscene outlier but a critique internal to the lawn. The stability, permanence, certainty and immobility of the lawn cannot hold up to determined and sustained analysis. The colonial landscape functions by attempting to fix spatial ambiguity and thereby resolve numerous tensions between humans and non-humans and, eventually, the problem of land. After apartheid, the lawn continues to deny not only its own politics, but also the political in general.

In 2011, Julius Malema, then the president of the African National Congress Youth League, declared: 'Citizens cannot complain about the lack of service delivery while watering the lawn in front of a RDP house.'[16] In the most literal manner, his statement deploys the concept of the lawn to discredit political grievances and political activity: after the lawn, what can there be to complain about? Malema's depoliticising discourse echoes Anton Kannemeyer's rhetorical question: how can anyone be unhappy who lives in such a 'splendid dwelling' (see Plate 3)? How can anyone be unhappy who owns a lawn? Malema is drawing on the colonial weight of the lawn in an attempt to resolve ambiguity. It functions as a 'system of aesthetic, conventional, and ideological ordering useful in the management of political contradictions' (Bunn 1994: 127).

What this chapter has shown is that it is very easy to be unhappy with a lawn. Indeed, part of what the lawn does, more often than it is recorded in the dominant archive, is to make people miserable. This process of immiseration – linked to capitalism, patriarchy and racial domination – is not an aberration; it is the proper historical trajectory of the lawn.

Conclusion: Saddening the Green

Sweet smiling village, loveliest of the lawn,
Thy sports are fled and all thy charms withdrawn;
Amidst thy bowers the tyrant's hand is seen
And desolation saddens all thy green ...

— Oliver Goldsmith, 'The Deserted Village'

What does the lawn want?

At the end of this book it is appropriate to return to a theoretical proposition that has been central to it: W. J. T. Mitchell's proposal that landscape should be considered a verb. I have argued that this notion holds promise for studying the landscape, especially as Mitchell has revised the verb concept in the second edition of *Landscape and Power* (2002) and *What Do Pictures Want?* (2005).

First, implicit in the shift from landscape-as-noun to landscape-as-verb is a move from *meaning* to *doing*. This book has asked not what the lawn – or, for that matter, the mine dump, the suburban swimming pool, the safari sunset, the hills of Marikana – *means*, or what it *is*, but rather what it *does*; what that doing does, what possibilities it opens up or closes down. Along these lines, the book has been asking what the lawn makes possible. Clearly, the lawn often forms the grounds of possibility for making certain claims on a respectable subjectivity. Put another way, the lawn is one of the grounds for the constitution of civilised human and non-human subjects. What the lawn does not provide grounds for is political annunciation. It reduces the political problem of *land* to the aesthetic question of *landscape*, thereby obscuring issues of ownership, labour, belonging and redress. The lawn is an 'anti-politics machine' (Ferguson 1990), distributing modernity but denying its own politics.

One key aspect of the lawn's modernity is the creation of regularity – the production of standardised, internationally (and especially nationally) recognised landscapes with historically established rules, by which it is possible to assess their conformity to norms. Here we are required to ask: what other kinds of diversity are denied, disallowed and misrecognised by this attempt at structural regularity? The lawn attempts to dematerialise itself, or deny its own materiality – as if it were not made out of living matter, as if there is no labour and no consequences to lawning a space – which is evident in how often it is described as clean, sanitary, flat, neat. These descriptions are profoundly non-botanical ways of thinking about an assemblage of living plants, deeply rooted and aggressively growing. The common-sense notion, linked to this, is of the lawn as an outdoor carpet, which, it is suggested, is hiding something underneath. That it does sometimes appear to be hiding truths beneath it detracts from a perhaps more interesting question: what is hidden by theorising the lawn as a thin surface – rather than, for instance, an assemblage, a rhizomatic vegetable machine? The tradition of the carpet draws on a painterly or decorative idea, like murals or interior wallpaper, and is structured by binaries: lies/truth, illusion/reality, surface/depth. The lawn as a theatrical backdrop or painterly background functions in much the same way by supposing that real biological life happens *in front of* the landscape. Challenging this conception makes it possible to disrupt the figure-ground relationship. The landscape does not recede into the background, framing human action, making a silhouette of our lives. Rather, we emphasise a dialectical relationship between the ground and figure or, indeed, an inversion of the relationship. Lawn becomes the subject, and human dramas and labour and pleasure become the background to more-than-human narrative.

One of the things that the lawn makes possible is a certain kind of playfulness and exuberance. This playfulness is often channelled into heteronormative, sporting and healthy activities, especially the production of a particular kind of childhood. The order of the lawn is powerfully aligned with a fruitful and positive teleology associated with the child. Nevertheless, the queer exuberance of the lawn is evident, too. If there is something we can say about the lawn, it is that it wants you to have fun with it. To be sure, what counts as fun is political, but the lawn indisputably does invite a kind of play.

The second important aspect of the verb thesis is that it accords agency – how much is debatable – to non-human matter, in this case, the lawn. This seems essential for understanding what is happening in the figure-ground relationship. To argue for the lawn's vibrant materiality does not necessarily require mobilising its patently dynamic matter, its growing and dying material, its expansive geographical reach, its botanically evolved response to disruptions such as trimming and mowing. Even in instances where the lawn is purely theoretical, or only literary, or essentially illustrative (for example, on an architectural plan that will never be built), there is convincing evidence of its liveliness. The possibility of the lawn as an active agent is a compelling idea. The lawn is very much at work.

Implicit in this formulation is the third aspect I wish to highlight: the idea that humans do not just create lawns but are co-created with them, are interpellated in 'some more or less determinate relation to its givenness as sight and site' (Mitchell 1994b: 2). The power of the landscape is the crux of the argument Mitchell puts forward: 'Landscape, we suggest, doesn't merely signify or symbolize power relations; it is an instrument of cultural power, perhaps even an agent of power that is (or often represents itself as) independent of human intentions' (1–2). As pointed out in the Introduction, Mitchell's current position is that if we are to insist on the power of the landscape, we have to admit that it is a 'relatively weak' or 'subtle' power, more of a 'passive force', which elicits a 'broad range of emotions and meanings that may be difficult to specify. This indeterminacy of affect seems, in fact, to be a crucial feature of whatever force landscape can have' (2002: vii). This interpretation emphasises the excesses and slippages that always occur in the production of subjects and signals a shift towards the question of desire, which Mitchell argues is better suited to grappling with the silences, powerlessness and ambivalence that characterise the landscape.

Rather than putting the landscape and the question of power in the background, Jill Casid argues that deploying queer analysis would reinvigorate the 'still haunting promise' (2011: 98) of the landscape as a verb. By summoning the performative, she argues, we can come closer to understanding the materialisation and sedimentation of the landscape. This approach – which emphasises process rather than the finished object – centres on *landscaping* rather than landscape. Casid proposes that instead of seeing landscape as a 'settled place or fixed point', we must reckon with it 'in the performative, landscaping the relations of ground to figure, the potentials of bodies, and the interrelations of humans, animals, plants, and what we call the "environment"'. Her critique of Mitchell has the value of foregrounding the categories of sex and gender in the postcolonial landscape and providing performativity as an explanation for materialisation. Casid advocates getting down and dirty, mucking around in the mud and taking matter seriously. Troubling the landscape, 're- or anti- or un-landscaping' (100), means accounting for 'landscaping as an act of erasure, evacuation, or abstraction' (111).

Lastly, Mitchell's turn to the notion of desire opens up a repertoire of conceptual tools for destabilising the monolithic landscape. His approach to desire is promiscuous; he is open to both the Freudian and Deleuzian 'pictures of desire', which include, on the one hand, desire as lack or longing and, on the other hand, desire as an 'experimental, productive force' (Ross 2010: 66–67). As Mitchell says, he is looking for the 'paradoxical double consciousness' that desire can open up. It is interesting to read what he says about images, if one thinks of the lawn as an image:

> We need to reckon with not just the meaning of images but their silence, their reticence, their wildness and nonsensical obduracy. We need to account for not just the power of images but their powerlessness, their impotence, their abjection. We need, in other words, to grasp *both* sides of the paradox of the image: that it is alive – but also dead; powerful – but also weak; meaningful – but also meaningless. The question of desire is ideally suited for this inquiry because it builds in at the outset a crucial ambiguity. To ask, what do pictures want? is not just to attribute to them life and power and desire, but also to raise the question of what it is they *lack*, what they do not possess, what cannot be attributed to them. To say, in other words, that pictures 'want' life or power does not necessarily imply that they *have* life or power, or even that they are capable of wishing for it. It may simply be an admission that they lack something of this sort, that it is missing or (as we say) 'wanting'. (Mitchell 2005: 10)

Mitchell's generative use of desire opens up the landscape to multiple lines of inquiry with the ability to account for both power and weakness, amenability and recalcitrance, silence and clamour, absence and presence.

This book has argued that ambiguity characterises the South African lawn (and potentially the postcolonial landscape more broadly). Here is the amazing paradox: the lawn appears to be singular, uni-coloured, monolithic, mono-botanical, formed by strict injunctions but, in fact, is not. Therefore, the lawn's desire for mastery over nature, modernity, respectability, domesticity and permanence cannot but fail.

Second, the lawn (and potentially the postcolonial landscape more broadly) is not a thing but a process of experimentation and materialisation, of placing, of the co-construction of humans and non-humans. To say that the lawn is not a thing is not, however, to deny its materiality; how it materialises and how we conceive of its materialism matters. But it is to say that the lawn is never finished and will always be tenuous and provisional.

A time after the lawn?

The anti-social turn in queer studies brings with it a concern with temporality, asserting that time is an essential component of spatial production. The critique of chrononormativity has attempted to demonstrate how the racial and sexual dimensions of time work to structure the lives of subjects in productive (capitalist) and reproductive (heterosexual) ways. This book has attempted to mobilise this critical line of questioning and direct it towards the problem of the landscape. The landscape takes place over time and the temporality of the lawn is essential to understanding how lawns do – or fail to do – what they do.

The lawn in South Africa has tended to dwell in a state of timelessness – it seems, on the face of it, to have no history and has generally appeared and still appears to be a suitable landscape for any place and any time. It is a measure of its presumed temporal neutrality that the lawn seemed – and, indeed, still seems – suitable for the Union Buildings, the Voortrekker Monument and Freedom Park; relevant for the plans of the unbuilt township for 20 000, for the NE 51 series and the Reconstruction and Development Programme house; apt in Joubert Park for promenading Edwardians and post-apartheid photographers; unquestionably relevant for the 1820 Settlers, the Randlords and the Reeftown elite. Historicising the lawn is essential because it confronts the fundamental discursive power of the lawn: its 'wonderful endurance and longevity' (Jekyll & Elgood 1904: 104).

However, far from being timeless or permanent, the lawn is very much of its time. Through the analysis of, for instance, the history of kikuyu – its colonial-era 'discovery', imperial propagation and Union-era planting – this book shows not only the dramatic movement of the lawn across space (which is important to demonstrate that lawns are far from sedate and immobile) but also the temporal specificity of lawn. It is essential to notice that the lawn derives at least part of its legitimacy from its alignment with historical points such as eighteenth-century enclosures in the United Kingdom, the colonial travel narrative, imperial botanical transfers, settler colonial aesthetics, post-Anglo-Boer War reconstruction politics, mid-twentieth-century modernist discourses, apartheid social engineering and postcolonial appropriation. The lawn has its own history, and the analysis of that history serves to challenge the ancientness and terrible permanence of the lawn. Furthermore, by enumerating the time(s) of the South African lawn, we are able to demonstrate connections between local and international lawn 'events' and so to contextualise aspects of the South African landscape within the broader ecological and political environment.

There are also very telling and satisfying moments when the lawn fails to stand the test of time, and thus to stand outside of time. For instance, the perceived and sometimes real degradation of public greens such as Welkom's Central Park, Sasolburg's green belts and Johannesburg's Joubert Park in the years after apartheid causes a great deal of consternation, not only because it provides supposed proof of the ineptitude of black governance, but also because these instances of failure reveal the lawn in its historical place and illustrate that lawn takes place over time.

It is clear how vital timely and continuous care of the lawn is for its growth and flourishing. As a botanical assemblage, the lawn must be kept in accordance with the rhythm of the seasons and the weather, which requires the knowledge and the physical and financial capacity to do so. Indeed, part of the choice to locate this book on the highveld is because its rainless, cold and frosty winters make apparent the lawn's seasonality, which is not as evident in many other parts of South Africa. In particular, keeping the lawn green out of season requires tremendous commitment, as well as access to water. Many lawns during winter are not green at all. In addition to these patterns of care, daily attention is required with regard to watering at the correct times, sometimes managed by automated sprinkler, and mowing frequently and to the right length, in order to stimulate growth. All this requires sensitivity to the time of the lawn.

Garden labourers are also, at least partly, determined chronologically. As I have argued, the 'garden boy' exists in a truncated childhood, unable to advance to manhood, linguistically at least. This retardation has to do with the expectations and logics of chrononormativity, which privileges the linear narrative of growth, procreation and development. The 'boy' is set in relation to black and white women and white men in precise ways. While delayed in boyhood, he is also a sex object, a body made up of parts – strong legs, big arms, thighs, bulges, huge cock. His strength and virility threaten white patriarchy but also make the South African lawn and garden possible in obvious practical ways. And while his generally unfulfilling and underpaid labour is part of the teleology of the lawn, there are occasions when that future-orientedness is challenged. For instance, in Diriye Osman's 'Shoga' (2011) and Chimamanda Ngozi Adichie's 'Apollo' (2015), the servant's presence in the home and garden disrupts the compulsory heteronormative progression of the young master. This postcolonial queering of domestic time provides relief from the punishing norms of healthy, positive, child-centred development. Instead of a compulsion towards productivity, the lawn can sometimes be seen to provide the possibility for a different kind of becoming, a kind of un-reproductive flourishing.

Attention to lawn care also highlights a key area to which this book has not been able to contribute substantially: the lived and embodied experience of the black garden worker. There is empirical research still to be done to flesh out an archive of black voices and experiences in order to answer some of the following questions: What knowledge transfers existed and continue to exist between master and servant, between garden workers themselves, between neighbours and within neighbourhoods? How have garden workers translated the knowledge, skills and tastes from their professional life into their own domestic spaces and their communities? How have rural–urban migration and international migrant labour patterns affected the transfers of botanical material, skills and tastes? What plants were and are disseminated as part of informal botanical transfers, and are these flows uni-, bi- or multidirectional? Lastly, would we be able to periodise 'native' or 'black' gardening before, during and after apartheid, and how would voices from below, as it were, differ from the authoritative literary texts I have examined?

The discourse analysis of 'scientific' lawn literature suggests the foundational and incontrovertible idea that the lawn is bounded – that it must, always, end somewhere. This argument seems both sensible and difficult to dispute; however, this book has described numerous instances where the lawn's ending is open to debate.

The normative lawn boundary, severe and impermeable, is epitomised by the suburban lawn in David Goldblatt's *Saturday Afternoon in Sunward Park. 1979* (see Plate 5) and John Buchan's cool lawn in *The African Colony* (1903). In Goldblatt's apartheid-era Boksburg, the muscled, white homeowner mows dead-straight lines, which mirror both the straight line of the road and the clear boundary with the veld beyond; and on Buchan's Haenartsburg after the Anglo-Boer War, the garden wall draws a strict line between the lawn and the nameless wilderness beyond. In addition, Joane Pim (1956) conceptualises the lawn itself as a kind of formal boundary, which greets the miner who emerges from the dark each day.

This orthodox lawn discourse is confronted by at least three other kinds of boundaries. The first type, an immutable but invisible boundary, is exemplified by the eighteenth-century ha-ha, which obscured the lawn's limits, visually blending the inside and outside. North American lawn discourse does something similar, visually integrating private front yards into a single 'public' lawn.

The second kind of boundary is, for lack of a better term, raised. As seen in KwaThema, in this instance the lawn is substantially higher than the swept earth around it and does not function as the boundary of the property. The sharp edges of the lawn frame the patch of grass as a discrete picture, as a small, manageable terrain; the lawn is not the canvas on which the house is created. This framing might inform how we interpret Kemang Wa Lehulere's *Do not go far they say* (see Plate 17). While obviously mobile, the lawn luggage in his installation calls to mind these particular township lawn treatments. The life of the 'raised' lawn and a whole number of 'vernacular' surface preferences, such as *lebala*, for instance – the belief that the area around houses should be open, devoid of vegetation and swept, indicating the tidiness of the household (Cilliers, Bouwman & Drewes 2009: 104) – require extended empirical fieldwork.

The third and last kind of boundary I wish to point out is the porous one. This confounds the notion that lawn is discreetly bounded and in a definite and stable relationship to a definable outside. The instability of the lawn is demonstrated in dramatic moments – as when Dorothea Fairbridge's lovely little lawn was penetrated by the mineshaft (1924) or when the Oosthuizens' home and garden were sucked up by the 1964 Blyvooruitzicht sinkhole. The threatening verticality of the lawn is evident also in Marlene van Niekerk's *Triomf*, where molehills punctuate the Benades' yellow lawn and Mol rightly worries that dangerous cavities in the earth below their home make their lives unstable. The rubble of Sophiatown persists, pushing up unpleasant reminders, too.

Above the ground, the lawn's coherence, integrity and enclosedness is also open to question. In Chapter 2, I offered a letter from the 'Clean Stand Lover and Lawn Proud Lady' to the Sasolburg municipal health department about the weeds growing at No. 10. Not only was the garden of her unrespectable neighbour overgrown, but also, as she complained, the weeds were 'coming into seed already and will of course blow into other stands and create a lot of extra work for people round about' (Sasolburg Town Clerk Files, 27 March 1968, quoted in Sparks 2012: 125). The Lawn Proud Lady's judgement about the contagious nature of other people's gardens – that is to say, the problem it causes for others – is demonstrated in Van Niekerk's *Triomf* by the noisy, disruptive, inappropriate and aggressive mowing at 127 Martha Street in the 'fuck-around' scene.

If the lawn's boundary can be shown to be troubled and permeable, unable to sustain its binary structure, then provocative non-binary or binary-challenging lines of inquiry are opened up. What would it mean if we could invert or upset the neat polarities in the study of landscape? It would mean that the lawn could be thought of as an outside – hot, nameless, unhealthy, dangerous, wild, violent, brown; and that the wildness could be considered as an interior – green, cool, soft, smooth, domestic, private, named. This intellectual manoeuvre would allow us to revisit our definition of the wilderness, of nature and of the problematic distinction between the human-made and the pristine.

It is my hope that this book shows that the lawn cannot conclusively and convincingly be depicted as finished. It is, at best, a provisional and temporary victory, an attempt at suspending flux by producing the illusion of completion. When taken as evidence for some kind of triumph over nature, as a manifestation of control over the wilderness, it suggests that wilderness is *out there.* And yet the notion of the lawn as a 'conquest over nature' relies on the most unimaginative, linear – and, indeed, often unsupportable – reading of human and non-human relationships. Even if the enchantment of a green, flat and soft lawn is almost universal, there are also unexpected moments when alternatives present themselves, occasions when people reject the politeness of the lawn, and situations in which we might glimpse a possible time *after* the lawn.

Notes

Introduction: The Lawn is Singing

1 For research focused on the United States, see, for example, Jackson (1985); Jenkins (1994b); Marusek (2012); Schroeder (1993); Steinberg (2006); and Teyssot (1999). For research on the United Kingdom, see, for example, Chevalier (1997); Fort (2001); Hitchings (2006); Moran (2011); and on the ex-British colonies, see Feagan & Ripmeester (2001); Hall (2010); Head & Muir (2006); and Sandberg & Foster (2005).

2 For international literature making arguments against the lawn, see Bogh & Schnetz (2014); Carson (1962); Flores (2006); Gift (2009); Haeg (2010); Penick (2013); Stein (1993); Wasowski & Wasowski (2004).

3 Mitchell is paraphrasing the first line of John Berryman's poem 'Dream Song 14': 'Life, friends, is boring. We must not say so.' See https://www.poetryfoundation.org/poems/47534/dream-song-14%20. Accessed 13 September 2018.

4 The first bowling club in South Africa was the Port Elizabeth Bowling Green Club founded on 14 August 1882, and the country's first green, 'Founder's Green', was opened on 5 January 1884 by A. C. Wylde, the resident magistrate.

5 The central proposition of the British Marxist art historians, cultural critics and geographers of the 1970s and 1980s who studied the 'dark side of the landscape' is that 'landscape is an ideological concept' (Harris 1999: 436), which 'represents a way in which certain classes of people have signified themselves and their world through their imagined relationship with nature' (Cosgrove 1984: 15); it hides the 'inhabitants' and their labours, delegitimising their 'struggles, achievements and accidents' and obscuring 'the forces and relations of production' (Daniels 1989: 206).

6 'Returning' by Mike Nicol, from *Staffrider* 6, no. 1 (1984), p. 6. Reprinted with permission of the author.

Chapter 1 The Lawn Discourse

1 The greenness of the lawn is axiomatic. Greenness is connected to 'relaxation' (King & Oudolf 1998: 22), 'peace' (Eliovson 1968: 113), described as 'natural and soothing' (Johnson 1979: 154) and as 'neutral' (King & Oudolf 1998: 22). John Loudon's *Encyclopaedia of Gardening* warns that nothing should be 'neglected to ensure that deep green colour and velvet texture which is, or ought to be, the characteristic of the British lawn, and which indeed is the pride of our island' (1825: 932).

2 The lawn is also described as a 'soft cushion to walk on' (Martin 1983: 467), without which a 'garden is somehow hard' (Smith 1940: 216). Hosea Omole describes kikuyu (*Pennisetum clandestinum*) as 'an attractive bright salad-green cover that is thick, soft and somewhat springy' (2011), as does Otto Stapf in 1921: 'a dense, soft and springy turf' (88). Joseph Burtt-Davy describes Florida grass (*Cynodon transvaalensis*) as having a 'soft springy nature' (1921: 281). In addition to noting that a lawn *is* soft, some authors have suggested meanings for the softness. For Johnson, something 'soft is more natural and more soothing' (1979: 154), and for Jackson Downing 'soft, verdant velvet lawn' is one of the most 'forcible illustrations of the *beautiful*' (1853: 62).

3 http://www.carolizejansen.com/Joane-Pim.html. Accessed 13 September 2018.

Chapter 2 Keeping the Lawn

1 From *Poetic Licence* by Mike Alfred (Johannesburg: Botsoto Publications, 2007). Reprinted with permission of the author.

2 The history of mowing and the invention of the lawnmower have been reliably covered elsewhere. See, for instance, Hoyles (1991, 2002); Jenkins (1994a); Macinnis (2009); Robbins (2007); Teyssot (1999).

3 Smuts was actively involved in the politics of botany. He published *The Grasses and Pastures of South Africa* in 1950, travelled with the chemist Rudolf Marloth as he did research for his *Flora of South Africa* and was closely aligned with bureaucrat and scientist Illtyd Buller Pole-Evans. Anker's *Imperial Ecology* (2001) provides an analysis of Smuts's patronage of botany and his involvement in the emergent concepts of 'Holism' and 'Ecological Idealism'.

4 Kipling's poem can be found at http://historymatters.gmu.edu/d/5478/. Accessed 18 September 2018.

5 For other complementary and contextual studies on the term 'boy', see Bosmajian (1969); Dube (1985); Hickson & Strous (1993); Ratele &

Laubscher (2013); Steinberg et al. (2010); Van Onselen (1982); Zabus (2013).

6 Notwithstanding the curtailment of vocational 'manhood', in his analysis of masculinity on the South African mines, Dunbar Moodie proposes that 'if the dominant mores of white society decreed that all black men, even senior mine supervisors were "boys" ... black workers themselves graduated from being "boys" for their fellow workers to being "men" with their own "boys" as they gained mine experience' (1994: 128).

7 Those who have read Vladislavić know his persistent concern for **walls**, **security**, **street addresses** and **gardens**. Those obsessions, along with others like **memorials**, **walking**, **old lives**, have been consolidated into a collection of 'itineraries' as an appendix to *Portrait with Keys* (2009; emphasis in original). The itineraries, which Vladislavić calls 'thematic pathways through the book' (205), provide an alternative approach to reading and exploring the city of Johannesburg, and perhaps also to analysing his texts. There is (curiously) no **lawn** itinerary. I have corrected that omission by arranging my own, first for *Portrait with Keys* as well as for *The Exploded View*, *The Restless Supermarket*, *Flashback Hotel*, *The Loss Library and Other Unfinished Stories*. 'Routes are classified as follows: L = Long, M = Medium, S = Short' (Vladislavić 2009: 205), with route numbers indicated in bold. A proposed itinerary for **lawns** in *Portrait with Keys* (2009) is (M): **2** – 'when some stranger who had lost his way might hail a man mowing his lawn' (13); **8** – 'In a standard Portuguese renovation' the entire garden may be 'cemented over, with the occasional porthole provided for a scrawny rosebush to stick out its neck' (20); **9** – Regarding 'another Portuguese modernization': 'In the left-hand corner of a severely cropped lawn sat a life-size statue of a German shepherd dog' (23); **19** – Dave the historian 'explains why certain kinds of landscape appeal so strongly. A meadow sweeping down to a river, a view from a patio over a rolling lawn, a spruit at the bottom of the yard, a koppie on which to loll, with the veld streaming away to the horizon – vistas like these call to our hunter-gatherer hearts' (37–38); **63** – Winter sports fields: 'Smells of dust and whitewash rise from the other side of the fence, reduced to red sand and straw this time of year' (86); **76** – 'The smell of grass is quenching' (102), 'We know this earth, this grass, this polished red stone with the soles of our feet. We will never be ourselves anywhere else' (103); **89** – 1981 Johannesburg snow: Snowmen fainting on the grass in Joubert Park; **90** – 'The cage of Max the Gorilla has the blatant charm of a garden in Meyerton. There is an expanse of rolling

kikuyu and a water feature on the left' (131); **94** – An attacker pushes Chas onto the lawn during a robbery; **95** – 'The path is a string of slate islands in a glistening sea of lawn' (140); **96** – 'Thief stumbling across the lawn below the window' (143); **126** – '*141 Kitchener* The Tiler who lives here has turned his yard into a chaotic catalogue of ornamental stone' (180); **138** – Security guard strike: commotion on the lawns of the Library Gardens (193). A proposed itinerary for **lawns** in *The Exploded View* (2004): (L) 35; 54; 73–74; 110; 120; 122; 136; 170; 177. For *The Restless Supermarket* (2006): (M) 15; 17; 181; 205; 320; 328. For *Flashback Hotel* (2010): (L) 9; 10; 12; 31; 37; 38; 42; 44; 68; 71; 114; 115; 116; 118; 202. For *The Loss Library* (2011): (S) 24; 67.

8 Koos Prinsloo authored a story called 'Huisbesoek', which includes the following erotic mowing passage: '*En op 'n warm somermiddag ry hulle deur die suburbs van Newcastle en gaan teken die pa 'n ornate hek na. By die huis langsaan sny 'n tienerseun ('n engel met 'n gebreekte vlerk?) in 'n boxer short die gras*.' (And on a warm summer afternoon they drive through the suburbs of Newcastle and the father makes a drawing of an ornate gate. At the house next door a teenage boy [an angel with a broken wing?] is mowing the grass in his boxer shorts) (2008: 283).

9 'Racialisation was explicit in the understanding of heavy labour – for instance in "representations of sweating, glistening bodies" (Bordo 1993: 195; Cranny-Francis 1995) belonging to slaves and colonised peoples' (Wolkowitz 2006: 40).

10 These images can be seen online: http://www.aphotostudent.com/james-pomerantz/2009/12/11/week-14-course-update-africa/(Mofokeng) and http://www.goodman-gallery.com/exhibitions/193 (Goldblatt). Accessed 15 October 2018.

11 Goldblatt's photograph *A resident of the white suburb of Boksburg spreads top dressing on his lawn on a Sunday afternoon* (1985) is an excellent example of the deprioritisation of other activities on the lawn. The colour photograph is not a well-known image, neither is it an especially beautiful one. It depicts a young white man (not unattractive) in navy blue Adidas shorts, shirtless, shovelling compost, towards the camera, over his yellowish lawn. His face-brick house in the background is inset with a white Catholic icon.

12 The photo can be seen at https://pamnogales.com/2014/11/25/exhibition-review-ernest-cole-photographer/. Accessed 15 October 2018.

13 See http://archive.stevenson.info/exhibitions/goldblatt/intersections20082/4_A0244.htm. Accessed 15 October 2018.

14 See http://collections.vam.ac.uk/item/O152869/ephraim-zulu-of-the-salvation-photograph-goldblatt-david/#. Accessed 15 October 2018.

Chapter 3 Planning the Modern Lawn

1 Blenheim Palace, Oxfordshire, is the ancestral seat of the Duke of Marlborough, given to the first duke, John Churchill, in *c.*1705. The gardens were designed by John Vanbrugh and master gardener to Queen Anne, Henry Wise, in the formal style: a steady avenue of trees, a formal military garden, a kitchen garden, a series of formal parterres leading to a hexagonal wilderness, a plantation of trees dissected by axial avenues, and Vanbrugh's Grand Bridge crossing a small lake and a linear canal (Booth 1996: 107). Those overly 'fussy and somehow out of scale' gardens (Turner 1985: 94) – while mourned later by some, like Vanbrugh's biographer Laurence Whistler (1939) – were transformed by the fourth duke and his gardener Lancelot Brown into one of the definitive English landscape gardens (Booth 1996: 107).

2 This peculiar eighteenth-century approach has also been noted by Thomas Adams and Peter Youngman (1939), Christopher Tunnard (1938), Jan Woudstra (2000) and David Jacques and Jan Woudstra (2009).

3 The *Collective Thesis* has five written chapters, each authored by one of the students: Jonas, 'Sociological Approach to Native Housing' (1–49); Wepener, 'Psychological Approach to Native Housing' (50–85); Kantorowich, 'Planning Native Housing' (86–122); Connell, 'Construction of Native Housing' (123–165); and Irvine-Smith, 'Financing Native Housing' (166–199). At the end of the thesis are plans, photographs of models and elevations of their design for 'Model Native Township' for 20 000 people. The models were shown at the Town Planning Congress and Exhibition and accompanied by three days of presentations.

4 The *South African Architectural Record* (Sept. 1938) published the following in relation to the 1938 moment: (a) Jonas's lecture 'The Architect in the Social System' (205–215); (b) Pearse's paper 'A Survey of Town Planning in South Africa' (231–242); (c) a message from Le Corbusier to the Congress: 'Do You Prefer to Wage War?', along with a beautiful green-and-black image of Plan Voisin (266–267); (d) an introduction by Jonas (268–269); (e) First Evening, 'Approach': B. A. Farrell on 'Sociological Approach to Town Planning' and S. Biesheuvel on 'Psychological Approach to Town Planning' (273–303); (f) interspersed images of the exhibition attributed to Irvine-Smith; (g) Second Evening, 'Thesis': W. G. McIntosh on 'The Task of the Architect' and L. W. Thornton-White on 'A Survey of 20th Century Town Planning' (312–341); (h) Third Evening, 'Demonstration': Kantorowich on 'A Model Native Township for 20,000 Inhabitants'

and Hanson on 'A New Business Centre for Capetown [*sic*]' (342–372); (i) Discussion (373–380).

5 For research on the 'urban native', see NBRI (1954) and Spence (1950).

6 For more on the 1944 City of Johannesburg Competition for Non-European Housing, see *South African Architectural Record* (Anon. 1944: 220–229); for the 1954 Institute of South African Architects Architectural Competition for Non-European Housing, see *South African Architectural Record* (Anon. 1954: 35–39); for high-rise prototypes, see Cutten (1952) and Van der Bijl (1944); and on Witbank, see Hector & Calderwood (1951) and Jennings (1951).

7 The Housing Act (No. 35 of 1920) created the Central Housing Board to 'regulate local authority housing developments for Africans, Coloured and Indians. The Board's mandate is to supervise/administer the lending of government funds for housing developments' (Lester et al. 2009: 17). During this period the central government, via the Housing Board, limited its financial responsibilities for 'implementing residential segregation in the urban areas, which devolved essentially to making subsidies available for the provision of very basic sub economic houses by the local authorities' (Wilkinson 1998: 218).

8 The approach to black labour in KwaThema has resonances with the descriptions of 'garden boys' we have seen before. Enormous amounts of energy were dedicated to academic scientific study of black labourers' productivity. 'It's no good treating the native artisan the way you would treat the European artisan. One has to bring him along like a child, with that attitude there will be success' (D. H. Darvill, City Engineer of Pietermaritzburg, quoted in Steenkamp 2008: 171). 'Our experience ... shows that the non-European, when he is employed on repetition and simple work, is quite capable of turning out first-class work' (H. V. Davies, Director of Public Works, Bechuanaland Protectorate, quoted in Steenkamp 2008: 171).

9 See Demissie (2004); Foster (2012, 2015); Godehart (2006); Haarhoff (2011); Japha (1998); Le Roux (2014); Steenkamp (2008); Vestbro (2012).

10 'The township of Welkom officially came into being on 15th April 1947, some six years after the first mining lease in the area was awarded to the St Helena Gold Mining Company, and was proclaimed a town on 23rd July 1948. Between 1937 and 1947 the early mining community consisted of about 500 people who lived at Uitzig Camp' (Welkom Publicity Association, quoted in Murray 2010: 87). The town was established to service six mines of the Orange Free State gold fields – Free State Geduld Mines, Western Holdings, Welkom Gold

Mining Company, President Steyn Gold Mining Company, President Brand Gold Mining Company and St Helena Gold Mines. The first five mines were under administrative control of Anglo American and the sixth by Union Corporation (Backhouse 1952: 13).

11 The images can be viewed at https://archive.org/details/observations-onth00rept/page/n31. Accessed 23 October 2018.

12 Welkom Dutch Reformed Church, 1964 Uytenbogaardt Manuscripts ZA UCT BC1264_H_H1, University of Cape Town Libraries: Special Collections (Manuscripts and Archives).

13 See 'Hier staan Welkom-Wes se N.G. Kerk' (*Huisgenoot*, 10 February 1967) and 'N.G. Kerk, Welkom, O.V.S' (*Credo* 1969).

14 David Goldblatt's *Dutch Reformed Church Edenvale, 1983* can be seen online at http://collections.vam.ac.uk/item/O199933/gereformeerde-kerk-edenvale-transvaal-28-photograph-goldblatt-david/. Accessed 23 October 2018.

Chapter 4 No Fucking up/on the Lawn

1 'i don't want that suburban house', from *i must show you my clippings* by Wopko Jensma (Johannesburg: Ravan Press, 1977). Reprinted with permission of Pan Macmillan.

2 One important terrain on which the production of colonial subjectivities is negotiated is the ceremonial and sporting fields of South African private schools. These sites function at the intersection of religious and pedagogic practices with the explicit intention of locating childhood positions in a moral, cultural, intellectual and sexual matrix that privileges white, patriarchal, heterosexual, Christian identities. The following list is an incomplete inventory, derived from recollections of teachers and students, of the more or less formal names and rules attached to lawns at South African private schools. Bishops Diocesan College (Cape Town): no student may walk on the first team rugby field called 'Piley Rees' and only prefects can walk on the grass paths that link classrooms and buildings; Hilton College (Pietermaritzburg): only Grade 12s may walk on the 'Main Lawn'; only the head boy may cross the lawn to the headmaster's office; only first team cricket and rugby players may cross those respective fields; certain punishments require students to 'stand early' on lawns; Kingsmead School for Girls (Johannesburg): 'The Green' is only accessible to prefects and only if wearing a blazer; the use of the 'Matric Green' is only for Grade 12s and only if sitting on a blanket; no students may take a short cut across lawns; Kingswood College (Grahamstown): the Matric

Lawn is for Grade 12s' use only; Roedean School (Johannesburg): the 'Bears Lawn' is only for Grade 12s' use; Rustenburg Girls' High (Cape Town): 'The Quad' may be traversed only by teachers; however, on Valedictory Day Grade 12s may use the lawn; Somerset College (Stellenbosch): the 'Matric Lawn' is for Grade 12s only, and for Grade 11s by invitation; St Andrews Girls (Johannesburg): the quadrangle in front of the library is for Grade 12s' use only; St David's Marist Inanda (Johannesburg): only Grade 12s may walk on the lawn of the 'senior quad'; the 'First Team Field' is only accessible to first team players; St John's College (Johannesburg): only Grade 12s may walk on the 'Clayton Quadrangle'; juniors may not walk across sports fields; all students to avoid walking on the grass of the 'David Quadrangle'; Saint Mary's Diocesan School for Girls (Pretoria): the 'Matric Lawn' is labelled as such with an official school sign; the front lawns outside the main building are never used; even though there is no official rule, it is assumed to be off limits to students; St Stithians College (Johannesburg): only prefects, the head boy and 'Duke of Cornwall' recipients (persons having saved a life or gone beyond the call of duty) may walk on the lawn of the 'Chapel Quad'; no one may walk across any first team fields; Treverton College (KwaZulu-Natal): outside the Hudson Reed Hall is a lawn with tables and benches for exclusive use of Grade 12s.

3 Family Poaceae; Genus *Pennisetum*: Latin *penna* (feather) and *seta* (bristle). The description of this species was published by Emilio Chiovenda in 1903, and acknowledges an earlier invalid description made by C. F. Hochstetter (Stapf 1921).

4 It is important to make clear that the analysis of Joubert Park is a very important but limited snapshot of gay life in parks in Johannesburg. It does not, for instance, address the question of where black males met in Soweto for sex. Also, Joubert Park was only one of the parks that served this function, with most of them reachable only by car and therefore effectively white. In Johannesburg alone, there were Zoo Lake, Emmarentia Park, Rhodes Park and the little park on top of the hill bordering Berea.

5 See http://deathofjohannesburg.blogspot.co.za/. Accessed 20 October 2018.

6 For Hugo's image, see http://archive.stevenson.info/exhibitions/hugo/kin/green_point_common_tree.html. Accessed 22 October 2018.

7 That these reminders of Sophiatown's past interrupt the family's garden has been noted by a number of scholars (see Buxbaum 2011: 34, 2014: 33–34; Devarenne 2006: 113; Jackson 2011: 347; Samuelson 2008: 71; Shear 2006: 76–77; Stotesbury 2004: 24; White 2007: 86–87).

8 Julia Kristeva's psychoanalytic concept of abjection has been taken up in analyses of *Triomf* by Buxbaum (2014: 12–15), Crous (2013) and Rossmann (2012).

9 The threat of the unstable underground is also figured through the trope of the sinkhole. Rosalind Morris (2006, 2008) analyses the 1964 Blyvooruitzicht sinkhole disaster in the mining community of Carletonville, where an entire white Afrikaner family, the Oosthuizens, and their domestic worker were swallowed up in their home by a 100-metre wide sinkhole. She argues that sinkholes 'are not merely the evidence of geological events, however; they are also potent metaphors' (2006: 63).

10 In 1962 the Non-European Affairs Department issued a pamphlet called *Your Bantu Servant and You: A Few Suggestions to Facilitate Happier Relations between Employer and Employee*, which presented brief guidelines for managing the 'human relationship factor' between the races. The short booklet pursues the argument that 'domestic servants are human' (1962: 5) and that for the sake of racial harmony, mutual respect in the home is necessary. Women are strongly warned to 'be exceptionally careful in their treatment of male servants' (1), and all employers are entreated not to use the appellation 'boy', which, the Department warns, 'gives more offence than is generally realised' (2). *Your Bantu Servant and You* offers advice on work hours, pay, transportation, accommodation, legal issues and food provision. Joseph Lelyveld notes that 'in most white households, the servants receive meat two or three times a week – "boysmeat," as the signs in the windows of the butcher shops describe the cheap cuts that white South Africans feed their help' (1967: 15).

11 'Ikoyi', from *Moonsongs* by Niyi Osundare (Ibadan: Spectrum, 1988). Reprinted with permission of the author.

12 Brandel-Syrier reports that black families built the rockeries but 'the trouble began when the pockets had to be filled with plants'. The researcher recounts how she was repeatedly asked for rock plants and she explained that 'the real fun of a rockery was in collecting your own rock plants from the *veld*'. The problem, she explains, is that 'upper-class Africans do not go on picnics and do not sit around the *veld*. Only Bantu herbalists searched for plants, and no self-respecting Reeftowner would want to be seen doing this. No wonder that the interest in rockeries soon waned and attention was directed to making neat borders, flower beds and lawns, regularly watered by sprinklers or servants' (1971: 101).

13 This includes research on the layout and function of the 'Tswana Tshimo' (Molebatsi et al. 2010) and the 'Zulu Muzi' (Nemudzudzanyi et al. 2010), gardening in the township of Ga-Rankuwa, Pretoria

(Coetzee et al. 2007), and gardening in rural Thohoyandou, Limpopo Province (McHale et al. 2013).

14 See also Goldblatt's *A gardener at rest outside his employer's home in Houghton, Johannesburg* (1977) and *A domestic worker's afternoon off, Sunninghill, Sandton, 23 July 1999* (https://collections.artsmia.org/search/artist:%22David%20Goldblatt%22), as well as Mlangeni's *Lwazi Mtshali 'Bigboy'* (2009) (http://archive.stevenson.info/exhibitions/mlangeni/countrygirls/countrygirls14.htm) and *Blooming flowers of summer* (2013) (http://archive.stevenson.info/exhibitions/mlangeni/no_problem/blooming_flowers_summer.html). Accessed 25 October 2018.

15 In *Small Circle of Beings* (2012) Damon Galgut writes about how Moses the gardener's mowing caused the narrator's mother great distress and so Moses mows the lawn at night – 'a strange and wonderful sight: the squat black man gliding across the moonlit lawn. While my mother, unsuspecting, sits in her room and dreams' (2012: 15).

16 'No Complaining from Lawn of RDP House: Malema', *The Times*, 7 May 2011. http://www.timeslive.co.za/local/2011/05/07/no-complaining-from-lawn-of-rdp-house-malema. Accessed 5 September 2014.

References

Adams, T. & G. P. Youngman. 1939. 'Gardens Will be More Free and Flowing'. In *Gardens and Gardening*, edited by F. A. Mercer, 14–15. London: The Studio.

Adichie, C. N. 2015. 'Apollo'. *The New Yorker*, 13 April. http://www.newyorker.com/magazine/2015/04/13/apollo. Accessed 5 August 2015.

Alfred, M. 2007. *Poetic Licence*. Johannesburg: Botsotso Publications.

Althusser, L. 1971. *Lenin and Philosophy and Other Essays*. London: New Left Books.

Anderson, E. N. 1972. 'On the Folk Art of Landscaping'. *Western Folklore* 31, no. 3: 179–188.

Anderson, K. 1997. 'A Walk on the Wild Side: A Critical Geography of Domestication'. *Progress in Human Geography* 21, no. 4: 463–485.

Andrews, M. 1999. *Landscape and Western Art*. Oxford: Oxford University Press.

Anker, P. 2001. *Imperial Ecology*. Cambridge, MA: Harvard University Press.

Anon. 1920. 'The Houseboy'. *The South African Woman* 1, no. 6: 1.

Anon. 1944. 'City of Johannesburg Competition for Non-European Housing'. *South African Architectural Record* (September): 220–229.

Anon. 1954. 'Architectural Competition for Non-European Housing'. *South African Architectural Record* (March): 35–39.

Appadurai, A. 1996. *Modernity at Large: Cultural Dimensions of Globalization*. Minneapolis: University of Minnesota Press.

Ashcroft, B., G. Griffiths & H. Tiffin, eds. 2007. *Key Concepts in Post-colonial Studies*. London: Routledge.

Backhouse, W. 1952. 'Welkom: A Town Planned'. *Optima* (March): 12–17.

Ballard, R. 2005. 'When in Rome: Claiming the Right to Define Neighbourhood Character in South Africa's Suburbs'. *Transformation: Critical Perspectives on Southern Africa* 57: 64–87.

Ballard, R. 2010. '"Slaughter in the Suburbs": Livestock Slaughter and Race in Post-apartheid Cities'. *Ethnic and Racial Studies* 33, no. 6: 1069–1087.

Ballard, R. & G. A. Jones. 2011. 'Natural Neighbours: Indigenous Landscapes and "Eco-estates" in Durban, South Africa'. *Annals of the Association of American Geographers* 101, no. 1: 131–148.

Barrell, J. 1983. *The Dark Side of the Landscape: The Rural Poor in English Painting 1730–1840*. Cambridge: Cambridge University Press.

Beall, J., O. Crankshaw & S. Parnell. 2002. *Social Differentiation and Urban Governance in Greater Soweto: A Case Study of Post-apartheid Reconstruction*. London: Crisis States Research Centre, London School of Economics and Political Science.

Beinart, W. & K. Middleton. 2004. 'Plant Transfers in Historical Perspective: A Review Article'. *Environment and History* 10: 3–29.

Bell, S. G. 1990. 'Women Create Gardens in Male Landscapes: A Revisionist Approach to Eighteenth-Century English Garden History'. *Feminist Studies* 16, no. 3: 471–491.

Beningfield, J. 2006a. *The Frightened Land: Land, Landscape and Politics in South Africa in the Twentieth Century*. London: Routledge.

Beningfield, J. 2006b. 'Telling Tales: Building, Landscape and Narratives in Post-apartheid South Africa'. *Architectural Research Quarterly* 10: 223–234.

Bennett, J. 2010. *Vibrant Matter: A Political Ecology of Things*. Durham: Duke University Press.

Berger, J. 1972. *Ways of Seeing*. London: Penguin.

Berlant, L. 2011. *Cruel Optimism*. Durham: Duke University Press.

Bermingham, A. 1986. *Landscape and Ideology: The English Rustic Tradition 1740–1860*. Berkeley: University of California Press.

Beukes, P. 1996. *Smuts the Botanist*. Cape Town: Human & Rousseau.

Bhabha, H. K. 1994. *The Location of Culture*. London: Routledge.

Blomfield, R. 1892. *The Formal Garden in England*. London: Macmillan. http://www.archive.org/details/cu31924012145060. Accessed 14 March 2013.

Boddam-Whetham, R. E. 1933. *A Garden in the Veld*. Wynberg: Speciality Press of South Africa.

Bogh, M. & B. Schnetz. 2014. *Life after Lawns*. San Bernardino: CreateSpace Independent Publishing Platform.

Booth, D. W. 1996. 'Blenheim Park on the Eve of "Mr. Brown's Improvements"'. *Journal of Garden History* 15, no. 2: 107–125.

Bordo, S. 1993. 'Reading the Male Body'. *Michigan Quarterly Review* 32, no. 4: 696–734.

Bosmajian, H. A. 1969. 'The Language of White Racism'. *College English* 31, no. 3: 263–272.

Brandel-Syrier, M. 1971. *Reeftown Elite: A Study of Social Mobility in a Modern African Community on the Reef*. London: Routledge & Kegan Paul.

Brandel-Syrier, M. 1978. *Coming Through: The Search for a New Cultural Identity.* Johannesburg: McGraw-Hill.

Bremner, L. 2004. 'Bounded Spaces: Demographic Anxieties in Post-apartheid Johannesburg'. *Social Identities* 10, no. 4: 455–468.

Broadbent, S. 1865. *A Narrative of the First Introduction of Christianity amongst the Barolong Tribe of Bechuanas, South Africa.* London: Wesleyan Mission House.

Brockway, L. H. 1979. 'Science and Colonial Expansion: The Role of the British Botanical Gardens'. *American Ethnologist* 6, no. 3: 449–465.

Bruwer, J. 2006. *Report on the Historic Layered Development of the Johannesburg Park Station Complex and Joubert Park Precinct.* Johannesburg: Johannesburg Development Agency.

Buchan, J. 1903. *The African Colony: Studies in Reconstruction.* The Gutenberg Project. http://www.gutenberg.org/files/34548/34548-h/34548-h.htm. Accessed 1 September 2012.

Bunn, D. 1994. '"Our Wattled Cot": Mercantile and Domestic Spaces in Thomas Pringle's African Landscapes'. In *Landscape and Power,* edited by W. J. T. Mitchell, 127–174. Chicago: University of Chicago Press.

Bunn, D. 2008. 'Art Johannesburg and its Objects'. In *Johannesburg: The Elusive Metropolis,* edited by S. Nuttall & A. Mbembe, 137–170. Durham: Duke University Press.

Burtt-Davy, J. 1915. 'Kikuyu Grass'. *Agricultural Journal of the Union of South Africa* 2, no. 10: 146–147.

Burtt-Davy, J. 1921. 'New or Noteworthy South African Plants: III'. *Bulletin of Miscellaneous Information, Royal Botanic Gardens, Kew* 7: 278–284.

Buxbaum, L. 2011. '"Embodying Space": The Search for a Nurturing Environment in Marlene van Niekerk's *Triomf, Agaat* and *Memorandum*'. *English in Africa* 38, no. 2: 29–44.

Buxbaum, L. 2014. '"To See Another Person's Face ... to Touch Another Person's Hand": Bodies and Intimate Relations in the Fiction of Marlene van Niekerk'. PhD thesis, University of the Witwatersrand.

Caccia, A. 1993. 'Moses Tladi (1906–1959): South Africa's First Black Landscape Painter?' *de arte* 28, no. 48: 3–22.

Calderwood, D. M. 1952. 'An Investigation into the Functional and Aesthetic Aspects of Garden Architecture, Vol. II'. Master's dissertation, University of the Witwatersrand.

Calderwood, D. M. 1953. 'Native Housing in South Africa'. PhD thesis, University of the Witwatersrand.

Calderwood, D. M. 1954. 'An Approach to Low Cost Urban Native Housing in South Africa'. *The Town Planning Review* 24, no. 4: 312–328.

Calderwood, D. M. 1955. *Native Housing in South Africa.* Cape Town: Cape Times.

Cane, J. 2010. 'Het Versamel: On Un-remembering'. http://www.jonathancane.com. Accessed 10 August 2016.

Carruthers, J. 2011. 'Trouble in the Garden: South African Botanical Politics 1870–1950'. *South African Journal of Botany* 77, no. 2: 258–267.

Carson, R. 1962. *Silent Spring*. Boston: Houghton Mifflin; Cambridge, MA: Riverside Press.

Casid, J. H. 2008. 'Landscape Trouble'. In *Landscape Theory: The Art Seminar 6*, edited by J. Elkins and R. DeLue, 179–186. New York: Routledge.

Casid, J. H. 2011. 'Epilogue: Landscape in, around, and under the Performative'. *Women & Performance: A Journal of Feminist Theory* 21, no. 1: 97–116.

Chevalier, S. 1997. 'From Woolen Carpet to Grass Carpet'. In *Material Cultures: Why Some Things Matter*, edited by D. Miller, 47–71. Chicago: University of Chicago Press.

Chipkin, C. 1993. *Johannesburg Style: Architecture & Society 1880s–1960s*. Cape Town: David Philip.

Cilliers, S., H. Bouwman & E. Drewes. 2009. 'Comparative Urban Ecological Research in Developing Countries'. In *Ecology of Cities and Towns: A Comparative Approach*, edited by M. McDonnell, A. Hahs & J. Breuste, 90–111. Cambridge: Cambridge University Press.

Coetzee, J. M. 1988. *White Writing: On the Culture of Letters in South Africa*. New Haven: Yale University Press.

Coetzee, M. M., W. van Averbeke, S. C. D. Wright & E. T. Haycock. 2007. 'Understanding Urban Home Garden Design in Ga-Rankuwa, Pretoria'. Unpublished paper, presented at the Institute of Environment and Recreation Management Conference, Pietermaritzburg, 5–6 October. http://www.inca.org.za/Portals/19/Documents/Convention%202007/Understanding%20urban%20home%20garden%20design%20in%20Ga-Rankuwa,%20Pretoria%20-%20Magriet%20Coetzee.pdf. Accessed 24 October 2018.

Cole, E., G. Knape, S. Robertson & I. Powell. 2010. *Ernest Cole: Photographer*. Göteborg: Hasselblad Foundation & Steidl.

Colvin, B. 1970. *Land and Landscape*. London: J. Murray.

Comaroff, J. & J. L. Comaroff. 1992. 'Home-made Hegemony: Modernity, Domesticity, and Colonialism in South Africa'. In *African Encounters with Domesticity*, edited by K. Hansen, 39–74. New Brunswick: Rutgers University Press.

Comaroff, J. & J. L. Comaroff. 1997. *Of Revelation and Revolution, Vol. II: The Dialectics of Modernity on a South African Frontier*. Chicago: University of Chicago Press.

Comaroff, J. & J. L. Comaroff. 2001. 'Naturing the Nation: Aliens, Apocalypse and the Postcolonial State'. *Journal of Southern African Studies* 27, no. 3: 627–651.

Comaroff, J. & J. L. Comaroff. 2012. *Theory from the South; or, How Euro-America is Evolving toward Africa*. Boulder: Paradigm Publishers.

Connell, P. H. 1947. *Sub-economic Housing Practice in South Africa*. Pretoria: Council for Scientific and Industrial Research (CSIR), National Building Research Institute.

Connell, P. H., C. Irvine-Smith, K. Jonas, R. Kantorowich & F. J. Wepener. 1939. *Native Housing: A Collective Thesis*. Johannesburg: Witwatersrand University Press.

Constant, C. 2012. *The Modern Architectural Landscape*. Minneapolis: University of Minnesota Press.

Cooper, F. 2005. *Colonialism in Question: Theory, Knowledge, History*. Berkeley: University of California Press.

Coppola, F. F., dir. *Apocalypse Now*. San Francisco: Omni Zoetrope, 1979.

Corner, J. 1999. 'Recovering Landscape as Critical Cultural Practice'. In *Recovering Landscape: Essays in Contemporary Landscape Architecture*, edited by J. Corner, 1–28. New York: Princeton Architectural Press.

Cosgrove, D. E. 1984. *Social Formation and Symbolic Landscape*. Sydney: Croom Helm.

Cran, M. D. 1927. *The Gardens of Good Hope*. London: H. Jenkins.

Cranny-Francis, A. 1995. *The Body in the Text*. Melbourne: Melbourne University Press.

Crosby, A. W. 1986. *Ecological Imperialism: The Biological Expansion of Europe, 900–1900*. Cambridge: Cambridge University Press.

Crous, M. 2013. 'Abjection in the Novels of Marlene van Niekerk'. PhD thesis, University of the Cape Town.

Cutten, A. J. 1952. 'Native Housing'. *South African Architectural Record* (May): 114–126.

Daniels, S. 1989. 'Marxism, Culture and the Duplicity of Landscape'. In *New Models in Geography, Vol. II*, edited by R. Peet and N. Thrift, 196–220. London: Unwin Hyman.

Darian-Smith, K., E. Gunner & S. Nuttall, eds. 1996. *Text, Theory, Space*. London: Routledge.

Das, V., A. Kleinman, M. Ramphele & P. Reynolds, eds. 2000. *Violence and Subjectivity*. Berkeley: University of California Press.

Dean, J. 1996. *Solidarity of Strangers: Feminism after Identity Politics*. Berkeley: University of California Press.

De Certeau, M. 1984. *The Practice of Everyday Life*. Berkeley: University of California Press.

De Crescentiis, P. 1305. *Liber ruralium commodorum.*

Deleuze, G. & F. Guattari. 1987. *A Thousand Plateaus: Capitalism and Schizophrenia*, translated by B. Massumi. Minneapolis: University of Minnesota Press.

Demissie, F. 2004. 'Controlling and "Civilising Natives" through Architecture and Town Planning in South Africa'. *Social Identities* 10, no. 4: 483–507.

Devarenne, N. 2006. '"In Hell You Hear Only Your Mother Tongue": Afrikaner Nationalist Ideology, Linguistic Subversion and Cultural Renewal in Marlene van Niekerk's *Triomf*'. *Research in African Literatures* 37, no. 4: 105–120.

DeWerth, A. F. 1961. *A Planning Guide for Home Landscaping.* College Station: Texas Agricultural Extension Service.

Dick, A. L. 2005. '"To Make the People of South Africa Proud of Their Membership of the Great British Empire": Home Reading Unions in South Africa, 1900–1914'. *Libraries & Culture* 40, no. 1: 1–24.

Dlamini, J. 2010. *Native Nostalgia.* Johannesburg: Jacana Media.

Drayton, R. 2000. *Nature's Government: Science, Imperial Britain, and the 'Improvement' of the World.* New Haven: Yale University Press.

Dreher, N. H. 1997. 'The Virtuous and the Verminous: Turn-of-the-Century Moral Panics in London's Public Parks'. *Albion* 29, no. 2: 246–267.

Dube, E. F. 1985. 'The Relationship between Racism and Education in South Africa'. *Harvard Educational Review* 55, no. 1: 86–100.

Dubow, N. 1998. 'Constructs: Reflections on a Thinking Eye'. In *The Structure of Things Then*, by D. Goldblatt, 22–33. Cape Town: Oxford University Press.

Dubow, S. 2006. *A Commonwealth of Knowledge: Science, Sensibility, and White South Africa, 1820–2000.* Oxford: Oxford University Press.

Dubow, S. 2014. *Apartheid, 1948–1994.* Oxford: Oxford University Press.

Edelman, L. 2004. *No Future: Queer Theory and the Death Drive.* Durham: Duke University Press.

Eden, W. A. 1935. 'The English Tradition in the Countryside, Part III: The Re-birth of the Tradition'. *Architectural Review* 77, no. 462 (March): 193–202.

Eisenstadt, S. N. 2000. 'Multiple Modernities'. *Daedalus* 129, no. 1: 1–29.

Eliovson, S. 1968. *The Complete Gardening Book for Southern Africa.* Cape Town: Howard Timmins.

Eliovson, S. 1983. *Garden Design for Southern Africa.* Johannesburg: Macmillan.

Evans, I. 1997. *Bureaucracy and Race: Native Administration in South Africa.* Berkeley: University of California Press.

Fairbanks, E. 2014. 'I Have Sinned against the Lord and against You! Will You Forgive Me?' *New Republic*. http://www.newrepublic.com/article/118135/adriaan-vlok-ex-apartheid-leader-washes-feet-and-seeks-redemption. Accessed 20 July 2014.

Fairbridge, D. 1924. *Gardens of South Africa*. London: A. & C. Black.

Fairclough, N. 1989. *Language and Power*. Essex: Longman.

Fanon, F. 1963. *The Wretched of the Earth*. New York: Grove Weidenfeld.

Fanon, F. 2008. *Black Skin, White Masks*. London: Pluto Press.

Feagan, R. & M. Ripmeester. 2001. 'Reading Private Green Space: Competing Geographic Identities at the Level of the Lawn'. *Philosophy and Geography* 4, no. 1: 79–95.

Ferguson, J. 1990. *The Anti-politics Machine: 'Development' and Bureaucratic Power in Lesotho*. Cambridge: Cambridge University Press.

Ferguson, J. 1999. *Expectations of Modernity: Myths and Meanings of Urban Life on the Zambian Copperbelt*. Berkeley: University of California Press.

Ferreira, H. J. V., V. Murtinho & L. Simões da Silva. 2013. 'The Legacy of the Modern Movement and its Adversities in the Face of the Current Development of Changeable Housing Construction Solutions'. In *Structures and Architecture: Concepts, Applications and Challenges*, edited by P. J. S. Cruz, 1168–1176. London: Taylor & Francis.

Findley, L. 2011. 'Red and Gold: A Tale of Two Apartheid Museums'. *The Design Observer Group*. http://places.designobserver.com/. Accessed 6 October 2012.

Flores, H. C. 2006. *Food Not Lawns: How to Turn Your Yard into a Garden and Your Neighborhood into a Community*. White River Junction: Chelsea Green Publishing Company.

Fort, T. 2001. *The Grass is Greener: An Anglo-Saxon Passion*. London: HarperCollins.

Foster, J. 2005. 'Northward, Upward: Stories of Train Travel, and the Journey towards White South African Nationhood, 1895–1950'. *Journal of Historical Geography* 31: 296–315.

Foster, J. 2008. *Washed with Sun: Landscape and the Making of White South Africa*. Pittsburgh: University of Pittsburgh Press.

Foster, J. 2009. 'From Socio-nature to Spectral Presence: Re-imagining the Once and Future Landscape of Johannesburg'. *Safundi: The Journal of South African and American Studies* 10, no. 2: 175–213.

Foster, J. 2012. 'The Wilds and the Township: Articulating Modernity, Capital, and Socio-nature in the Cityscape of Pre-apartheid Johannesburg'. *Journal of the Society of Architectural Historians* 71, no. 1: 42–59.

Foster, J. 2015. 'Modernity, Mining and Improvement: Joane Pim and the Practice(s) of "Landscape Culture" in Mid-Twentieth-Century South Africa'. In *Women, Modernity, and Landscape Architecture*, edited by S. Dümpelmann & J. Beardsley, 122–142. New York: Routledge.

Freeman, E. 2010. *Time Binds: Queer Temporalities, Queer Histories*. Durham: Duke University Press.

Freschi, F. 2009. 'A Modernist in Arcadia: Edoardo Villa's "Changing Worlds" at the Nirox Sculpture Park'. In *Edoardo Villa: Changing Worlds*, edited by K. Nel, 17–59. Johannesburg: Everard Read Gallery.

Froude, J. A. 1886. *Oceana, or England and Her Colonies*. London: Longmans, Green.

Gaitskell, D. 1979. '"Christian Compounds for Girls": Church Hostels for African Women in Johannesburg, 1907–1970'. *Journal of Southern African Studies* 6, no. 1: 44–69.

Galgut, D. 2012. *Small Circle of Beings*. London: Penguin.

Galli, P. & L. Rafael. 1995. 'Johannesburg's "Health Clubs"'. In *Defiant Desire: Gay and Lesbian Lives in South Africa*, edited by M. Gevisser & E. Cameron, 134–140. New York: Routledge.

Gandy, M. 2012. 'Queer Ecology: Nature, Sexuality, and Heterotopic Alliances'. *Environment and Planning D: Society and Space* 30: 727–747.

Gaonkar, D. P. 2001. 'On Alternative Modernities'. In *Alternative Modernities*, edited by D. P. Gaonkar, 1–23. Durham: Duke University Press.

Garb, T. 2008. 'A Land of Signs'. In *Home Lands – Land Marks: Contemporary Art from South Africa*, by O. Enwezor, I. Vladislavić & T. Garb, 8–39. London: Haunch of Venison.

Garb, T. 2011. *Figures and Fictions: South African Photography in the Present Tense*. Göttingen: Steidl; London: V&A Publishing.

The Gardeners' Magazine of Botany, Horticulture, Floriculture, and Natural Science, Volumes I–II. 1850. London: W. S. Orr & Company.

Gardiner, N. 1991. *Beautiful Gardens of South Africa*. Cape Town: Struik Timmins.

Gevisser, M. 1995. 'A Different Fight for Freedom: A History of Gay and Lesbian Organisation from the 1950s to the 1960s'. In *Defiant Desire: Gay and Lesbian Lives in South Africa*, edited by M. Gevisser and E. Cameron, 14–87. New York: Routledge.

Gevisser, M. 2014. *Lost and Found in Johannesburg*. Johannesburg: Jonathan Ball.

Gibson, D. J. 2009. *Grasses and Grassland Ecology*. Oxford: Oxford University Press.

Gift, N. A. 2009. *A Weed by Any Other Name: The Virtues of a Messy Lawn, or Learning to Love the Plants We Don't Plant*. Boston: Beacon Press.

Godehart, S. 2006. 'The Transformation of Townships in South Africa: The Case of KwaMashu, Durban'. PhD thesis, University of Dortmund.

Goldblatt, D. 1975. *Some Afrikaners Photographed*. Sandhurst: M. Crawford.

Goldblatt, D. 1982. *In Boksburg*. Cape Town: The Gallery Press.

Goldblatt, D. 1998. *The Structure of Things Then*. Cape Town: Oxford University Press.

Goldblatt, D. & N. Gordimer. 1973. *On the Mines*. Cape Town: C. Struik.

Goldsmith, O. 1770. 'The Deserted Village'. https://www.poetryfoundation.org/poems/44292/the-deserted-village. Accessed 23 October 2018.

Gordillo, G. R. 2014. *Rubble: The Afterlife of Destruction*. Durham: Duke University Press.

Gordimer, N. 1994. *Occasion for Loving*. New York: Viking Press.

Gordimer, N. 2001. 'Sudden Life, Never Seen or Expected Before: David Goldblatt's Photographs'. In *Fifty-one Years: David Goldblatt*, 431–443. Barcelona: Museu d'Art Contemporani de Barcelona.

Greene, D. 1970. 'The Gardener's Notebook'. *Architectural Digest* (August): 385–387.

Gropius, W. 1956. *Scope of Total Architecture*. London: George Allen & Unwin.

Grove, R. 1995. *Green Imperialism: Colonial Expansion, Tropical Island Edens, and the Origins of Environmentalism, 1600–1860*. New York: Cambridge University Press.

Haarhoff, E. J. 2011. 'Appropriating Modernism: Apartheid and the South African Township'. *ITU Journal of the Faculty of Architecture, Istanbul, Turkey* 8, no. 1: 184–199.

Haeg, F. 2010. *Edible Estates: Attack on the Front Lawn*. New York: Metropolis Books.

Halberstam, J. 2005. *In a Queer Time and Place: Transgender Bodies, Subcultural Lives*. New York: New York University Press.

Halberstam, J. 2007. 'Notes on Failure'. In *The Power and Politics of the Aesthetic in American Culture*, edited by K. Benesch & U. Haselstein, 69–90. Heidelberg: Universitatsverlag.

Halberstam, J. 2008. 'The Anti-social Turn in Queer Studies'. *Graduate Journal of Social Science* 5, no. 2: 140–156.

Halberstam, J. 2011. *The Queer Art of Failure*. Durham: Duke University Press.

Hall, T. 2010. *The Life and Death of the Australian Backyard*. Collingwood: CSIRO Publishing.

Haney, D. 2010. *When Modern was Green: Life and Work of Landscape Architect Leberecht Migge*. New York: Routledge.

Hanson, N. 1943. 'Vote of Thanks'. *South African Architectural Record* (July): 144–147.

Hardy, G. W. 1912. *The Black Peril*. London: Holden & Hardingham.

Harris, D. 1999. 'The Postmodernization of Landscape: A Critical Historiography'. *The Journal of the Society of Architectural Historians* 58, no. 3: 434–443.

Harris, W. C. 1839. *Wild Sports of South Africa: Being the Narrative of an Expedition from the Cape of Good Hope*. London: H. G. Bohn.

Harrison, B. 1982. *Peaceable Kingdom: Stability and Change in Modern Britain*. New York: Oxford University Press.

Harrison, D. 1983. *The White Tribe of Africa: South Africa in Perspective*. Johannesburg: Macmillan.

Hart, D. & G. Pirie. 1984. 'The Sight and Soul of Sophiatown'. *Geographical Review* 74, no. 1: 38–47.

Hartman, S. 1997. *Scenes of Subjection: Terror, Slavery, and Self-making in Nineteenth-Century America*. Oxford: Oxford University Press.

Haywood, E. 1745. *The Female Spectator*. London: T. Gardner.

Head, L. & P. Muir. 2006. 'Suburban Life and the Boundaries of Nature: Resilience and Rupture in Australian Backyard Gardens'. *Transactions of the Institute of British Geographers, New Series* 31, no. 4: 505–524.

Hector, A. R. & D. M. Calderwood. 1951. 'A New Native Township for Witbank'. *South African Architectural Record* (May): 122–128.

Henshaw, P. 2003. 'John Buchan from the "Borders" to the "Berg": Nature, Empire and White South African Identity, 1901–1910'. *African Studies* 62, no. 1: 3–32.

Hickson, J. & M. Strous. 1993. 'The Plight of Black South African Women Domestics: Providing the Ultraexploited with Psychologically Empowering Mental Health Services'. *Journal of Black Studies* 24, no. 1: 109–122.

Hitchings, R. 2006. 'Expertise and Inability: Cultured Materials and the Reason for Some Retreating Lawns in London'. *Journal of Material Culture* 11, no. 3: 364–381.

Holston, J. 1989. *The Modernist City: An Anthropological Critique of Brasília*. Chicago: University of Chicago Press.

Howie, W. D. 1943. 'Housing'. *South African Architectural Record* (October): 235–240.

Hoyles, M. 1991. *The Story of Gardening*. London: Journeyman Press.

Hoyles, M. 2002. 'English Gardens and the Division of Labour'. *Cabinet* 6. http://cabinetmagazine.org/issues/6/hoyles.php. Accessed 11 August 2013.

Huggins, M. 2000. 'More Sinful Pleasures? Leisure, Respectability and the Male Middle Classes in Victorian England'. *Journal of Social History* 33, no. 3: 585–600.

Hyslop, J. 1995. 'White Working-Class Women and the Invention of Apartheid: "Purified" Afrikaner Nationalist Agitation for Legislation against "Mixed" Marriages, 1934–9'. *Journal of African History* 36, no. 1: 57–81.

Imbert, D. 1993. *The Modernist Garden in France.* New Haven: Yale University Press.

Imbert, D. 2007. 'The AIAJM: A Manifesto for Landscape Modernity'. *Landscape Journal* 26: 219–235.

Imbert, D. 2009. *Between Garden and City: Jean Canneel-Claes and Landscape Modernism.* Pittsburgh: University of Pittsburgh Press.

Isaacson, M. 1990. 'Whose Triomf?' *Staffrider* 9, no. 2: 12–18.

Jackson, J. 2011. 'Going to the Dogs: Enduring Isolation in Marlene van Niekerk's *Triomf*'. *Studies in the Novel* 43, no. 3: 343–362.

Jackson, K. T. 1985. *Crabgrass Frontier: The Suburbanization of the United States.* New York: Oxford University Press.

Jackson, L. 2005. *Surfacing Up: Psychiatry and Social Order in Colonial Zimbabwe, 1908–1968.* Ithaca: Cornell University Press.

Jackson Downing, A. 1849. *A Treatise on the Theory and Practice of Landscape Gardening.* New York: George Putnam.

Jackson Downing, A. 1853. *Horticulturist and Journal of Rural Art and Rural Taste, Vol. III.* Rochester: James Vick.

Jacques, D. & J. Woudstra. 2009. *Landscape Modernism Renounced: The Career of Christopher Tunnard (1910–1979).* London: Routledge.

Jansen, E. 2015. *Soos Familie: Stedelike Huiswerkers in Suid-Afrikaanse Tekste.* Pretoria: Protea Boekhuis.

Janssen, D. F. 2007. 'BOY – Linguistic Anthropological Notes'. *Thymos* 1, no. 1: 43–67.

Janssen, D. F. 2008. 'Discipline, Suppress, or Kill: From "Ages of Man" to Masculine Temporalities'. *Journal of Men's Studies* 16, no. 1: 97–116.

Japha, D. 1986. 'The Birth of the State Housing Policy'. *Metropolis: Architectural Students Congress*, 74–101. University of the Witwatersrand, April.

Japha, D. 1998. 'The Social Programme of the South African Modern Movement'. In *Blank____Architecture, Apartheid and After*, edited by I. Vladislavić & H. Judin, 423–437. Rotterdam: NAi.

Jayawardane, M. N. & A. Edoro. 2015. '(Gay) Sexuality and African Writers: Adichie, Osman'. *Africa is a Country.* http://africasacountry.com/2015/07/gay-sexuality-and-african-writers-adichie-osman/. Accessed 31 July 2015.

Jeffs, W. 1964. *Good Morning Gardeners.* Cape Town: Howard Timmins.

Jekyll, G. 1899. *Wood and Garden: Notes and Thoughts, Practical and Critical, of a Working Amateur.* London: Longmans, Green, and Co.

Jekyll, G. & G. S. Elgood. 1904. *Some English Gardens*. London: Longmans, Green, and Co.

Jenkins, V. S. 1994a. 'Green Velvety Carpet: The Front Lawn in America'. *Journal of American Culture* 17, no. 3. https://onlinelibrary.wiley.com/doi/10.1111/j.1542-734X.1994.t01-1-00043.x. Accessed 2 October 2018.

Jenkins, V. S. 1994b. *The Lawn: A History of an American Obsession*. Washington, D.C.: Smithsonian Press.

Jennings, J. E. 1951. 'Building Research in Relation to the Architect and Quantity Surveyor'. *South African Architectural Record* (August): 186–192.

Jensma, W. 1977. 'i don't want that suburban house'. In *i must show you my clippings*, by W. Jensma, 17. Johannesburg: Ravan Press.

Johnson, E. A. & K. Miyanishi. 2007. *Plant Disturbance Ecology: The Process and the Response*. Amsterdam: Elsevier/AP.

Johnson, H. 1979. *The Principles of Gardening*. London: Mitchell Beazley.

Jonas, K. 1939. 'Sociological Approach to Native Housing'. In *Native Housing: A Collective Thesis*, edited by P. H. Connell, C. Irvine-Smith, K. Jonas, R. Kantorowich & F. J. Wepener, 1–48. Johannesburg: Witwatersrand University Press.

Kantorowich, R. 1939. 'Planning Native Housing: Sociological Approach to Native Housing'. In *Native Housing: A Collective Thesis*, edited by P. H. Connell, C. Irvine-Smith, K. Jonas, R. Kantorowich & F. J. Wepener, 86–122. Johannesburg: Witwatersrand University Press.

Kellaway, H. J. 1907. *How to Lay Out Suburban Home Grounds*. New York: J. Wiley & Sons.

Kentridge, W. 2010. 'Meeting the World Halfway: A Johannesburg Biography'. The 2010 Kyoto Prize Commemorative Lectures: Arts & Philosophy. Kyoto International Conference Centre, 10 November. https://www.kyotoprize.org/en/laureates/william_kentridge/. Accessed 24 October 2018.

King, M. & P. Oudolf. 1998. *Gardening with Grasses*. Warnsweld: Terra Publishing.

Klapp, E. 1897. *The House Beautiful* 2 (July): 42–45.

Kurgan, T. 2003. 'Public Art/Private Lives'. *Cultural Studies* 27, no. 3: 462–481.

Kuzwayo, M. 2007. *There's a Tsotsi in the Boardroom: Winning in a Hostile World*. Johannesburg: Jacana Media.

Kwon, M. 2002. *One Place after Another: Site-Specific Art and Locational Identity*. Cambridge, MA: MIT Press.

Latour, B. 1991. *We Have Never Been Modern*. Cambridge, MA: Harvard University Press.

Le Corbusier. 1987. *The City of To-morrow and its Planning*. New York: Dover Publications.

Lefebvre, H. 1991. *The Production of Space*. Cambridge: Blackwell.

Lelyveld, J. 1967. 'One of the Least-Known Countries in the World'. In *House of Bondage*, edited by E. Cole & T. Flaherty, 7–19. New York: Random House.

Le Roux, H. 2005. 'Foreign Parts'. In *Modern Architecture in East Africa around Independence, July 27–29 2005, Dar es Salaam, Tanzania*, 43–52. Utrecht: ArchiAfrika.

Le Roux, H. 2007. 'The Congress as Architecture: Modernism and Politics in Post-war Transvaal'. *Architecture South Africa* (Jan/Feb): 72–76.

Le Roux, H. 2014. 'Lived Modernism: When Architecture Transforms'. PhD thesis, Catholic University of Leuven.

Lessing, D. 1994. *The Grass is Singing*. London: Flamingo.

Lester, N., F. Menguele, G. Karuri-Sebina & M. Kruger. 2009. *Township Transformation Timeline*. Pretoria: Department of Cooperative Governance and Traditional Affairs in collaboration with the European Commission.

Liebenberg, D. 2014. 'Modernism and Anti-modernism in the Afrikaner Protestant Churches during the Twentieth Century'. *South African Journal of Cultural History* 28, no. 2: 75–92.

Loudon, J. 1825. *An Encyclopaedia of Gardening, Comprising the Theory and Practice of Horticulture, Floriculture, Arboriculture and Landscape-gardening, Including a General History of Gardening in All Countries*. London: Longman, Hurst, Rees, Orme, Brown, and Green.

Lynch, D., dir. *Blue Velvet*. Santa Monica: MGM Home Entertainment, 1986.

Mabey, R. 2010. *Weeds: In Defense of Nature's Most Unloved Plants*. London: HarperCollins.

Mabin, A. & M. Oranje. 2014. 'The 1938 "Town Planning Exhibition and Congress": Testament, Monument and Indictment'. In *Exhibitions and the Development of Modern Planning Culture*, edited by R. Freestone & M. Amati, 97–110. Burlington: Ashgate.

Mabin, A. & S. Parnell. 1995. 'Rethinking Urban South Africa'. *Journal of Southern African Studies* 21, no. 1: 39–61.

MacDougall, E. 1986. *Medieval Gardens*. Washington, D.C.: Dumbarton Oaks Research Library & Collection.

Macinnis, P. 2009. *The Lawn: A Social History*. London: Pier 9.

Malcomess, B. & D. Kreutzfeldt. 2013. *Not No Place: Johannesburg. Fragments of Spaces and Times*. Johannesburg: Jacana Media.

Mamdani, M. 1996. *Citizen and Subject: Contemporary Africa and the Legacy of Late Colonialism*. Princeton: Princeton University Press.

Marks, L. U. 2010. 'Vegetable Locomotion: A Deleuzian Ethics/Aesthetics of Traveling Plants'. Connect, Continue, Create, Third Annual

Deleuze Studies Conference, University of Amsterdam, 14 July. https://nanopdf.com/download/vegetable-locomotion-a-deleuzian-ethics-aesthetics-of-traveling-plants_pdf. Accessed 24 October 2018.

Martens, J. C. 2002. 'Settler Homes, Manhood and "Houseboys": An Analysis of Natal's Rape Scare of 1886'. *Journal of Southern African Studies* 28, no. 2: 379–400.

Martin, E. 1983. *Landscape Plants in Design: A Photographic Guide*. New York: Van Nostrand Reinhold.

Marusek, S. 2012. 'Lawnscape: Semiotics of Space, Spectacle, and Ownership'. *Social Semiotics* 22, no. 4: 447–458.

Mattera, D. 1971. 'Sophiatown'. *Izwi* 2: 27–44.

Mavor, W. F. 1806. *New Description of Blenheim the Seat of His Grace the Duke of Marlborough*. Oxford: Munday & Slatter.

Maylam, P. 1990. 'The Rise and Decline of Urban Apartheid in South Africa'. *African Affairs* 89, no. 354: 57–84.

Mbembe, A. 2001. *On the Postcolony*. Berkeley: University of California Press.

McClintock, A. 1995. *Imperial Leather: Race, Gender and Sexuality in the Colonial Conquest*. London: Routledge.

McClintock, A. 2009. 'The White Family of Man: Colonial Discourse and the Reinvention of Patriarchy'. In *Theories of Race and Racism: A Reader*, edited by L. Back & J. Solomos, 356–370. New York: Routledge.

McCulloch, J. 2000. *Black Peril, White Virtue: Sexual Crime in Southern Rhodesia, 1902–1935*. Bloomington: Indiana University Press.

McHale, M., D. Bunn, S. Pickett & W. Twine. 2013. 'Urban Ecology in a Developing World: Why Advanced Socioecological Theory Needs Africa'. *Frontiers in Ecology and the Environment* 11, no. 10: 556–564.

Mda, Z. 2007. *Cion*. Johannesburg: Penguin.

Mears, P. T. 1970. 'Kikuyu (*Pennisetum clandestinum*) as a Pasture Grass: A Review'. *Tropical Grasslands* 4, no. 2: 139–152.

Meehan, T., ed. 1868. *The Gardeners' Monthly and Horticulturist*. Philadelphia: Brinckloe & Marot.

Mellon, J. G. 2009. 'Visions of the Livable City: Reflections on the Jacobs–Mumford Debate'. *Ethics, Place & Environment: A Journal of Philosophy & Geography* 1, no. 1: 35–48.

Mercer, K. 1991. 'Looking for Trouble'. *Transition* 51: 184–197.

Merrifield, A. 2006. *Henri Lefebvre: A Critical Introduction*. New York: Routledge.

Merrington, P. 1995. 'Pageantry and Primitivism: Dorothea Fairbridge and the "Aesthetics of Union"'. *Journal of Southern African Studies* 21, no. 4: 643–656.

Merrington, P. 1999. 'Fairbridge, Dorothea (Ann)'. In *The Cambridge Guide to Women's Writing in English*, edited by L. Sage, 230. Cambridge: Cambridge University Press.

Mhlongo, N. 2010. 'Zwakal'eMsawawa'. In *Soweto*, edited by J. Bieber & N. Mhlongo, 11–15. Johannesburg: Jacana Media.

Miller, W. 1909. *Garden Magazine*. 9 March: 75–78.

Miller, W. 1913. *What England Can Teach Us about Gardening*. New York: Doubleday, Page & Company.

Miller, W. 2000. 'Gardening with Trees, Shrubs, and Roses'. In *The Once and Future Gardener: Garden Writing from the Golden Age of Magazines, 1900–1940*, edited by V. T. Clayton, 47–56. Boston: David R. Godine.

Mitchell, D. 1998. *Cultural Geography: A Critical Introduction*. Oxford: Basil Blackwell.

Mitchell, J. C. & A. L. Epstein. 1959. 'Occupational Prestige and Social Status among Urban Africans in Northern Rhodesia'. *Africa* 29, no. 1: 22–40.

Mitchell, W. J. T. 1994a. 'Imperial Landscape'. In *Landscape and Power*, edited by W. J. T. Mitchell, 5–34. Chicago: University of Chicago Press.

Mitchell, W. J. T. 1994b. 'Introduction'. In *Landscape and Power*, edited by W. J. T. Mitchell, 1–4. Chicago: University of Chicago Press.

Mitchell, W. J. T. 2002. 'Preface'. In *Landscape and Power: Second Edition*, edited by W. J. T. Mitchell, vii–xii. Chicago: University of Chicago Press.

Mitchell, W. J. T. 2005. *What Do Pictures Want?* Chicago: University of Chicago Press.

Mogren, M. 2012. 'Lawns: Botanical Garden Design as Colonial Domination'. In *Ecology and Power: Struggles over Land and Material Resources in the Past, Present, and Future*, edited by A. Hornborg, B. Clark & K. Hermele, 143–152. London: Routledge.

Molebatsi, L., S. Siebert, S. Cilliers, C. Lubbe & E. Davoren. 2010. 'The Tswana Tshimo: A Homegarden System of Useful Plants with a Particular Layout and Function'. *African Journal of Agricultural Research* 5, no. 21: 2952–2963.

Moodie, D. 1994. *Going for Gold: Men, Mines and Migration*. Berkeley: University of California Press.

Moran, J. 2011. 'The Poetry of Lawnmowers'. *The Guardian*, 10 June. https://www.theguardian.com/commentisfree/2011/jun/10/growing-awareness-lawns-grass. Accessed 12 December 2012.

Moreno, M. P. 2003. 'Consuming the Frontier Illusion: The Construction of Suburban Masculinity in Richard Yates's *Revolutionary Road*'. *Iowa Journal of Cultural Studies* 3: 84–95.

Morrell, R. 1998. 'Of Boys and Men: Masculinity and Gender in Southern African Studies'. *Journal of Southern African Studies* 24, no. 4: 605–630.

Morris, R. C. 2006. 'The Mute and the Unspeakable: Political Subjectivity, Violent Crime, and "the Sexual Thing" in a South African Mining Community'. In *Law and Disorder in the Postcolony*, edited by J. Comaroff & J. L. Comaroff, 57–101. Chicago: University of Chicago Press.

Morris, R. C. 2008. 'The Miner's Ear'. *Transition* 98: 96–115.

Mortimer-Sandilands, C. & B. Erickson. 2010. 'Introduction: A Genealogy of Queer Ecologies'. In *Queer Ecologies: Sex, Nature, Politics, Desire*, edited by C. Mortimer-Sandilands & B. Erickson, 1–49. Bloomington: Indiana University Press.

Mosse, G. 1985. *Nationalism and Sexuality*. Madison: University of Wisconsin Press.

Mumford, E. 2000. *The CIAM Discourse on Urbanism, 1928–1960*. Cambridge, MA: MIT Press.

Munroe, J. 2006. 'Gender, Class, and the Art of Gardening: Gardening Manuals in Early Modern England'. *Prose Studies* 28, no. 2: 197–210.

Murray, J. 2012. 'The Layered Gaze: Reading Lesbian Desire in Selected South African Fiction'. *Current Writing: Text and Reception in Southern Africa* 24, no. 1: 88–97.

Murray, N. 2007. 'Remaking Modernism: South African Architecture in and out of Time'. In *Desire Lines: Space, Memory and Identity in the Post-apartheid City*, edited by N. Murray, N. Shepherd & M. Hall, 43–66. London: Routledge.

Murray, N. 2010. 'Architectural Modernism and Apartheid Modernity in South Africa: A Critical Inquiry into the Work of Architect and Urban Designer Roelof Uytenbogaardt, 1960–2009'. PhD thesis, University of Cape Town.

Murray, S. 2006. 'The Idea of Gardening: Bewilderment and Indigenous Identity in South Africa'. *English in Africa* 33, no. 2: 45–65.

Mvoko, V. 2006. 'Intolerance and Slaughter: The Dry White Heart of SA's Suburbs'. *Business Day*, 3 July. https://mybroadband.co.za/forum/threads/intolerance-and-slaughter-the-dry-white-heart-of-sa%E2%80%99s-suburbs.47038/. Accessed 24 October 2018.

Nassauer, J. I. 1995. 'Messy Ecosystems, Orderly Frames'. *Landscape Journal* 14, no. 2: 161–170.

NBRI (National Building Research Institute). 1949. *Research Committee on Minimum Standards of Accommodation: Interim Report of the Main Committee*. Pretoria: Council for Scientific and Industrial Research (CSIR).

NBRI (National Building Research Institute). 1954. *Final Report of the Socio-economic Survey at Payneville Location, Springs, Undertaken to Collect Necessary Data for the Design of the New Native Township of Kwathema*. Pretoria: Council for Scientific and Industrial Research (CSIR).

Ndebele, N. 1998. 'Game Lodges and Leisure Colonialists'. In *Blank____ Architecture, Apartheid and After*, edited by I. Vladislavić & H. Judin, 119–123. Rotterdam: NAi.

Nemudzudzanyi, A., S. Siebert, A. Zobolo & L. Molebatsi. 2010. 'The Zulu Muzi: A Homegarden System of Useful Plants with a Specific Layout and Function'. *Indilinga: African Journal of Indigenous Knowledge Systems* 9, no. 1: 57–72.

Nicol, M. 1984. 'Returning'. *Staffrider* 6, no. 1: 6.

Nieftagodien, N. 1996. 'The Making of Apartheid in Springs during the Sixties: Group Areas, Urban Restructuring and Resistance'. Seminar paper presented at the University of the Witwatersrand, Institute for Advanced Social Research, 15 April.

Non-European Affairs Department. 1962. *Your Bantu Servant and You: A Few Suggestions to Facilitate Happier Relations between Employer and Employee*. Johannesburg: Non-European Affairs Department.

Norwich, O. I. 1986. *A Johannesburg Album: Historical Postcards*. Johannesburg: Ad. Donker.

Nuttall, S. 2001. 'Subjectivities of Whiteness'. *African Studies Review* 44, no. 2: 115–140.

Nuttall, S. & A. Mbembe. 2008. 'Introduction: Afropolis'. In *Johannesburg: The Elusive Metropolis*, edited by S. Nuttall & A. Mbembe, 1–36. Durham: Duke University Press.

O'Doherty, B. 1999. *Inside the White Cube: The Ideology of the Gallery Space*. Berkeley: University of California Press.

O'Gorman, R. & M. Werry. 2012. 'On Failure (on Pedagogy): Editorial Introduction'. *Performance Research: A Journal of the Performing Arts* 17, no. 1: 1–8.

Olwig, K. R. 2003. 'Natives and Aliens in the National Landscape'. *Landscape Research* 28, no. 1: 61–74.

Omole, H. 2011. 'Understanding Lawn Grass'. *The Standard*, 24 March. https://www.standardmedia.co.ke/business/article/2000031780/understanding-lawn-grass. Accessed 24 October 2018.

Osman, D. 2011. 'Shoga'. http://www.diriyeosman.com/post/18990200939/shoga. Accessed 5 August 2015.

Osundare, N. 1988. *Moonsongs*. Ibadan: Spectrum.

O'Toole, S. 2003. 'Looking at the Land with David Goldblatt'. *Artthrob*. http://www.artthrob.co.za/03dec/news/goldblatt.html. Accessed 21 September 2011.

O'Toole, S. 2014. 'Caught Between: South African Photography after 1994'. In *Apartheid & After*, by E. Barents & S. O'Toole, 8–11. Amsterdam: Huis Marseille, Museum voor Fotografie.

Penick, P. 2013. *Lawn Gone! Low-Maintenance, Sustainable, Attractive Alternatives for Your Yard.* Berkeley: Ten Speed Press.

Peters, W. & P. Kotze 2013. 'N. G. Kerk Welkom-Wes: Reforming Unity Temple'. *Architecture South Africa* (March/April): 35–46.

Pevsner, N. 1955. *The Englishness of English Art.* New York: Frederick A. Praeger.

Pim, J. 1956. 'Creating a Landscape for a Mining Town'. *Optima* (March): 26–31.

Pim, J. 1971. *Beauty is Necessary.* Cape Town: Purnell & Sons.

Pollan, M. 1998. 'Beyond Wilderness and Lawn'. *Harvard Design Magazine* 4 (Winter/Spring): 1–7.

Pollan, M. 2003. *Second Nature: A Gardener's Education.* New York: Grove Press.

Polsky, N. 1969. *Hustlers, Beats and Others.* Middlesex: Penguin.

Posel, D. 1999. 'Whiteness and Power in the South African Civil Service: Paradoxes of the Apartheid State'. *Journal of Southern African Studies* 25, no. 1: 99–119.

Posel, D. 2000. 'A Mania for Measurement: Statistics and Statecraft in the Transition to Apartheid'. In *Science and Society in Southern Africa*, edited by S. Dubow, 116–139. Manchester: Manchester University Press.

Posel, D. 2001. 'Race as Common Sense: Racial Classification in Twentieth-Century South Africa'. *African Studies Review* 44, no. 2: 87–113.

Posel, D. 2011. 'The Apartheid Project, 1948–1970'. In *The Cambridge History of South Africa, Vol. II*, edited by R. Ross, A. Kelk Mager & B. Nasson, 319–368. Cambridge: Cambridge University Press.

Powell, I. 2002. *Exploding Heads: Brett Murray and the Aesthetics of Whiteness.* Cape Town: Bell Roberts.

Powell, I. 2007. 'Inside and Outside of History'. *Art South Africa* 5, no. 4: 32–38.

Pratt, M. L. 1991. 'Arts of the Contact Zone'. *Profession*: 33–40.

Pratt, M. L. 2007. *Imperial Eyes: Travel Writing and Transculturation.* London: Routledge.

Price, U. 1794. *Essays on the Picturesque, as Compared with the Sublime and the Beautiful: And, on the Use of Studying Pictures, for the Purpose of Improving Real Landscape, I.* London: J. Mawman.

Price, U. 1810. *Essays on the Picturesque, as Compared with the Sublime and the Beautiful: And, on the Use of Studying Pictures, for the Purpose of Improving Real Landscape, II.* London: J. Mawman.

Prinsloo, K. 2008. *Verhale.* Cape Town: Human & Rousseau.

Quattrocchi, U. 2006. *CRC World Dictionary of Grasses: Common Names, Scientific Names, Eponyms, Synonyms, and Etymology, Vol. I: A–D*. Boca Raton: CRC/Taylor & Francis.

Rabinow, P. 1989. *French Modern: Norms and Forms of the Social Environment*. Cambridge, MA: MIT Press.

Rabinow, P. 1992. 'France in Morocco: Technocosmopolitanism and Middling Modernism'. *Assemblage* 17: 53–54.

Raeburn, M., dir. *Triomf*. Johannesburg: Giraffe Creations, G. H. Films, 2008.

Randeria, S. 2002. 'Entangled Histories of Uneven Modernities: Civil Society, Caste Solidarities and Legal Pluralism in Post-colonial India'. In *Unraveling Ties: From Social Cohesion to New Practices of Connectedness*, edited by Y. Elkana, I. Krastev, E. Macamo & S. Randeria, 284–311. Frankfurt: Campus.

Ratele, K. 2009. 'Sexuality as Constitutive of Whiteness in South Africa'. *NORA: Nordic Journal of Feminist and Gender Research* 17, no. 3: 158–174.

Ratele, K. & L. Laubscher. 2010. 'Making White Lives: Neglected Meanings of Whiteness from Apartheid South Africa'. *Psychology in Society* 40: 83–99.

Ratele, K. & L. Laubscher. 2013. 'Archiving White Lives: Historicising Whiteness'. In *Race, Memory and the Apartheid Archive: Towards a Transformative Psychosocial Praxis*, edited by G. Stevens, N. Duncan & D. Hook, 109–127. Hampshire: Palgrave Macmillan.

Read Lloyd, A. 2009. *The Artist in the Garden: The Quest for Moses Tladi*. Cape Town: Print Matters.

Reynolds, R. 2012. 'Guerrilla Gardening: Why People Garden without Boundaries'. https://www.youtube.com/watch?v=mQPZsD8nKu4. Accessed 5 August 2015.

Robbins, P. 2007. *Lawn People: How Grasses, Weeds, and Chemicals Make Us Who We Are*. Philadelphia: Temple University.

Robbins, P., A. Polderman & T. Birkenholtz. 2001. 'Lawns and Toxins: An Ecology of the City'. *Cities: The International Journal of Urban Policy and Planning* 18, no. 6: 369–380.

Rogers, R. 1995. 'More Work for Father and Son: The Problems of the Perfect Lawn in the U.S.A.'. *EASST Review* 14, no. 2. http://dare.uva.nl/document/43044. Accessed 10 April 2013.

Rönnbäck, K. 2014. '"The Men Seldom Suffer a Woman to Sit Down": The Historical Development of the Stereotype of the "Lazy African"'. *African Studies* 73, no. 2: 211–227.

Ross, A. 2010. 'Desire'. In *The Deleuze Dictionary*, edited by A. Parr, 56–67. Edinburgh: Edinburgh University Press.

Ross, E. 1985. '"Not the Sort That Would Sit on the Doorstep": Respectability in Pre-World War I London Neighborhoods'. *International Labor and Working-Class History* 27: 39–59.

Ross, R. 1999. *Status and Respectability in the Cape Colony, 1750–1870: A Tragedy of Manners*. Cambridge: Cambridge University Press.

Rossmann, J. 2012. 'Martha(martyr)dom: Compassion, Sacrifice and the Abject Mother in Marlene van Niekerk's *Triomf*'. *Current Writing: Text and Reception in Southern Africa* 24, no. 2: 159–168.

Ruskin, J. 1862. *Unto This Last*. London: University Tutorial Press.

Russell, M. 2003. 'Are Urban Black Families Nuclear? A Comparative Study of Black and White South African Family Norms'. *Social Dynamics: A Journal of African Studies* 29, no. 2: 153–176.

Samuelson, M. 2008. 'The Urban Palimpsest: Re-presenting Sophiatown'. *Journal of Postcolonial Writing* 44, no. 1: 63–75.

Sandage, S. 2005. *Born Losers: A History of Failure in America*. Cambridge, MA: Harvard University Press.

Sandberg, L. A. & J. Foster. 2005. 'Challenging Lawn and Order: Environmental Discourse and Lawn Care Reform in Canada'. *Environmental Politics* 14, no. 4: 478–494.

Schiller, G., dir. *The Man Who Drove with Mandela*. New York: Cinema Guild, 1999.

Schoeman, K. 1991. *Another Country*. London: Picador.

Schroeder, F. E. H. 1993. *Front Yard America: The Evolution and Meanings of a Vernacular Domestic Landscape*. Bowling Green: Bowling Green State University Popular Press.

Schweik, S. 2009. *The Ugly Laws: Disability in Public*. New York: New York University Press.

Scott, J. C. 1998. *Seeing Like a State: How Certain Schemes to Improve the Human Condition Have Failed*. New Haven: Yale University Press.

Shear, J. 2006. 'Haunted House, Haunted Nation: *Triomf* and the South African Postcolonial Gothic'. *Journal of Literary Studies/Tydskrif vir Literatuurwetenksap* 22, no. 1/2: 70–95.

Sheat, B. & G. Schofield. 1995. *Complete Gardening in Southern Africa*. Cape Town: Struik.

Sheat, W. G. 1956. *Standard Garden Practice for Southern Africa*. Johannesburg: Central New Agency.

Shepherd, N. & S. Robins. 2008. *New South African Keywords*. Johannesburg: Jacana Media; Athens: Ohio University Press.

Silberman, L. 1943. 'Social Postulates of Planning'. *South African Architectural Record* (September): 215–240.

Silverman, M. 1998. '"Ons Bou vir die Bank": Nationalism, Architecture and Volkskas Bank'. In *Blank____Architecture, Apartheid and After*, edited by I. Vladislavić & H. Judin, 128–143. Rotterdam: NAi.

Silverman, M. & M. Myeza. 2005. 'Four Spaces'. In *Johannesburg Circa Now: Photography and the City*, edited by T. Kurgan & J. Ractliffe, 44–51. Johannesburg: T. Kurgan and J. Ractliffe.

Skeggs, B. 1997. *Formations of Class and Gender: Becoming Respectable*. Thousand Oaks: Sage.

Smith, C. W. 1940. *Home Gardening in South Africa*. Cape Town: Central News Agency.

Smith, T. 2012. 'The Big Interview: What Doctors Ordered'. *The Times*. http://www.timeslive.co.za. Accessed 15 September 2012.

South African Congress Alliance. 1955. 'The Freedom Charter'. http://www.historicalpapers.wits.ac.za/inventories/inv_pdfo/AD1137/AD1137-Ea6-1-001-jpeg.pdf. Accessed 23 October 2018.

Southall, R. 2016. *The New Black Middle Class in South Africa*. Suffolk: James Currey.

The Southern African Garden Manual. Cape Town: The Speciality Press, 1958.

Sparks, S. J. 2012. 'Apartheid Modern: South Africa's Oil from Coal Project and the History of a South African Company Town'. PhD thesis, University of Michigan.

Spence, B. 1950. 'How Our Urban Native Lives'. *South African Architectural Record* (October): 221–236.

Stapf, O. 1921. 'Kikuyu Grass (*Pennisetum clandestinum*, Chiov.). *Royal Botanic Gardens Kew Bulletin of Miscellaneous Information*, 85–93. London: Her Majesty's Stationery Office.

Steenkamp, A. 2008. 'Space, Power and the Body: The Civil and Uncivil as Represented in the Voortrekker Monument and the Native Township Model'. PhD thesis, Delft University of Technology.

Stein, S. B. 1993. *Noah's Garden: Restoring the Ecology of Our Own Back Yards*. Boston: Houghton Mifflin.

Steinberg, J. 2004. *The Number: One Man's Search for Identity in the Cape Underworld and Prison Gangs*. Cape Town: Jonathan Ball.

Steinberg, S. R., M. Kehler & L. Cornish, eds. 2010. *Boy Culture: An Encyclopedia, Vol. I*. Santa Barbara: Greenwood.

Steinberg, T. 2006. *American Green: The Obsessive Quest for the Perfect Lawn*. New York: W. W. Norton & Company.

Stevens, G. 2007. 'Tactical Reversal or Re-centring Whiteness? A Response to Green, Sonn, and Matsebula'. *South African Journal of Psychology* 37, no. 3: 425–430.

Steyn, M. 2007. 'As the Postcolonial Moment Deepens: A Response to Green, Sonn, and Matsebula'. *South African Journal of Psychology* 37, no. 3: 420–424.

Stoler, A. 1989. 'Making Empire Respectable: The Politics of Race and Sexual Morality in 20th-Century Colonial Cultures'. *American Ethnologist* 16, no. 4: 634–660.

Stoler, A. 2013. '"The Rot Remains": From Ruins to Ruination'. In *Imperial Debris: On Ruins and Ruination*, edited by A. Stoler, 1–38. Durham: Duke University Press.

Stotesbury, J. A. 2004. 'Urban Erasures and Renovations: Sophiatown and District Six in Postapartheid Narratives'. *Scrutiny2* 9, no. 2: 18–27.

Sutton, D. & D. Martin-Jones. 2011. *Deleuze Reframed: A Guide for the Arts Student*. London: I. B. Tauris.

Taylor, H. A. 1995. 'Urban Public Parks, 1840–1900: Design and Meaning'. *Garden History* 23, no. 2: 201–221.

Taylor, L. 2008. *A Taste for Gardening: Classed and Gendered Practices*. Hampshire: Ashgate.

Teige, K. 2002. *The Minimum Dwelling*. Cambridge, MA: MIT Press.

Teppo, A. B. 2004. *The Making of a Good White: A Historical Ethnography of the Rehabilitation of Poor Whites in a Suburb of Cape Town*. Helsinki: University of Helsinki.

Teyssot, G., ed. 1999. *The American Lawn*. New York: Princeton Architectural Press & Canadian Centre for Architecture.

Thacker, C. 1985. *The History of Gardens*. Berkeley: University of California Press.

Thompson, G. 1827. *Travels and Adventures in Southern Africa: Comprising a View of the Present State of the Cape Colony; with Observations on the Progress and Prospects of British Emigrants*. London: Henry Colburn.

Thornton-White, L. W. 1938. 'A Survey of 20th Century Town Planning'. *South African Architectural Record* (September): 312–341.

Thwing, W. E. 1948. *The Home Garden* 11.

Tlali, M. 1975. 'Sophiatown or Triomf?' In *Sophiatown Renaissance: A Reader*, edited by N. Masilela, 136–144. https://www.scribd.com/document/156116199/Sophiatown-Reader. Accessed 25 October 2018.

Tunnard, C. 1938. *Gardens in the Modern Landscape*. London: Architectural Press.

Turner, J. 1979. *The Politics of Landscape*. Oxford: Basil Blackwell.

Turner, R. 1985. *Capability Brown and the Eighteenth-Century English Landscape*. New York: Rizzoli.

Union of South Africa. 1938. *Report of the Commission of Inquiry into the Question of Mixed Marriages between Europeans and Non-Europeans*. Pretoria: Government Printing Office.

Union of South Africa. 1947. *National Housing: A Review of Policy and Progress*. Pretoria: Government Printing Office.

Union of South Africa. 1950. *Population Registration Act (No. 30 of 1950)*. Pretoria: Government Printing Office.

Van der Bijl, H. 1944. 'Native Housing: Experimental House, Johannesburg'. *South African Architectural Record* (November): 286–288.

Van der Spuy, U. 1953. *Gardening in Southern Africa (The Flower Garden)*. Cape Town: Juta.

Van der Spuy, U. 1971. *Wild Flowers of South Africa for the Garden*. Johannesburg: H. Keartland.

Van der Walt, J. & P. Birkholtz. 2012. 'Phase 1 Heritage Impact Assessment for the Proposed Development of the ERPM Mine Village, Boksburg, Gauteng'. http://www.sahra.org.za/sahris/heritage-reports/phase-1-heritage-impact-assessment-erpm-mine-village-boksburg-gauteng. Accessed 10 June 2018.

Van Niekerk, M. 1999. *Triomf*. Translated by L. de Kock. Johannesburg: Jonathan Ball.

Van Niekerk, M. 2007. 'Labour'. In *Omnibus of a Century of South African Short Stories*, edited by M. Chapman, 852–868. Johannesburg: Ad. Donker.

Van Onselen, C. 1982. *New Babylon New Nineveh: Everyday Life on the Witwatersrand 1886–1914*. Johannesburg: Jonathan Ball.

Van Rensburg, C., et al. 1986. *Johannesburg: One Hundred Years*. Johannesburg: Chris Van Rensburg Publications.

Van Selms, A. 1954. *Beginsels van Protestantse Kerkbou*. Cape Town: HAUM.

Van Sittert, L. 2003. 'Making the Cape Floral Kingdom: The Discovery and Defence of Indigenous Flora at the Cape *ca*.1890–1939'. *Landscape Research* 28, no. 1: 113–129.

Veblen, T. 2007. *The Theory of the Leisure Class*. Oxford: Oxford University Press.

Vestbro, D. 2012. 'Housing in the Apartheid City'. *Izgradnja: Journal of the Association of Civil Engineers, Geotechnical Engineers, Architects and Town Planners* 66, no. 7/8: 349–355.

Vice, S. 2010. 'How Do I Live in This Strange Place?' *Journal of Social Philosophy* 41, no. 3: 323–342.

Vladislavić, I. 2001. *The Restless Supermarket*. Cape Town: David Philip.

Vladislavić, I. 2009. *Portrait with Keys: Joburg & What-What*. Cape Town: Umuzi.

Vladislavić, I. 2010. *Flashback Hotel: Early Stories*. Cape Town: Random House Struik.

Vladislavić, I. & H. Judin, eds. 1998. *Blank____Architecture, Apartheid and After*. Rotterdam: NAi.

Walpole, H. 1780. *On Modern Gardening*. Canton: Kirgate Press.

Warf, B. 2006. *Encyclopedia of Human Geography*. Thousand Oaks: Sage.

Wasowski, S. & A. Wasowski. 2004. *Requiem for a Lawnmower: Gardening in a Warmer, Drier World*. Lanham: Taylor Trade Publications.

Watts, H. L. & H. J. Sibisi. 1969. *Urban Bantu Housing: A Detailed Study and Re-appraisal of the Position in South Africa*. Durban: Institute for Social Research.

Waugh, F. A. 1926. *Book of Landscape Gardening*. New York: Orange Judd.

Webb, R. H., D. E. Boyer & R. M. Turner. 2010. *Repeat Photography: Methods and Applications in the Natural Sciences*. Washington, D.C.: Island Press.

Wepener, F. J. 1939. 'Planning Native Housing: Psychological Approach to Native Housing'. In *Native Housing: A Collective Thesis*, edited by P. H. Connell, C. Irvine-Smith, K. Jonas, R. Kantorowich & F. J. Wepener, 50–85. Johannesburg: Witwatersrand University Press.

Whistler, L. 1939. *Sir John Vanbrugh: Architect and Dramatist 1664–1726*. New York: Macmillan.

White, L. 2007. 'Renegotiating the Land Covenant in Marlene van Niekerk's *Triomf*'. *Scrutiny2* 12, no. 2: 84–95.

Wicomb, Z. 1998. 'Five Afrikaner Texts and the Rehabilitation of Whiteness'. *Social Identities* 4, no. 3: 363–383.

Wiesmeyer, E. M. 2007. *Joane Pim: South Africa's Landscape Pioneer*. Pinegowrie: The Horticultural Society.

Wigley, M. 1999. 'The Electric Lawn'. In *The American Lawn*, edited by G. Teyssot, 154–195. New York: Princeton Architectural Press & Canadian Centre for Architecture.

Wilkinson, P. 1998. 'Housing Policy in South Africa'. *Habitat International* 22, no. 3: 215–229.

Williams, R. 1975. *The Country and the City*. New York: Oxford University Press.

Wittenberg, H. 2004. 'The Sublime, Imperialism and the African Landscape'. PhD thesis, University of the Western Cape.

Wolkowitz, C. 2006. *Bodies at Work*. London: Sage.

Woudstra, J. 2000. 'The Corbusian Landscape: Arcadia or No Man's Land?' *Garden History* 28, no. 1: 135–151.

Wylie, D. 2011. 'Playing God in Small Spaces? The Ecology of the Suburban Garden in South Africa and the Poetry of Mariss Everitt'. *Journal of Literary Studies/Tydskrif vir Literatuurwetenskap* 27, no. 4: 71–90.

Wylie, J. 2007. *Landscape*. New York: Routledge.

Yates, R. 2008. *Revolutionary Road*. New York: Knopf Doubleday.

Zabus, C. 2013. *Out in Africa: Same-Sex Desire in Sub-Saharan Literatures and Cultures*. Woodbridge: James Currey.

Žižek, S. 1995. 'The Lamella of David Lynch'. In *Reading Seminar XI: Lacan's Four Fundamental Concepts of Psychoanalysis*, edited by R. Feldstein, B. Fink & M. Jaanus, 205–220. New York: State University of New York Press.

Index

F

G

P

Printed and bound by CPI Group (UK) Ltd, Croydon, CR0 4YY

09/06/2025

14685802-0002